1989

University of St. Francis
S0-BBT-199
3 0301 00054573 7

Jung and Eastern Thought

SUNY Series in Transpersonal and Humanistic Psychology
Richard D. Mann and Jean B. Mann, Editors

Jung and Eastern Thought

LIBRARY
College of St. Francis
JOLIET, ILLINOIS

Harold Coward

University of Calgary

with contributions by

J. Borelli, College of Mount Saint Vincent
J. F. T. Jordens, Australian National University
J. Henderson, Stanford University

State University of New York Press

Published by
State University of New York Press, Albany

© 1985 State University of New York

All rights reserved

Printed in the United States of America

No part of this book may be used or reproduced in any manner whatsoever without written permission except in the case of brief quotations embodied in critical articles and reviews.

For information, address State University of New York Press, State University Plaza, Albany, N.Y., 12246

Library of Congress Cataloging in Publication Data

Coward, Harold G.
Jung and Eastern thought.

(SUNY series in transpersonal and humanistic psychology)
Includes index.
1. Jung, C. G. (Carl Gustav), 1875–1961. 2. Yoga. 3. East and West. 4. Psychology and religion. I. Title. II. Series.
BF173.J85C612 1985 150.19'54 85–2784
ISBN 0–88706–052–8
ISBN 0–88706–051–X (pbk.)

10 9 8 7 6 5 4 3 2 1

150.1954
C 874

Contents

132,777

To Rachel

Preface

Along with the strong and continuing interest in the psychology of Carl Jung is the growing awareness of the extent to which Eastern thought—especially from India—influenced his thinking. Jung's own followers have not shown a readiness to examine the Eastern contribution to his thinking, tending instead to focus on his Western roots. This book is a serious scholarly attempt to fill that gap—to identify where Jung received Eastern influence, when he drew the line and drew back from the East, and to assess the overall impact of Eastern thought on his life and teaching.

Although the main body of the book (Chapters 1–3 and 5–7) is the result of my own research, I have included two excellent articles by Professor Jordens, and one article and an annotated bibliography by Dr. J. Borelli. Although he worked quite independently from me, Professor Jordens has taken a very similar line of analysis and provides findings which in general support my own, although on one important point differ—namely in giving Jung, at times, a more positive attitude towards the practice of yoga, and a more positive assessment of the nature of the highest yogic states. Dr. Borelli's article also addresses the same issue but from a different angle. His annotated bibliography is a helpful resource for scholars wanting to do further work in this area.

Professor Joseph Henderson is a senior and highly respected student of Carl Jung. It is a privilege to have him introduce this volume. He is one of the few Jungians to have given recognition to the important influence of the East on Jung's thinking.

Thanks are due to the University of Calgary for providing me with a research grant which enabled the collection of source materials to take place. My former secretary Joan Barton, and my current Administrative Assistant Gerry Dyer, both saw to the careful typing and retyping of the manuscript. Finally, much gratitude is due to William Eastman, Publisher, and his staff at the State University of New York Press for their encouragement and publication of this volume.

Harold Coward
Director
The Calgary Institute for the Humanities
University of Calgary

Introduction

In his chapters on Jung and Yoga, Harold Coward has presented a much needed, clear, and comprehensive account of C.G. Jung's relation to the religious traditions of India and, to some extent, of other forms of oriental spirituality. Together with follow-up essays by Dr. J. Jordens and Dr. J. Borelli, he has maintained throughout a healthy balance between approval and disapproval of Jung's point of view in reference to the usefulness of Eastern religion for Western people. There is considerable agreement that Jung's insistence on his empiricism may be justified, but there is disagreement where it seems he rejected certain values the East seems to offer the West. Did Jung protest too much and too often that Eastern mysticism of the kind represented by Patañjali's *Yoga Sūtras* was bad for Western adepts? Had he not, himself, borrowed from that source many of his own psychological concepts, or at least used them to support his own? Why did he fall short of acknowledging the attainment of *samādhi* as the ultimate achievement of spiritual awakening? These are questions the answers to which the reader may discover in varying degrees, as the authors pursue their observations and speculations. This is made easier by the welcome inclusion of Dr. Borelli's annotated bibliography which indicates what others have thought of Jung's apparent polarization between the claims of psychologists and religious mystics. To clarify this, Coward has provided an excellent redefinition of mysticism.

If I have anything to add to this discussion it is because it was my good fortune to be a frequent member of Jung's English seminars in the Zurich of the 1930s, and during that period I absorbed a good deal of Jung's thought on the subject of religion and its relation to psychology. Subsequently, becoming a Jungian analyst, I have frequently found my patients in a conflict engendered by the collision between psychology and religion, where they require in the course of therapy a special understanding that cannot be found in any philosophical system. I learned from Jung that if psychology does not learn to resolve such conflicts, probably nothing else in our culture will.

I remember Jung saying to me, on his return from a trip to India, that he saw the religions of the East as a great challenge to our Western psychology as therapy. I was impressed by the deep earnestness of his response to this challenge; he did not merely think about it. I am therefore grateful to Dr. Borelli in his chapter, "Jung's Criticism of Yoga Spirituality," for emphasizing that Jung's identity as a psychotherapist is mainly what prevented him from responding to the metaphysical dimension of Eastern mysticism. He was interested above all in healing the sick mind rather than in teaching it to think differently.

However, I do not believe Jung would have wished to be excused from criticism because of this. His own mind was too keenly attuned to the philosophical questions involved in a meeting of East and West, and he entered into the theological aspect of this challenge with his customary vigor. One of the seminars he gave in 1932 illustrates this particularly well. This was a joint seminar with Professor Hauer, a German Indologist, on the subject of Kuṇḍalinī Yoga. Professor Hauer presented this material in the traditional Indian way which honored the methods prescribed by the Patañjali *Yoga Sūtras.* He tended to think the lower *chakras* were successively to be left behind in the quest for a transcendent position from which to awaken the higher centers of consciousness, namely the *Viśuddha, Ājña,* and *Sahasrāra chakras.* In this presentation the lower centers associated with earth, water, fire and air, that is, *Mūlādhāra, Svādiṣṭhāna, Maṇipūra* and *Anāhata* respectively, were subtly put down as inferior, embodying all that is purely instinctual, materialistic, emotionally disturbing and obsessive, except for *Anāhata* where a certain benevolent detachment first appears.

When it was Jung's turn to comment on this introduction to the subject, he expressed great appreciation for Professor Hauer's viewpoint which he described as coming like the yogin from above. Admirable as this was, he acknowledged that he presented his own point of view as coming from below. Far from seeing the lower *chakras* as inferior, he described them as necessary parts of the whole experience of psychic reality, or as regions of the psyche and soma into which we must periodically descend to find those elements we need to give depth to our spiritual evolution. He noticed that certain members of the seminar were all too prone to identify with what they imagined it would be like to experience the higher centers as utterly detached from egoconsciousnes, and accordingly became somewhat inflated. Then, in response to Jung's cautionary remarks, these same people were quite ready to reverse their imagined experience and return to the reductive interpretation of reality offered by the instinct psychologists such as Freud or Adler, where the lower *chakras* are synonymous with sex or power drives. This, from Jung's point of view, was just as bad as aspiring prematurely to the heights of Eastern enlightenment.

In the end, I think, he arrived at a point of balance between two complementary opposites with regard to mystical experience. He saw one of them as real as climbing a ladder from a lower to higher level of consciousness; but he also saw the other equally as real as a wheel that always revolves upon its own axis. The image of the ladder does justice to the *Yoga Sūtras* of Patañjali, so well described by Harold Coward, as well as his redefinition of the mystical experience in general. The image of the wheel is used by Dr. Jordens in the sense in which it is found in the *Kauṣītakī Upaniṣad,* where "the hub always refers to the essential central principle out of which the other elements emerge." This center is *prāṇa* and, "In this connection it is important to recall that in this particular *Upaniṣad,* Brahman is presented as an immanent, intra-cosmic force and is not referred to as transcendent, extra-cosmic principle" (Ch. IX).

In appreciating these differences I feel that the disagreement between the psychologists and the religious mystics may be considerably lessened. Jung as an empirical psychologist honored an evolutionary process of becoming in accordance with the basic principles of the *Yoga Sūtras,* but he always felt close to the mystical tradition of being as that religious sense of immanence represented by the Upaniṣads as an eternal process of self-centering. Because he had to remain true to both these principles he could not totally satisfy the adherents of any one of them as *traditions*. He had to remain true to his own "reality of the psyche."

A particularly relevant account of one of Jung's followers, Dr. Esther Harding, is to be found in her paper *The Reality of the Psyche,* delivered as a lecture at the International Congress of Analytical Psychologists in 1966. She said of Kuṇḍalinī Yoga:

> And so the realization begins to dawn on one in whom this transformation is taking place that the psyche is an energic system. . . . In the heart region it is represented by the Lord, the Purusha, a symbol [the Self] corresponding to the Christian teaching that Christ would dwell in the heart of every Christian. But until the consciousness that *Viśudda* represents has been achieved, or rather, one should say, evolved in the individual, not in his ego-consciousness, his intellect or character but in the instinctive *Urgrund* of his being, it is not possible for him to appreciate . . . the actual reality of the psyche. . . . For, as Jung put it: "*Viśudda* means full recognition of the psychical essences or substances as the fundamental essences of the world, and not by speculation but by virtue of fact, namely as experience." P. 184, *The Kuṇḍalinī Yoga.* Notes on the Seminar given by Prof. J.W. Hauer with Psychological Commentary by Dr. C.G. Jung, Zurich, 1932.

Perhaps this may convey something of the paradoxical quality of Jung's attitude as he sought to bridge the chasm that existed and still exists, though less today, between our behavioral use of psychology, its gross or *stūla* aspect, as they would say in India, and its subtle or *sūkṣma* aspect as represented by the psychology of the self. It is with this concept that Jung approached the golden temple of Eastern wisdom, but also by which he refrained from entering as an adept. Because of this need to bridge these opposites as well as to acknowledge the validity of both traditions of mysticism, the transcendent and the immanent, he was not able to enter that temple in a personal quest of *samādhi.* Although he had certain attributes of the *guru* he basically remained a healer in the tradition of Western science.

Joseph L. Henderson M.D.
Stanford University

PART I

Jung and Eastern Cultures

I. Jung's Encounter with Yoga*

I. Yoga as Inclusive of the East in Jung's Thought

For Carl Jung, yoga is a general term indicating all of Eastern thought and psychological practice. In his writings yoga is used to designate Eastern traditions as diverse as Hinduism, Indian Buddhism, Tibetan Buddhism, Japanese Buddhism and Chinese Taoism. For Jung, therefore, yoga should not be confused with the narrow and technical definitions of the term which are encountered in Eastern thought itself. In Indian philosophy, for example, yoga refers to one of the six classical schools of thought—the yoga viewpoint systematized by Patañjali in his *Yoga Sūtras.*[1] Although Jung was aware of this technical usage of yoga as early as 1921,[2] (and based his 1939 Lectures[3] given at the Eidgenössiche Technische Hochschule, Zurich, on Patañjali's *Yoga Sūtras*) his interest from the beginning was not with Patañjali's technical definitions but with the spiritual development of the personality as the goal of all yoga.[4] In his lectures Jung observes that in India the practice of yoga involves both psychology and philosophy. To be a philosopher in the East requires that one has undergone the spiritual development of yoga. It is in this sense that Jung sees yoga as a general term (inclusive of psychology as well as philosophy), which is the foundation of everything spiritual not only for India, but also for Tibet, China and Japan. Consequently in writing his

---

* First published in *The Journal of Analytical Psychology,* vol. 23, No. 4, 1978.

Tibetan commentaries,[5] Jung talks about Tibetan yoga. In his commentary on the Taoist text, *The Secret of the Golden Flower,*[6] he refers to Chinese yoga and in his *Psychology of Eastern Meditation*[7] (actually a commentary on the Pure Land Buddhist Text, *Amitāyur-dhyana Sūtra*), Jung speaks of the Japanese practice of yoga.

Although yoga in Eastern thought often has a very technical meaning, it is also employed in a general way similar to Jung's usage. Mircea Eliade, in his well-known book, *Yoga: Immortality and Freedom,* observes that yoga is one of the basic motifs of Eastern thought.[8] And T. H. Stcherbatsky, the Russian scholar of Buddhism, maintains that yogic trance *(samādhi)* and yogic courses for the training of the mind in the achievement of the goal of release from suffering *(mokṣa,* or *nirvāṇa)* appear in virtually all Eastern schools of thought—be they Hindu or Buddhist.[9] It is exactly this sense of yoga as a way to release and self-realization that Jung has taken as the general theme of all Eastern thought and practice. However, the conception of the nature of the self-realization to be achieved, and the proper method to follow, are points on which Jung and the East show significant differences. An analysis of these differences and similarities is undertaken in the following chapters. For now, all that is required is that the reader be aware of the broad general way in which Jung uses the term yoga.

II. The Attitude (or Worldview) which Jung Brought to Yoga

If we are to understand Jung's encounter with yoga, a firm grasp of the viewpoint from which Jung began is required. Although the period of Jung's life with which we are concerned was very turbulent both personally and professionally,[10] through it all one thing remained firm his mind—namely, that he was an empiricist, grounded completely on observation and experience. Jung understood his whole encounter with the contents of his unconscious as a scientific experiment. In Jung's view, the possibility of being an objective psychological observer of others required first that the observer be sufficiently informed about the nature and scope of his own personality: "He can, however, be sufficiently informed only when he has in a large measure freed himself from the levelling influence of collective opinions and thereby arrived at a clear conception of his own individuality." [12] It is Jung's view that as one goes further back in his history and as one goes East, the individual is more and more swallowed up in the collectivity of the society. Only in recent times has there been sufficient individual awareness to make possible impartial observation and objective psychology.[13]

From a scientific point of view, Jung's purpose in opening himself to the contents of his unconscious was twofold. In the first place, it was necessary that he gain awareness of these contents with their warping needs and biases if he was to become an objective observer of others. Secondly, the contents of the unconscious are, for Jung, empirically real, and therefore proper objects for the scientific study of psychology. With regard to yoga, this means that Jung saw his approach as that of an objective observer who had encountered certain psychic realities in his own self-analysis, and then looked elsewhere (including to the East) for supporting evidence. This is made quite clear in Jung's September 1935 letter to Paster Jahn in Berlin. Jung says:

> . . . you seem to forget that I am first and foremost an empiricist, who was led to the question of Western and Eastern mysticism only for empirical reasons. For instance, I do not by any means take my stand on Tao or any yoga techniques, but I have found that Taoist philosophy as well as yoga have very many parallels with the psychic processes we can observe in Western man.[14]

In his *Memories, Dreams, Reflections,* Jung offers two examples of how the study of yoga can provide verification or support for something already encountered in Western consciousness. The first has to do with Jung's 1918–1920 discovery of the psychic development of the self occuring in a circular rather than linear fashion. He found that this new insight could best be expressed in paintings such as his "Window on Eternity." Several years later Jung reports an event that provided for him confirmation of his experience of the self. He received a letter from Richard Wilhelm enclosing the Taoist treatise, *The Secret of the Golden Flower,* with the request that Jung write a commentary on it.

> I devoured the manuscript at once, for the text gave me undreamed-of confirmation of my ideas about the mandala and the circumambulation of the center. That was the first event which broke through my isolation. I become aware of an affinity; I could establish ties with something and someone.[15]

The second example comes out of Jung's struggle with the contents of his unconscious. In the course of his self-analysis one of the several dream figures he encountered was Elijah (called by Jung Philemon). Psychologically, says Jung, Philemon came to represent superior insight. He was a guide through the inner darkness.[16] Many years later, in a conversation with an Indian friend, the role of the Indian *guru* in the process of education was discussed. When Jung's friend admitted that Śaṅkara, the eighth century philosopher-saint, had been his personal *guru,* Jung made the discovery that in yoga there are "spirit *gurus*". Jung reports the conversation as follows:

> "You don't mean the commentator on the Vedas who died centuries ago?," I asked.
> "Yes, I mean him," he said to my amazement.
> "Then you are referring to a spirit?," I asked.
> "Of course it was his spirit," he agreed.
> At that moment I thought of Philemon.
> "There are ghostly gurus too," he added.
> "Most people have living gurus. But there are always some who have a spirit for a teacher." [17]

To Jung this did not signify that he had experienced an Indian spirit *guru.* Only that, as he put it, "Evidently, then I had not plummeted right out of the human world, but had only experienced the sort of thing that could happen to others who made similar efforts." [18] It was confirmation only in the sense of confirming that Jung's experience of Philemon was a true human experience and not an idiosyncratic fantasy of Jung's own mind. But the content of Jung's Philemon remained resolutely Western, understandable not through the teachings of Eastern yoga, but through the wisdom of Western alchemy. As we shall see, this principle of finding confirmation in form rather than content, typifies most of Jung's contacts with yoga.

But the principle of looking for "confirmation in form" of psychic experience is too narrow. For Jung, yoga was not just an after-the-fact confirmation of his Western discoveries. Yoga often played the role of broadening and heightening one's experience of consciousness, by stimulating one to an increased awareness. This does not mean, warns Jung, that Western science should be belittled or given up—only that one must not become so encapsulated in the Western scientific approach as to claim that it is the only approach there is. In his Commentary on *The Secret of the Golden Flower,* Jung says, "The East teaches us another broader, more profound, and higher understanding—understanding through life." [19] The difficulty the typical Westerner has in experiencing this higher understanding arises from two things: his attachment to Western science as the only valid way of knowing; and his difficulty in identifying with the strangeness of Eastern texts such as *The Secret of the Golden Flower.* This means that the Westerner approaching Eastern yoga must not give in to his first reaction which will be to quickly dispose of it by calling it "Eastern wisdom," in quotation marks, or by relegating it to the obscurity of religion or superstition. Nor must he make the mistake of attempting to cope with the strangeness of Eastern ideas by becoming an uncritical imitator of yoga practices. Through a shallow imitating of yoga practices, says Jung, Western man "abandons the one safe foundation of the Western mind, and loses himself in a mist of words and ideas which never would have originated in European brains, and which can never be profitably grafted upon them." [20] The increased awareness, which Jung values as a result of his contact with the East, comes not through mindless imitation. It comes, rather, as a result of critical study of the East as a parallel to our human experience in West—a parallel which reawakens Western man to aspects of his own experience that in modern times he had lost touch with, namely, the intuitive, the spiritual.

A careful study of Eastern texts such as *The Secret of the Golden Flower* stresses the importance of having a balance between opposites in one's experience. When the opposites balance one another, says Jung, that is a sign of a high and stable culture. "Onesidedness, though it lends momentum, is a mark of barbarism." [21] This, in Jung's view, is the difficulty in which the modern West finds itself. After having placed great value on the spiritual and the intuitive during the Middle Ages, the intellect has come to a position of overwhelming dominance in modern man. But now there is a reaction in the West against the onesidedness of the overstressing of intellect to the virtual exclusion of the other aspects of human experience. At this point, study of the East is helpful in presenting an approach to life which includes all of the aspects or opposites and attempts to hold them in tension—intellect balanced with intuition. The truth of the East is not in the Eastern way itself, but in the demonstrated need for a balance between intellect and intuition, between thinking and feeling. And this serves to provide parallel confirmation of the reaction in the modern West in favor of feeling and intuition as a cultural advance or "a widening of consciousness beyond the narrow limits set by a tyrannical intellect." [22] The wisdom of Eastern yoga for the West is that one must "yoke" these extreme oscillations from intuition to intellect and now back again towards intuition, into a creative tension or balance. To be overbalanced in any one aspect of consciousness is a sign of immaturity and "barbarism", to use Jung's word for it. Consequently, it is not the case that the modern West should give up its highly developed scientific intellect—only that the intuitive and feeling aspects of psychic function must achieve an equally high development in Western consciousness so that a creative balance can be achieved, and a widening of consciousness result.

While Jung openly admired the Eastern yoga principle of inclusiveness and balance between the opposing aspects of psychic function, it is clear that he felt that the East had overstressed the intuitive, just as the modern West had overdeveloped the scientific. As Jung put it in his Commentary on *The Tibetan Book of the Great Liberation*, "In the East, the inner man has always had such a firm hold on the outer man that the world had no chance of tearing him away from his inner roots; in the West, the outer man gained ascendancy to such an extent that he was alienated from his innermost being." [23] Jung illustrated this contention by observing the following difference in Eastern versus Western religious practice. In the

West, the spiritual is associated with something external and lifted up, thus the high and raised up place of the altar and cross in Christian churches. In an Eastern Śiva temple, however, the spiritual symbol, the lingam, is often sunk in a deep shaft several meters below ground level. To Jung this indicated that in Eastern experience, the spiritual is to be found in the inward direction, in the deepest and darkest place.[24] In his *Psychology of Eastern Meditation,* Jung makes the same point:

> The West is always seeking uplift, but the East seeks a sinking or deepening. Outer reality, with its bodiliness and weight, appears to make a much stronger and sharper impression on the European than it does on the Indian. The European seeks to raise himself above this world, while the Indian likes to turn back into the maternal depths of Nature.[25]

The principle of all Eastern yoga is that the pairs of opposites *(dvandva),* the extremes, must be transcended or held in creative tension.[26] They must not exclude or devalue one another. From the East, therefore, the West needs to rediscover or resensitize itself to the interior aspects of intuition and feeling—but without letting go of its strong grip on exterior scientific consciousness. The East, on the other hand, needs the science, industry, and technology of the West, but not at the expense of its sensitivity to the inner man.

On both sides, said Jung, a balanced, widened, and inclusive consciousness needs to be achieved. But on the question of how this balancing was to be achieved, Jung was emphatic. The West must not simply attempt to copy the Eastern spiritual yoga, or the East blindly adopt Western science. Each should study the other and gain inspiration from its example, but each must pursue its own development within its own historical consciousness. As E.A. Bennet put it, "A race with an ancient cultural heritage, in Jung's opinion, had a collective experience not available to other races." [27] The modern West, says Jung, cannot graft Eastern yoga on to its scientific consciousness as so many misled individuals naively attempt to do.[28] In his letters the question of the practice of Eastern yoga frequently arises, and Jung's response is always emphatic and always the same. Yoga is suitable to the Eastern but not to the Western mind.[29] The occidental world should leave it alone and instead develop or rediscover its own spiritual practice. While yoga is the spiritual foundation of everything in the East, on no account is it a suitable practice for the West.[30] Although Jung admits to having practiced yoga himself on a few occasions during his turbulant period of self-analysis, he states that his purpose was quite different from that of an Easterner.

> I was frequently so wrought up that I had to do certain yoga exercises in order to hold my emotions in check. But since it was my purpose to know what was going on within myself, I would do these exercises only until I had calmed myself enough to resume my work with the unconscious. As soon as I had the feeling that I was myself again, I abandoned this restraint upon the emotions and allowed the images and inner voices to speak afresh. The Indian, on the other hand, does yoga exercises in order to obliterate completely the multitude of psychic contents and images.[31]

This is not the place to critically examine the correctness of Jung's analysis of the Easterner's experience of yoga. For the present our concern is to understand the attitude which Jung brought to his study of it. It is quite clear that for Jung the study of yoga served two important purposes. First it provided confirming evidence that others had had similar experiences to those of his own. Secondly, it suggested that consciousness was wider than the typical modern Western fixation on the scientific intellect. The study of Eastern yoga highlighted the intuitive side of psychic functioning, and encouraged modern Western man to redevelop his sensitivity to this aspect which had been so dominant in Western experience during the Middle Ages. For Jung personally, as we shall see, the role Eastern yoga played in the development of his thinking was brief but influential. Although Eastern ideas lingered on throughout his thinking, Jung's main fascination with yoga occurred during the 1920s and 1930s, culminating with his journey to India in 1938. By the end of his visit, however, the focus of his interest had already returned West, so that when his boat docked at Bombay he had no desire to leave the ship to see the city. "Instead", reports Jung, "I buried myself in my Latin alchemical texts."[32]

Indeed it may well be that in the development of Jung's thinking yoga lead him on from his early fascination with Western gnosticism and then back to Western alchemy, which then remained the keystone for the rest of his life.

III. Jung's Approach to Yoga Through Western Gnosticism

In a conversation with Richard Evans a few years before his death, Jung recalled the way he had come upon the notions of archetypes and the collective unconscious. He noticed that in primitive groups, as well as the great religious traditions, there exist certain typical patterns of behavior, often supported by mythological tales. In religions there are the codes of conduct as well as the examples set by the saints. In Greek mythology there are the poetic models of fine men and women. As he thought about the notion of archetypes, Jung asked himself whether anyone else in the history of the world had studied that problem. Casting his 'scholarly net' widely, Jung's first finding was "that nobody except a peculiar spiritual movement that went together with the beginning of Christianity, namely, the Gnostics. . ." had concerned themselves with the problem of archetypes.[33] The Christian Gnostics, who lived in the first, second, and third centuries, had come across structural elements in the unconscious psyche and made a philosophic system out of it. In his autobiography Jung notes that between 1918 and 1926 he seriously studied the Gnostic writers.[34]

It is in his *Psychological Types,* first published in 1921, that Jung's analysis of Gnosticism is clearly seen. Jung points out that the further we go back into history, the less the individuality and the more of the collective we encounter. In primative peoples, says Jung, we find no trace of the concept of the individual. Indeed, the very idea of individuality is fairly recent in the history of human thought. Jung felt that the development of the notion of individuality went hand in hand with the differentiation of man's psychological functioning.[35] The Gnostics caught Jung's eye because they were one group in classical Western literature that did differentiate between basic types of psychological functioning, and stressed the individual development of the personality even to the point of perfection.[36] As we shall see, this notion of the perfectibility of man's nature is also found in Eastern yoga, although it is a premise which Jung never accepted. The Gnostic dual emphasis on perfectibility and the need for disciplined individual development, both of which are shared by yoga, may well have paved the way for the movement in Jung's thinking to the East.

Gnostic philosophy established three basic types: the *pneumatikoi* or "thinking type," the *psychikoi* or "feeling type," and the *hylikoi* or "sensation type." [37] In addition to their perception of different psychological types, the Gnostics, says Jung, lay before us "man's unconscious psychology in full flower, almost perverse in its luxuriance; it contained the very thing that most strongly resisted the *regula fidei,* that Promethean and creative spirit which will bow only to the individual soul and to no collective ruling." [38] For Jung, therefore, the Gnostic evidenced awareness not only of different psychological types, but also the importance of individuality. In Jung's view, such psychological knowledge set the Gnostics apart from the collective psychology characteristic of the centuries before and after them right up to the modern period. Jung expressed it in these words, "Although in crude form, we find in Gnosticism what was lacking in the centuries that followed: a belief in the efficacy of individual revelation and individual knowledge." [39]

It is clear that the foundations for several of Jung's major theoretical concepts may have originated or at least received strong support from the early Christian Gnostics, that is, the psychic functions of thinking, feeling, sensing, and the process of individuation. The Gnostics were also fascinated with symbols and the question of how to release these symbols (e.g., God, Sophia, and Christ) from the entrapment of the baser instincts. While all of this fascinated Jung as a parallel providing his thinking with historical support, he became increasingly frustrated by the lack of material available due to the suppression of the Gnostics by the early Christian Church. In his autobiography he summarizes his Gnostic studies in the following words:

> But the Gnostics were too remote for me to establish any link with them in regard to the questions that were confronting me. As far as I could see, the tradition that might have connected Gnosis with the present seemed to have been

> severed, and for a long time it proved impossible to find any bridge that led from Gnosticism—or neo-Platonism—to the contemporary world.[40]

That bridge from Gnosticism to the modern world Jung later discovered to be medieval alchemy. But Jung made this discovery through his study of Eastern yoga.

It is quite natural that Jung's study of early Christian Gnosticism should have led him to the East. One of the Gnostics who most fascinated him was Origen,[41] and of course Origen was much influenced by Eastern thought. In addition Jung was also reading the contemporary philosopher Schiller. Schiller was strongly influenced by Schopenhauer who championed Eastern yoga as it is presented in the Hindu scriptures, the Upanisads. It is not surprising then to find Jung putting aside Gnosticism and immersing himself in Eastern thought, beginning with the Indian Brahmanical tradition of the Upanisads.

IV. Jung's Encounter with *Dvandva* or the Pairs of Opposites of Yoga

In his memoir, Jung reports that very early in life he had become aware of a kind of split within his personality, as if two opposing souls were housed in the one breast.[42] And when, as a young man, Jung read Goethe's *Faust,* it awakened in him the problem of opposites, of good and evil, of mind and matter, of light and darkness.[43] Faust, and his inner shadow Mephistopheles, presented to Jung in dramatic form his own inner contradictions. "Later", says Jung, "I consciously linked my work to what Faust had passed over: respect for the external rights of man, recognition of 'the ancient,' and the continuity of culture and intellectual history." [44] Although Jung's search into the 'ancient sources' first took him to the Gnostic experience of the opposites of matter and spirit, it was in the Eastern approach to the problem that he found the first real "light."

Dvandva is the Sanskrit term for the pairs of opposites in classical Indian thought.

Dvandva includes one's individual experience of opposites such as hot and cold, love and hate, honor and disgrace, male and female, as well as the encounter with universal cosmic opposites such as good and evil. In Hindu thought, it is frequently through creating of the pairs of opposites (or more explicitly, by separating them from one another) that the universe itself comes into being.[45] The experience of *dvandva* is psychologically analyzed by Jung as being caused by a split in the deployment of psychic energy at the level of the unconscious.[46] There is an infinite variety in the amounts of psychic energy that could be contained on either side of the split, for example, 50–50, 60–40, 70–30, etc. In Jung's view, however, an unbalanced deployment of psychic energy on one side can only go on for so long until finally the opposite tendency will reassert itself and swing the pendulum in the other direction. Jung said that this is exactly what is occurring in modern Western experience: the psyche has developed in too one-sided a fashion with an over-emphasis on the scientific intellect, thus robbing the intuitive function of its power. Now the intuitive side is reasserting itself (witness the contemporary Western fascination with the East) and the movement is beginning to flow in the opposite direction.

In Jung's view any unbalance in the split of psychic energy, while it may produce the short-term gains of rigorous specialization (e.g., modern Western technology), will, in the long run, prove detrimental.

> Naturally this split is a hindrance not only in society but also in the individual. As a result, the vital optimum withdraws more and more from the opposing extremes and seeks a middle way, which must naturally be irrational and unconscious, just because the opposites are rational and conscious. Since the middle position, as a function of mediation between the opposites, possesses an irrational character and is still unconscious, it appears projected in the form of a mediating god, a Messiah.[47]

The projection of a mediating Messiah, says Jung, is indicative of the more primative nature of Western religion—primative because it lacks insight into the psychological balancing of the opposites that is occurring, and instead blindly accepts the whole thing as the action of God's grace. By contrast, the East has for thousands of years known of the processes required to balance the opposites, and has made them into paths *(marga)* of liberation or release.[48]

In his *Psychological Types,* Jung reviews the teaching of the Vedas, Upaniṣads and *Yoga Sūtras* on the problem of the pairs of opposites[49] and reaches the following conclusions. In Hindu or Brahmanical thought, the pairs of opposites are experienced as a continuum extending from external opposites such as heat and cold to the fluctuations of inner emotion and the conflict of ideas such as good and bad. The Hindu *marga* or path, aims at freeing the individual completely from entanglement in the opposites, which seem inherent in human experience, so that he can experience oneness with Brahman *(mokṣa).* What is meant, says Jung, is a union of opposites in which they are cancelled out. ". . .Brahman is the union and dissolution of all opposites, and at the same time stands outside them as an irrational factor. It is therefore wholly beyond cognition and comprehension." [51] The specific psychological process the yogi uses to realize this transcendence of opposites involves the systematic withdrawing of libido or attention from both external objects and internal psychic states—in other words, from the opposites. This eventually results in the elimination of sense-perception and the disappearance of conscious contents (rational ideas), which opens the way for rising up of images from the collective unconscious. These, says Jung, are the archetypes, ". . . primordial images, which, because of their universality and immense antiquity, possess a cosmic and suprahuman character." [52] The great images of the Vedas, such as *ṛta* (divine cosmic order) and *dharma* (the universal moral law), are symbols with the power to regulate and unite the destructive tensions of the pairs of opposites.

In Indian thought *ṛta* acts as a principle of dynamic regulation by withdrawing energy from any imbalance existing between the pairs of opposites until a balance or middle path is achieved. As Jung put it, "The optimum can be reached only through obedience to the tidal laws of the libido, by which systole alternates with diastole—laws which bring pleasure and the necessary limitations of pleasure, and also set us those individual life tasks without whose accomplishment the vital optimum can never be attained." [53] It is this psychological vital optimum that is symbolized in Indian concepts such as *ṛta. Ṛta* and *dharma* function to bring out the inherent fundamental laws of human nature which, when followed, guide the natural flow of libido into the middle path through the conflict of opposites. Although Jung finds close agreement between his own personal experience and the Indian view of the dynamic relationship between the pairs of opposites, there is one point on which he sharply differs. In a letter to his friend V. Subrahamanya Iyer, *guru* of the Maharajah of Mysore, and with whom Jung had searching talks during his visit to India in 1938, Jung discusses the impossibility of getting beyond the pairs of opposites in this life. Whereas to the orthodox Hindu *mokṣa* means a complete freedom or transcendence from the tensions of the pairs of opposites, Jung argued that without the dynamic tension between the opposites there is no life.

> It is certainly desirable to liberate oneself from the operation of the opposites but one can only do it to a certain extent, because no sooner do you get out of the conflict than you get out of life altogether. So that liberation can only be a very partial one. It can be the construction of a consciousness just beyond the opposites. Your head may be liberated, your feet remain entangled. Complete liberation means death.[54]

The basis of Jung's disagreement is rooted in his typically Western view of ego. Since the experience of oneself as an individual ego is fundamentally an experience of separation of oneself from other objects and persons, and since separation is the cause of the pairs of opposites, the complete overcoming of the pairs of opposites would also require the eradication of the ego and its sense of separation. But if there is no ego, there is no knower and therefore no consciousness. Abolishing the ego to transcend the opposites leaves only unconsciousness. In response to Subrahamanya Iyer's suggestion that there is, at the highest level, a consciousness without ego. Jung replies, "I'm afraid this supreme consciousness is at least not one we could possess. Inasmuch as it exists, we do not exist." [55]

In contrast with the very idealistic approach of Hindu yoga, Jung found the attitude of Chinese yoga more realistic in its perception of the problem of the pairs of opposites. Jung observed that like Hindu *ṛta,* the Chinese *Tao* is a uniting symbol for the pairs of opposites. Jung uses the fact that uniting symbols are found independently in Chinese and Indian thought as evidence for the existence of a uniting archetype in the collective unconscious. In Jungian theory this uniting archetype comes to be known as the self. For Lao-tsu, author of the *Tao Te Ching,* the *Tao* is hidden, nameless and yet at the same time the source of all creation. The *Tao* manifests the created universe by being divided into a fundamental pair of opposites named *yang* and *yin.* All of the other pairs of opposites can be grouped under *yang,* on the one side, and *yin,* in the other. *Yang,* for example, includes warmth, light and maleness, while *yin* is cold, darkness and femaleness.[56] The Taoist view is that psychic danger occurs when there comes to be too great a split between the opposites thus resulting in a serious imbalance. In his commentary on *The Secret of the Golden Flower,* Jung says that this is exactly what has happened to the psyche of the modern West. As contemporary Western man's conscious scientific intellect achieved more independence and power, his intuitive unconscious was thrust into the background to a corresponding degree. This made it even easier for the evolving emphasis upon consciousness to emancipate itself from the unconscious archetypal patterns. Gaining in freedom, the modern Western scientific intellect has burst the bonds of mere instinctuality and reached a condition of instinctual atrophy.[57]

The overdeveloped conscious intellect of today's Western man not only suffers from being cut off from his instinctive roots in the collective unconscious, but, due to this very rootlessness, he experiences a false sense of mastery over and freedom from nature—to the point of proclaiming himself god.[58] Jung points to Nietzsche as an example of just such a result.[59] Jung also takes up the Chinese insight that when one of the opposites reaches its greatest strength the other will begin to reassert itself. Quoting from the *I Ching* he says, "When *yang* has reached its greatest strength, the dark power of *yin* is born within its depths, for night begins at midday when *yang* breaks up and begins to change into *yin.*" [60] For Jung, the Dionysian eruption of Nietzsche's unconscious, with its intuitive and instinctive qualities, was confirming evidence of the correctness of the ancient Chinese insight.

Jung also saw the split of psychic energy into varying levels of imbalance throughout the pairs of opposites as a helpful theoretical model for understanding mental breakdown. Speaking as a psychiatrist of his typical patients, Jung says,

> . . . a consciousness heightened by an inevitable one-sidedness gets so far out of touch with the primordial images that a breakdown ensues. . . . Medical investigation then discovers an unconscious that is in full revolt against the conscious values, and that therefore cannot possibly be assimilated to consciousness, while the reverse is altogether out of the question.[61]

Modern Western man and his physicians thus stand confronted with the chronic problem of a severe imbalance and disunity within the psyche. The Easterner, by contrast, through the practice of his various yogas has kept a better balance between the pairs of opposites and thus does not as yet suffer from the same chronic problems as his Western colleague. Here Jung again sounds his warning that the solution for the Westerner cannot be found by taking up the direct practice of Eastern yoga. Says Jung, the neurosis or split within consciousness would then simply be intensified.[62] But what can be learned from the East is a general approach to be adopted so that the split, the imbalance between the opposites may be brought into harmony.

Although during 1918 and 1920, Jung had received from the analysis of his own unconscious a clue that the way to psychic integration was not linear but circular, it was not until his encounter with *The Secret of the Golden Flower* several years later that his therapeutic concept of "circumambulation of the self" was crystalized and confirmed.[63] In his commentary on *The Secret of the Golden Flower,* Jung points out that "the union of opposites on a higher level of consciousness is not a rational thing, nor is it a matter of will; it is a process of psychic development that expresses itself in symbols."[64] Jung maintains that in Western as well as Eastern experience the symbols of integration that appear are chiefly of the *mandala* type. *Mandala* means circle, and implies a circular movement focused on the center. It is a mental image or a ritually acted-out symbol which aims at engaging all sides of one's personality—all the positive and the negative opposites of one's nature.

In Jungian theory, the unifying psychological process of symbol formation is usually described as the raising or individuating of an archetype from the level of the collective unconscious to the level of conscious awareness. This may occur with varying degrees of psychic intensity from a relatively ordinary insight experience to the most extraordinary mystical experience (e.g., Paul's visionary experience of Christ). In conformity with much Eastern yoga, Jung admits that such a symbolic unity cannot be achieved by a determined effort of the conscious will—because the will is by nature, biased in favor of one of the sides of the opposites, namely, the conscious side. It is necessary that the appropriate cultural image, through the psychic process of intuition, be allowed to speak to and engage the contents of the collective unconscious in a manner that defies definitive expression.

It is the purpose of the various meditational techniques of Eastern yoga to make possible and promote this process. In the West this same goal of psychic unity should be pursued, not by imitating Eastern yoga, but by developing parallel Western practices such as the culture of what Jung calls active imagination. By such means, the contents of deeply unconscious layers can be raised and brought into fertile contact with ego-consciousness. Human history, too, may be seen to progress and unfold by such moments. When this happens, a pair of opposites may, momentarily at least, be said to be in balance and harmony.[65]

V. The Place of Religion in Jung's Encounter with Yoga

Jung, in the "Late Thoughts" section of his biography, observes that religious symbols "by their very nature, can so unite the opposites that these no longer diverge or clash, but mutually supplement one another and give meaningful shape to life." [66] This insight, which is nowhere more necessary than in reconciling the inevitable internal contradictions in any conception of God or Absolute Reality, Jung encountered in a highly refined form in Tibetan Buddhism. While writing his Commentary on *The Tibetan Book of the Great Liberation,* he notes that in the Tibetan meditations the different gods are nothing but symbolic representations of various aspects of the pairs of opposites which when taken together, constitute the whole.[67] In Indian and Chinese thought too, any representation of the divine in either philosophical or artistic forms almost always includes the various aspects of the pairs of opposites. The Hindu gods, for example, are balanced and completed by their goddesses (e.g., *Śiva-Śakti*). Indeed this balancing and fulfilling union between the male and female aspects of the absolute Brahman is the dominant symbolism in medieval Indian art.[68] The same theme may be found in the Tibetan *yab-yum* images,[69] the Taoist *yin-yang* symbol[70] and the many different ways in which Zen art represents the finite in the infinite.[71] This aspect of Eastern religious symbolism seems to have made a profound impact upon Jung. It provided a bridge for his return to Western thought in that he discovered the same sort of symbolizing of the opposites in Western alchemy.[72] However, perhaps even more important, it provided him with a theoretical structure for the Christian experience of God by means of which "the unavoidable internal contradictions in the image of a Creator-god can be reconciled in the unity and wholeness of the self as the *coniunctio oppositorum* of the alchemists or as a *unio mystica*." [73] It is clear that Jung's most significant religious experience did not have to do with the reconciling of God and man, but rather with the reconciliation of the opposites within the God-image itself. Although Jung's theological solution takes its content from Western alchemy, its form was largely shaped in his earlier encounter with Eastern religion. In his Commentary on *The Secret of the Golden Flower,* Jung summarized the significance of this encounter as bringing God within the range of his own experience of reality. By this he did not mean that he was adopting the metaphysics of Eastern yoga, for this he explicitly rejects. By seeing God, not as an absolute beyond all human experience, but as a powerful impulse within my personality, says Jung, "I must concern myself with him, for then he can become important, even unpleasantly so, and can affect me in practical ways. . . ." [74]

While analyzing the differences he found between East and West Jung noticed that in the East the religions received great respect because they provided the paths or yogas by which entrapment in the tensions of the pairs of opposites could be overcome. By contrast, Western forms of contemplation are little developed and in general are not respected. Contemplative religious orders are often judged to be worthless because they spend their time meditating and doing nothing, rather than in helping the needy. Jung states it concisely. "No one has time for self-knowledge or believes that it could serve any sensible purpose . . . We believe exclusively in doing and do not ask about the doer. . . ." [76] This leads Jung to conclude that the religious attitude of the West is extraverted while that of the East is introverted.[77] While Western religion sees God at work in the historical events of the external world, and acting through grace in his transcendental separation from the world, Eastern religion finds spiritual information and guidance mainly through introspection.[78] Here Jung would probably admit that he is overemphasizing for the purpose of making his point. Eastern religions such as Hinduism do not receive spiritual information and guidance *only* through introspection. For the Hindu, the encounter with his scriptural revelation, the Veda, which comes to him from the external world, is essential for his eventual realization of *mokṣa* or release. Similarly, the Western Christian, for example, has some sense of the presence of the Holy Spirit within. But the general insight Jung stated as a result of his encounter with Eastern yoga still receives credance today. Recent Western commentators such as Jacob Needleman[79] and Theodore Roszak[80] still stress the necessity of an "inward turn" exactly as Jung prescribed it some forty years ago.

Yet another aspect of Eastern religion which attracted Jung was that it was based on an experiential knowledge of man's own consciousness, and not on the blind faith or otherworldly grace that he felt characterized much Western religion. If the Eastern approach were adopted by the West, not only would this remove religion from the realms of otherworldly superstition, it would also do away with the conflict between religion and science. As long as science is based on empirical fact, and religion on blind faith, the barrier between the two will remain and the psychic split within Western man will deepen into still more of Nietzsche's madness. In the West both science and religion have to become less dogmatic and expand their awareness. "There is no conflict between religion and science in the East," says Jung, "because no science is there based upon the passion for facts, and no religion upon mere faith. . . ." [81] Of course Jung realized that he was referring here to traditional Eastern science and not to the imported brands of Western science that one now encounters in contemporary Eastern universities.[82]

VI. Jung's View of the Limits (Benefits and Dangers) in the Western Encounter with Yoga

There is little doubt that Jung's encounter with the various Indian, Tibetan, and Chinese forms of yoga had a significant and beneficial impact upon his life. But it was an impact that he found difficult to communicate to his Western readers. Jung was only too aware of the strong possibility that any such attempt would run the risk of promoting misunderstanding at many different levels—same relatively harmless, others quite dangerous. He realized that because the Westerner typically does not know his own unconscious, it is quite likely that when he finds the East strange and hard to understand he will project onto it everything he fears and despises in himself. Anyone who has had the experience of teaching the East to the general public of the West can confirm this insight of Jung. The other type of typical Western reaction, and perhaps the one which Jung feared most, is to be quickly attracted to the East, to give up one's own heritage, and, with little or no understanding of the psychic processes involved, to become a surface imitator of Eastern yoga—in a word, to mindlessly ape the East. As Jung put it, "The usual mistake of Western man when faced with this problem of grasping the ideas of the East is like that of the student in *Faust.* Misled by the devil, he contemptuously turns his back on science and, carried away by Eastern occultism, takes over yoga practices word for word and becomes a pitiable imitator." [83] The reason Jung feared this so much was that he felt the direct practice of yoga by a Westerner would only serve to strengthen his will and consciousness and so further intensify the split with the unconscious. This would simply add more aggravation to the already chronic Western ailment—overdevelopment of the will and the conscious aspect of the psyche. The outcome would be just as disastrous for the Western neurotic who suffers from the opposite problem of a lack of development of the conscious and a predominance of the unconscious. Since the thrust of yoga is inward, it would only plunge such a neurosis further into the depths.[84] In addition to these considerations, Jung pointed out that if we try to snatch spiritual techniques directly from the East "we have merely indulged our Western acquisitiveness, confirming yet again that 'everything good is outside,' whence it has to be fetched and pumped into our barren souls." [85]

When the above limitations and dangers are taken seriously, Jung felt that the West could obtain substantial benefits from encounter with the East. One of the major contributions of Western contact with the various spiritual disciplines of Eastern yoga is that they serve to remind the West that something similar may be found in its own cultural heritage. As examples of authentic spiritual practices which have been forgotten by the modern West, Jung points frequently to the Spiritual Exercises of Ignatius Loyola,[86] but with deepest interest to Western medieval alchemy.[87] And in addition to helping the West recover these most valuable aspects of its own tradition, contact with the East also has the effect of directing the attention of modern Western man to the importance of his inner nature and its intuitive function. As Jung clearly demonstrates in his last essay, *Approaching the Unconscious,* scientific as well as artistic and religious creativity may directly depend on sensitivity to the intuitive process of the unconscious.[88] Even in his own day Jung looked upon the growing interest in Eastern yoga as a sign that the West was beginning to relate to the intuitive elements within itself. Were he alive today Jung would probably judge the even greater fascination with the East in the same optimistic way. But he would surely repeat again and again his warning to the West that denial of its own historical foundations and its contemporary scientific advances would be sheer folly and the best way to bring about yet another uprooting of consciousness.[89]

> You cannot be a good Christian and redeem yourself, nor can you be a Buddha and worship God. It is much better to accept the conflict. . . .
> . . . we must get at Eastern values from within and not from without, seeking them in ourselves, in the unconscious. . . .[90]

Jung believed that the science of modern psychology would provide the necessary means for the contemporary West to seek within successfully.[91]

Notes and References

1. *Patañjali-Yogadarsanam* (Varanasi: Bhāratiya Vidhyā Prakāśana, 1963). A readable English translation is by Rama Prasada entitled *Patañjali's Yoga Sūtras* (Allahabad: Bhuvaneswari Asrama, 1924), although the version offered by J.H. Woods in the Harvard Oriental Series (vol. 17) entitled *The Yoga-System of Patañjali* is probably more generally available.
2. C.G. Jung, "Psychological Types." *Collected Works* (hereafter C.W.), volume 6 (Princeton: Princeton University Press, 1971; first published 1921), p. 196.
3. Barbara Hannah, "Notes on Lectures given at the Erdgenössische Technische Hochschule, Zurich, by Prof. C.G. Jung." Unpublished manuscript, 1938–1939. (Hereafter referred to as E.T.H. Lectures.)
4. *Ibid.,* Lecture II.
5. For Jung's Commentaries on "The Tibetan Book of the Great Liberation" and "The Tibetan Book of the Dead," see C.W. 11, *Psychology and Religion: West and East* (Princeton: Princeton University Press, 1958).
6. For Jung's Commentary on *The Secret of the Golden Flower,* see C.W. 13, "Alchemical Studies" (Princeton: Princeton University Press, 1967).
7. The "Psychology of Eastern Meditation" is found in C.W. 11.
8. Mircea Eliade, *Yoga: Immortality and Freedom* (Princeton: Princeton University Press, 1958), p. 3.
9. T.H. Stcherbatsky, *The Central Conception of Buddhist Nirvāṇa* (London: Mouton, 1965), pp. 16–19.
10. The period of Jung's life referred to is approximately 1914–1940. The turbulence and struggle is especially evident in Chapter Six, "Confrontation with the Unconscious" in Jung's *Memories, Dreams, Reflections,* ed. by Aniela Jaffé (New York: Vintage, 1965).
11. Ibid.
12. "Psychological Types," C.W. 6, op. cit., p. 10.
13. Ibid., p. 8.
14. *C.G. Jung: Letters* ed. by G. Adler (London: Routledge and Kegan Paul, vol. I, 1973), p. 195.
15. *Memories, Dreams, Reflections,* op. cit., p. 197. This "establishing of ties with something and someone" through finding parallels reallly allows Jung's method to be called "historical." Jung states his method most clearly in the 1957 "Preface" which he wrote for *Psyche and Symbol* (New York: Doubleday Anchor, 1958, p. xiii): ". . . we must ask whether our experiences are the only ones on record and, if not, where can we find comparable events. There is no difficulty in finding them; plenty of parallels exist, for instance, in the Far East . . ."
16. Ibid., pp. 182–183.
17. Ibid., p. 184.
18. Ibid.
19. 'The Secret of the Golden Flower,' in "Alchemical Studies," C.W. 13, p. 7.
20. Ibid.

21. Ibid, p. 9.
22. Ibid.
23. "Psychological Commentary on The Tibetan Book of the Great Liberation," *C.W.* II, p. 492.
24. E.T.H. Lectures by Professor C.G. Jung, Oct. 1938-June 1939, pp. 121–122.
25. "The Psychology of Eastern Meditation," *C.W.* II, p. 570.
26. "Psychological Types," *C.W.* 6, pp. 195–198; and "The Secret of the Golden Flower," *C.W.* 13.
27. E.A. Bennet, *What Jung Really Said* (London: Macdonald, 1966), pp. 68–69.
28. "Two Essays on Analytical Psychology," *C.W.* 7, pp. 149 fn. 8, and 171 ff.
29. See, for example, the letter to "Pater X", 17 Jan., 1942 in *C.G. Jung: Letters,* vol. I, edited by G. Adler (London: Routledge & Kegan Paul, 1973), p. 310.
30. E.T.H. Lectures, pp. 11, 13, 42.
31. *Memories, Dreams, Reflections,* p. 177.
32. Ibid., p. 284.
33. Richard I. Evans, *Conversations with Carl Jung and Reactions from Ernest Jones* (New York: Van Nostrand, 1964), pp. 48–9.
34. *Memories, Dreams, Reflections,* p. 200.
35. "Psychological Types," *C.W.* 6, p. 10.
36. John Passmore, *The Perfectibility of Man* (New York: Charles Scribners, 1970), pp. 83–88. In one of his letters Jung makes clear that in his view man is not perfectible, but will inevitably have to cope with the problem of suffering. Walter Uhsadel reports Jung as saying, "The Oriental wants to get rid of suffering by casting it off. Western man tries to suppress suffering with drugs. But suffering has to be overcome, and the only way to overcome it is to endure it." (*C.G. Jung: Letters,* vol. I, op. cit., p. 236.)
37. "Psychological Types," *C.W.* 6, p. 11.
38. Ibid., pp. 241–2.
39. Ibid., p. 242.
40. *Memories, Dreams, Reflections,* p. 201.
41. "Psychological Types," *C.W.* 6, pp. 16 ff.
42. *Memories, Dreams, Reflections,* p. 234.
43. Ibid., p. 235
44. Ibid.
45. For example, see *Ṛg Veda* X: 120. English translation can be found in *A Sourcebook in Indian Philosophy* ed. by S. Radhakrishnan and C.A. Moore (Princeton: Princeton University Press, 1967), p. 23.
46. "Psychological Types," *C.W.* 6, p. 194.
47. Ibid.
48. In this context Jung uses the term "salvation." This term seems to me so loaded with a Western Christian meaning that I find it unsuitable for expressing the quite different Eastern concepts of *mokṣa* or *nirvāṇa.* I find the English terms "release," "liberation," or "freedom" much better in conveying the Eastern concept of escaping the bondage of the pairs of opposites in everyday life *(samsāra).*

132,777
LIBRARY
College of St. Francis
JOLIET, ILLINOIS

49. "Psychological Types," *C.W.* 6, pp. 195–97.
50. Ibid., p. 197.
51. Ibid., p. 198.
52. Ibid., p. 202.
53. Ibid., p. 213.
54. *C.G. Jung: Letters,* vol. I, op. cit., p. 247.
55. Ibid.
56. As quoted by Jung in his "Psychological Types," *C.W.* 6, pp. 214–15.
57. "The Secret of the Golden Flower," *C.W.* 13, p. 12.
58. Ibid., p. 12.
59. "Psychological Types," *C.W.* 6, pp. 136–146.
60. "On the Secret of the Golden Flower," *C.W.*, p. 13.
61. Ibid.
62. Ibid., p. 14.
63. *Memories, Dreams, Reflections,* pp. 196–197.
64. "On the Secret of the Golden Flower," *C.W.*, 13, p. 21.
65. For Jung's own description of the above process, see "On the Secret of the Golden Flower," *C.W.* 13, pp. 22–28.
66. *Memories, Dreams, Reflections,* p. 338.
67. "Psychological Commentary on The Tibetan Book of the Great Liberation," *C.W.* 11, p. 495.
68. See, for example, H. Zimmer's *Myths and Symbols in Indian Art and Civilization,* ed. by J. Campbell (New York: Harper Torchbooks, 1962).
69. E. Obermiller, *History of Buddhism by Bu-ston* (Heidelberg: O. Harrassowitz, 1931).
70. L.G. Thompson, *The Chinese Way in Religion* (Belmont, California: Dickinson, 1973), pp. 63–76.
71. D.T. Suzuki, *Zen and Japanese Culture* (New York: Pantheon, 1959).
72. See, for example, the hermaphrodite images in Jung's "Paracelus as a Spiritual Phenomenon," *C.W.* 13, pp. 152 ff.
73. *Memories, Dreams, Reflections,* p. 338.
74. Ibid.
75. "On the Secret of the Golden Flower," *C.W.* 13, p. 50.
76. "Mysterium Coniunctionis," *C.W.* 14, p. 498.
77. "On the Tibetan Book of the Great Liberation," *C.W.* 11, p. 488.
78. Ibid., p. 506.
79. Jacob Needleman, *The New Religions* (Richmond Hill: Simon & Schuster, 1972).
80. Theodore Roszak, *Where the Wasteland Ends* (New York: Anchor Books, 1973).
81. "On the Tibetan Book of the Great Liberation," *C.W.* 11, p. 480.
82. For example, during a visit to India the author's experience of the Philosophy and Psychology Departments of the Banaras Hindu University showed them to be faithful copies of similar departments in any modern Western university. The philosophers were quite caught up in linguistic analysis and had little time for the Upaniṣads; the psychologists were busy with American Behaviorism and had no interest in Patañjali's *Yoga Sūtras.*
83. "On the Secret of the Golden Flower," *C.W.* 13, p. 7.

84. Ibid., p. 14.
85. "On the Tibetan Book of the Great Liberation," *C.W.* 11, p. 483.
86. See the references listed in the Index of *C.W.* 11.
87. See especially volumes 13, 14 and 15 of Jung's *C.W.*
88. In *Man and His Symbols,* ed. by C.G. Jung (New York: Dell, 1964).
89. "On the Secret of the Golden Flower," *C.W.* 13, p. 49.
90. "On the Tibetan Book of the Great Liberation," *C.W.* 11, pp. 483–484.
91. "On the Secret of the Golden Flower," *C.W.* 13, p. 43.

II. The Influence of Yoga on Jungian Psychology

On May 30, 1930, Carl Jung was the main speaker at a memorial service for Richard Wilhelm, translator of *The Secret of the Golden Flower* and the *I Ching*. In his memorial address, Jung made several observations about the way in which Eastern yoga should influence Western thought.[1] Jung noted that the typical Western specialist type of mind is intellectually narrow and not open to foreign influence. Wilhelm, on the other hand, showed an open and receptive mind which could understand and reshape the strangeness of the East into a more familiar form. By bringing to the West his deep experience of Chinese yoga, Wilhelm was inoculating the West with the "living germ" of the Chinese spirit which was capable of causing a fundamental change in the modern Western worldview. In this way, said Jung, we are no longer reduced to being merely admirers or critical observers, but we are able to in some sense participate in the spirit of the East.[2] However, Jung is quick to define the nature of such participation. Those in the West are not to participate after the fashion of beggars, being too ready "to accept the alms of the East in bulk and to imitate its ways unthinkingly." [3] If the West is to possess what has taken the East thousands of years to build, this cannot be done quickly, easily, or by theft. The inoculation of Eastern wisdom must be allowed to work within the Western mind in such a way that the danger of shallow "spiritual infection" from the East is avoided, and that the way forward to new spiritual growth on the old Western foundations is opened. Exposure to Eastern wisdom, therefore, is not so much the taking in of new knowledge, but rather the encounter with another way of understanding and living life which jars the Westerner loose from his own narrow-minded encapsulation. His awareness of consciousness is expanded, opening the door to experience of the unconscious. Clues are offered to the perceptive Western student as to what sort of things may be discovered within his own consciousness. But then he must experience these things for himself.

The above approach to the East, which is evidenced in the life and teachings of Richard Wilhelm, Jung also felt himself to be following. Jung's encounter with the East helped him to enlarge the awareness of his own unconscious and provided him with clues (such as the Eastern use of *maṇḍalas*) as to how to better make present its contents. Specifically, Jung felt that Eastern yoga could help modern Western psychology to avoid traps, such as becoming fixated in the sexual theories of Freudian psychoanalysis. Under the influence of yoga, the sensitive student would become aware that there is more to the unconscious than just the sexual libido, or as the Tibetans call it the *sidpa bardo.*[4] Jung saw his contact with the East as enabling him to discover, beneath the very real differences between East and West, a common basis or psyche shared by both.[5] In this chapter an examination will be made of those psychological concepts of Eastern yoga which Jung found to be basic or common and so incorporated in his own theorizing.

I. *Citta* and Psyche

Citta is the technical term used in Eastern yoga to refer to consciousness including both the level of awareness and the level of the unconscious.[6] *Citta* has empirical reality and may be controlled or experimented with in the same fashion as any other material reality. But because the material composing *citta* is of a finer or more subtle nature than the quality of matter in the physical environment, special scientific techniques suited to the nature of *citta* must be devised. These are the yoga techniques, one systematic formulation of which is found in the *Yoga Sūtras* of Patañjali. In ordinary experience, *citta* is experienced as a series of particular mental states *(citta vṛtti)*. A thought or *citta vṛtti* for yoga is understood as a specific shaping of psychic matter or *citta* in the same way as an external object, such as a chair, is a specific shaping of physical matter. In the Eastern view both are equally real. Jung shared this perception of the reality of psychic matter. As he put it, "It seems to me far more reasonable to accord the psyche the same validity as the empirical world, and to admit that the former has just as much 'reality' as the latter." [7]

Writing his autobiography, Jung refers to the turbulent years of confrontation with his unconscious as a period of scientific experimentation out of which his basic psychological insights arose.[8] Influence from the East came in a most welcome form, namely, in providing independent confirmation of what, to that point, had been merely his own experience. The full reality of the psyche, as Jung technically called it, was confirmed by the yoga conception of *citta* with its long and unquestioned history of psychological validity in a wide range of Eastern thought (Indian, Tibetan, Chinese, and Japanese). Like *citta,* Jung defines psyche as the totality of all psychic processes, conscious as well as unconscious.[9] Although the way in which Jung subdivides the psyche does not completely parallel the various stages in the evolution of *citta,*[10] there is one concept, namely, libido or psychic energy, that is shared by both Jung and Eastern thought. And from the way he develops the concept, it seems clear that Jung's view of libido is definitely influenced by Eastern thought. The receiving of support from Eastern yoga for his notion of libido was most important to Jung, for it was this concept that first caused the loss of his friendship with Freud. With the publication in 1912 of his book on the concept of libido, Jung reports that all his friends and acquaintances dropped away and the book was declared to be "rubbish." Jung's view differed from that of Freud in that for Jung libido "is not the sexual instinct, but a kind of neutral energy, which is responsible for the formation of such symbols as light, fire, sun, and the like." [12] Jung argues that this neutral energy can be canalized into many different expressions of desire, of which sexuality is an important one but not the only one. Another and perhaps equally strong expression of libido is found in the human experience of creativity.[13] The influence of the East on Jung is very evident here in that throughout his analysis of the different ways in which the neutral energy of libido has been canalized, Indian Vedic and Upaniṣadic symbols often dominate the text.[14] Jung's conclusion is "that the concept of libido in psychology has functionally the same significance as the concept of energy in physics. . . ."[15]

Jung found further support for his view of psyche and its neutral energy or libido in the classical Indian Sāṇkhya-Yoga conception of *citta*. In his 1939 lectures on "The Process of Individuation" given at the Zurich Eidgenössische Technische Hochschule, Jung spent considerable time analyzing the Sāṇkhya-Yoga theory of *citta*.[16] Jung's idea of the expression of the psyche as arising or being canalized from a pool of neutral energy (libido) fits very well with the Sāṇkhya-Yoga conception of *citta* as evolving from the latent energy pool of *prakṛti* (nonintelligent matter, one side of the Sāṇkhya-Yoga metaphysical duality). *Prakṛti* is composed of three aspects or substantive qualities *(guṇas)*, each of which can be found in an analysis of one's ordinary experience of consciousness: *sattva*, which is brightness or intelligence; *rajas*, which is energy or movement; and *tamas*, which is dullness or inertia. Although each of these *guṇas* keeps its own separate identity, no individual *guṇa* ever exists independently. Rather, the three *guṇas* are always necessarily found together like three strands of a rope. However, the proportionate composition of *citta* or consciousness assigned to each of the *guṇas* is constantly changing.[17] Only the predominant *guṇa* will be easily recognized in a particular thought. The other two *guṇas* will be present but subordinate. Jung found confirmation and support for his concept of libido or psychic energy in the yoga idea of *rajas*. *Rajas* is energy or movement of any kind. Passionate or lustful activity which leads one astray is *rajas*, as is the spiritual discipline of a saint or the highest thoughts of the greatest philosopher. Thus, in itself *rajas*, like Jung's libido, is neutral psychic energy. The value component is added by the way in which the energy is canalized by the constantly evolving psyche. Just as in Patañjali's yoga nothing would function without *rajas* (the other two *guṇas* of *sattva* and *tamas* would simply remain static), so also in Jungian theory the dynamic functioning of the psyche, the tension between the pairs of opposites and the process of individuation could not take place without the impetus of libido.[18]

In addition to supporting his notion of libido with the *guṇas* aspect of *citta,* Jung also appeals to the creative impulse inherent in the Hindu conception of the absolute or *Brahman.* Jung correctly points out that the Hindu scriptures (the Vedas) describe *Brahman* as the creative principle within the cosmos, the life force which fashions all of the organs and their respective instincts, and the uniting impulse which attempts to harmoniously tie all things together.[19] All strength, all energy, and all unity comes from Brahman. Jung concludes his study of the various Hindu scriptures with the following words: "It is clear from these examples, which could be multiplied indefinitely, that the Brahman concept, by virtue of its attributes and symbols, coincides with that of a dynamic or creative principle which I have termed libido." [20] But Jung foresaw the danger of a misunderstanding of this interpretation and so added a postscript: "In order to avoid all vitalistic misunderstandings, one would do well to regard this essence in the abstract, as simply *energy.*" [21] Jung goes on to cite the Sanskrit scholar W.D. Whitney and notes that the word *Brahman* comes from the root *barh* which means 'to swell.' This derivation he found to be quite significant. It "indicates a particular psychological state, a specific concentration of libido, which through overflowing innervations produces a general state of tension associated with the feeling of swelling." [22] Thus in day-to-day speech phrases such as "overflowing with emotion" or "bursting" are frequently used. One of the forms that such a "bursting-forth" takes in the *Yoga Sūtras* is that of the *kleśas.*[23] In his *Psychological Commentary on Kundalini Yoga* Jung describes *kleśas* as "urges, the natural instinctive forms in which libido first appears out of the unconscious; they represent psychological energy or libido in its simplest form of manifestation." [24] Although Patañjali confines *kleśas* to the "afflicting" processes of ignorance *(avidyā),* egoism *(aṣmitā),* attachment to sensuous pleasure *(rāga),* aversion or dislike *(dveṣa),* and shrinking from death or clinging to life *(abhiniveśa),* Jung follows the lead of Tantric yoga and includes desire for intellectual discrimination as yet another *kleśa.* This last Jung interprets as "an urge to produce a personality, something that is centered, and divided from other things . . . . It is what one would describe in Western philosophical terms as an urge or instinct toward individuation." [26] In addition to the more negative *kleśas* of the *Yoga Sūtras,* then, Jung highlights the very important *kleśa* of individuation, without which one could never develop an individual personality. Individuality is given to each human, animal, or plant by the very fact that *Brahman* had to separate into these many manifestations for the cosmos to be created. This is the root cause of the pairs of opposites discussed in Chapter 1. When a whole is divided into parts, such as male and female, says Jung, this causes the polarization which results in energy or libido tension between the opposites.[27] Even though everyone is physically separated out from the unity or whole in this way from the beginning of life, psychological individuation only occurs when one becomes conscious of one's separate existence. As young children or primitive people we identify strongly with the whole, in what Jung refers to as the *participation mystique*,[28] but maturity and psychic integration is realized only when our balanced unity in the center of the pairs of opposites is achieved. All of this Jung found well illustrated and supported in both the Brahmanical teachings of Hinduism and the practices of Tantric yoga.

II. *Tapas* and Active Imagination

Tapas is described in the *Yoga Sūtras* as that which burns up psychic impurities. It is the yoga or psychological technique by which one who is afflicted with a mind addicted to materialistic and sensuous goals for the purpose of satisfaction of the common urges (for example, food, sex, ego-aggrandizement, etc.) may purify himself of these psychic disturbances *(kleśas)*.[29] Jung's understanding of this yogic process runs as follows:

> The Indian conception teaches liberation from the opposites, by which are to be understood every sort of affective state and emotional tie to the object. Liberation follows the withdrawal of libido from all contents resulting in a state of complete introversion. This psychological process is, very characteristically, known as *tapas*, a term which can best be rendered as "self-brooding." [30]

In Jung's view the yogi practicing *tapas* seeks to concentrate his psyche by accumulating libido. This he accomplishes by withdrawing libido from both sides of the psychic opposites—that is from both external sense objects and interior thoughts. "The elimination of sense-perception and the blotting out of conscious contents enforce a lowering of consciousness (as in hypnosis) and an activation of the contents of the unconscious, that is, the primordial images, which, because of their universality and immense antiquity, possess a cosmic and suprahuman character." [31] It should be recorded immediately that the above interpretation of *tapas* and its goal is significantly different than the explanation found in Pantañjali's *Yoga Sūtras.* This difference will be explored in detail in subsequent chapters. For the present, however, our purpose is to show the degree to which Jung's thinking was influenced by the yogic conception of *tapas.*

It has been noted above that one of the translations of *tapas* offered by Jung was "self-brooding." Jung took this notion from *Ṛg Veda* X, 121, which contains the phrase *sa tapo atapyata,* and which the Sanskrit scholar Paul Deussen translated as "he brooded his own brooding." [32] In the Vedic hymns, Prajapati, the Lord of Creation, is depicted as the cosmic germ incubating himself in the form of a golden egg from which is hatched the world of diverse forms. Prajapati's *tapas* or "self-brooding" was a form of self-incubation which enabled him to penetrate into the unconscious and individuate the many separate forms of the cosmos. In this sense *tapas* is also a means to creativity. Jung also termed this process "active imagination." Just as in yoga, meditation upon an image is prescribed as an aid to *tapas,*[33] so also Jung found the use of an image helpful in cultivating active imagination. One of Jung's earliest descriptions of active imagination occurs in his essay *The Relations Between the Ego and the Unconscious.*[34] For Jung, active imagination was a therapeutic process opening the way for an exchange of contents, and therefore a shifting of the psychic integration, between the conscious level of ego awareness on the one hand, the the unconscious on the other. The patient fastens onto an image, which may be external or internal, and allows the workings of fantasy or imagination to operate until a vision, like the visions of the biblical prophets, results. Jung describes the process as follows: "Not a 'vision seen in a dream', but a vision perceived by intense concentration on the background of consciousness, a technique that is perfected only after long practice." [35] Unlike Patañjali's *Yoga Sūtras,* Jung does not specify a set series of exercises to be followed, for he finds that different patients use different methods. Jung leaves it to the patient to discover by trial and error the method that is most suitable. Jung's approach is well illustrated in *The Tavistock Lectures* description of the development of active imagination in a young artist he was treating.[36] The young man tried all sorts of things until he finally hit on the method suitable to himself. He used to take a train to see Jung, and on the wall of the train station was a poster advertising Mürren in the Bernese Alps—a colorful picture of the waterfalls, of a green meadow and a hill in the center with cows on it. The young artist finally succeeded in active imagination by sitting in the station, staring at the image the poster presented, and imagining himself in the poster walking up the hill among the cows and then looking down on the other side. By "seeing" what was behind the hill in his imagination, he was able to bridge the gap to the contents of his unconscious.[37]

The reason that Jung was so leery of any set formula, such as the yoga exercises prescribed by Patañjali, is that he felt the modern Western mind tended to be too tightly controlled by the conscious side—"the cramp in the conscious mind," as he called it.[38] This high degree of conscious cramp or control obstructs the free flow of materials between the conscious and unconscious levels of the psyche. Jung warned against Westerners practicing Patañjali's type of yoga for he felt that its highly structured and prescribed approach would only encourage more development of the already overdeveloped conscious control of the psyche and so serve to further intensify the "cramp." On this point Jung seems to have found the flexible and individualistic approach of Chinese Taoist yoga more to his liking. In his Commentary on *The Secret of the Golden Flower,* Jung comments on the Taoist practice of *wu-wei* (action through inaction) with the following words: "The art of letting things happen, action through non-action, letting go of oneself as taught by Meister Eckhart, became for me the key that opens the door to the way." [39] In Jung's view the most important thing for the West to learn today is the art of just letting things happen in the psyche. This is also the most difficult for the Westerner since from birth his conscious level is overemphasized and trained to interfere, to help, to correct, to negate, and to never allow psychic processes to grow in peace.[40] In overcoming this difficulty Jung felt that the West could learn a good deal from the East. From the Indian practice of *tapas,* the aspect of concentrating on an image often proves useful. From the Chinese Taoist yoga the notion of *wu-wei* or action through non-action, when combined with Meister Eckhart's "letting go of oneself," is most beneficial. Like the Chinese Taoist figure in meditation with the "flames" of a single consciousness being split up first into five and then further into twenty-five, so also personality growth requires dissociation of the previous consciousness so that an expanded consciousness may be achieved.[41] Jung felt that the use of active imagination would fulfill the same role for the West that yoga does for the East. It would help the unconscious to reach the conscious mind. Active imagination, says Jung, consists in a switching off of conscious awareness, at least to a relative extent, so as to make room in our conscious minds for new impressions and ideas. This makes possible the arising of new contents from the unconscious to the conscious level of the mind.[42]

III. *Buddhitattva* and the Collective Unconscious

Eastern yoga not only influenced Jung's perception of the methods by which the unconscious could be reached, it also played a great role in confirming and filling out Jung's own initial discovery of the collective unconscious. Here again Eastern influence was helpful in supporting Jung's divergence from Freud's position. Jung reports that his concept of the collective unconscious originated in one of the many dreams he had while on the 1909 trip to the United States with Freud.[43]

> This was the dream. I was in a house I did not know, which had two stories. It was "my house." I found myself in the upper story, where there was a kind of salon furnished with fine old pieces in rococo style. On the walls hung a number of precious old paintings. I wondered that this should be my house, and thought, "not bad." But then it occurred to me that I did not know what the lower floor looked like. Descending the stairs, I reached the ground floor. There everything was much older, and I realized that this part of the house must date from about the fifteenth or sixteenth century.

> The furnishings were medieval; the floors were of red brick. Everywhere it was rather dark. I went from one room to another thinking, "Now I really must explore the whole house." I came upon a heavy door, and opened it. Beyond it, I discovered a stone stairway that led down into the cellar. Descending again, I found myself in a beautifully vaulted room which looked exceedingly ancient. Examining the walls, I discovered layers of brick among the ordinary stone blocks, and chips of brick in the mortar. As soon as I saw this I knew that the walls dated from Roman times. My interest by now was intense. I looked more closely at the floor. It was of stone slabs, and in one of these I discovered a ring. When I pulled it the stone slab lifted, and again I saw a stairway of narrow stone steps leading down into the depths. These, too, I descended, and entered a low cave cut into the rock. Thick dust lay on the floor, and in the dust were scattered bones and broken pottery, like the remains of a primitive culture. I discovered two human skulls, obviously very old and half disintegrated. Then I awoke.[44]

Jung tells us that Freud was unable to interpret the meaning of the different levels of the house and instead concentrated his attention on the two skulls as representing death-wishes Jung had for two members within his own family. While Jung agreed to Freud's interpretation, he says that he did so only to avoid a break in their relationship at that time.[45] In his own mind, however, Jung was aware that the essence of the dream was something quite different. "It was plain to me that the house presented a kind of image of the psyche—that is to say, of my then state of consciousness, with hitherto unconscious additions." [46] The salon on the upper floor, represented conscious awareness; the ground floor stood for the first level of the unconscious, the personal unconscious; and the yet lower and darker levels represented depths of the collective unconscious which were as yet unknown to Jung. Jung reports that the dream had the effect of reviving his interest in archaeology, and eventually led him on to anthropology, comparative religion and medieval alchemy.[47] The dream itself recurred, over several years with Jung discovering new parts of "his house" that he did not know existed.[48] The interpretation of this dream led Jung first to an investigation of primitive mythology, and then to a study of the early Christian Gnostic writers which, he says, ended in total confusion. Although in the end it was the discovery of medieval alchemy which finally solved the confusion and put a stop to the recurring dream motif, Jung's detailed study of Eastern mythology and psychology was an important intermediary step.

The notion of a collective unconscious and the split it caused between Freud and Jung resulted in Jung's thinking being declared nonsense by most other psychoanalysts of the day. Without a group of supportive colleagues to confirm or reject his findings, Jung began a wide search for parallel evidence. The idea that there could be contents in the unconscious which are not those of a particular mind or person but belong instead to mankind in general, took Jung first to North America to examine the dreams of pure-blooded Negroes and American Indian tribes. His first idea was that such collective contents might be due to racial inheritance, but, reports Jung, "I was able to satisfy myself that these images have nothing to do with so-called blood or racial inheritance, nor are they personally acquired by the individual. They belong to mankind in general, and therefore they are of a *collective* nature." [49] As a trained physician Jung did not think this finding at all surprising. Just as people are born with bodies containing anatomical parts belonging to various fishes and animals, so also our mind or psyche, in its unconscious part, is a storehouse containing relics and memories of the past.[50] It is a common psychic basis that all humans share just as they share a common anatomical structure. In young children and in primitive peoples where little individual development has taken place, this collective level in which the individual differentiates little, if at all, between himself and other persons or objects, stands out. As further evidence for his contention Jung cites the French ethnologist Lucien Lévy-Brühl. Pointing to this lack of distinctiveness in the primitive mentality between the primitive and other humans, animals, or plants, Lévy-Brühl coined the term *participation mystique.*[51] Just as the primitive person may identify himself with a wild animal or a tree, so also the new-born twentieth century child begins by failing to distinguish between himself and his mother. To Jung, all of this was evidence that if each of us were introspectively to examine (through the use of dreams and active imagination) the inner levels of our psyches, we would reach a "layer where man is no longer a distinct individual, but where his mind widens out and merges into the mind of mankind—not the conscious mind, but the unconscious mind of mankind, where we are all the same." [52]

In Jung's judgment, the ordinary experience of "falling in love" is also a kind of *participation mystique*.[53] At first when two people fall in love they seem to be almost identical. It is as if the individual layers of consciousness no longer exist and together they share a common unconsciousness. The hatred which later appears has the function of "forcing them off" from one another so that, as the poet Kahlil Gibran put it:

> Ay, you shall be together even in the silent memory of God.
> But let there be spaces in your togetherness,
> And let the winds of the heavens dance between you. . . .
> For the pillars of the temple stand apart,
> And the oak tree and the cypress grow not in each other's shadow.[54]

Although Jung's studies of primitive psychology, analysis of his patients and his own dreams, and his appeals to common everyday experience lent support to his notion of the collective unconscious, the greatest confirmation came with his discovery of the abundant parallels in many schools of Eastern yoga. In Eastern thought the Sanskrit term *buddhitattva* suggests a pure collective or universal consciousness containing within it all the individual minds. Although the *buddhitattva* notion is not completely parallel to Jung's collective unconscious, and although the exact understanding of *buddhitattva* varies considerably from one school of Eastern thought to the next, Jung found in it much that was sympathetic to his point of view. The similarity is easily seen in the *Bṛhadāranyaka Upaniṣad* where the universal Brahman divides and subdivides until all the various gods, goddesses and beings are but individualized expressions of the One.[55] It was of course upon this insight that the Indian philosopher Śaṅkara built his Advaita Vedānta (non-dualist) philosophy. The parallel was also evident to Jung in his study of Buddhist texts such as the *Amitāyur-dhyāna Sūtra*. In the symbolism of this text Jung found that the levels of ego-consciousness and the personal unconscious were traversed until the background consciousness of the universal Amitābha land appeared with ever increasing intensity.[56] A recent Buddhist scholar, Ryukyo Fujimoto, points out that Jung's interpretation of this text is compatible with the more technical Yogācāra notion of *Ālaya*—conceived of as a storehouse or repository consciousness in which all individual experience is grounded.[57] Commenting on *The Tibetan Book of the Great Liberation,* Jung notes that it conceives of the *buddhitattva* as a Universal Mind which is *arupaloka* (without form). Yet it is the creative source of all forms. Similarly the collective unconscious is to be conceived as "the matrix mind," the birthplace of all thought forms.[58]

To justify his calling it the "collective" unconscious, Jung points out that, "unlike the personal unconscious and its purely personal contents, the images in the deeper unconscious have a distinctly mythological character." [59] Jung's study of both Hindu and Buddhist myths conformed to what he had previously observed in his study of primitive peoples—namely, that the human psyche possesses a common substratum containing, in seed-form, the myths and legends of all peoples regardless of differences in culture or personal experience.[60] In a letter dated January 1932, Jung underlines this same theme by describing how Eastern yoga had gotten into his way of looking at things.

> The intrusion of the East is rather a psychological fact with a long history behind it. The first signs may be found in Meister Eckhart, Leibniz, Kant, Hegel, Schopenhauer, and E. von Hartmann. It is not, however, the actual East we are dealing with but the collective unconscious, which is omnipresent. You have seen very rightly that I have landed in the Eastern sphere, so to speak through the water of this unconscious; for the truths of the unconscious can never be thought up, they can be reached only by following a path which all previous cultures right down to the most primitive level have called the way of initiation.[61]

Jung was aware that the idea of a collective unconscious containing in seed-form the universal images of mankind was very foreign to the Western mind—at least to the modern West where each person is thoroughly conditioned to think of his unconscious as his own.[62] Jung, therefore, found great encouragement in the discovery that in Eastern yoga the basic psychological processes of the *buddhitattva*—the *saṁskāra*—were a clear parallel to the seed-forms or archetypes which he saw as composing the collective unconscious.[63] In yoga these seed-forms of thought and behavior are technically termed *saṁskāras. Saṁskāra* is perhaps best described as a memory trace that has the dynamic quality of a seed constantly ready to sprout. In much Eastern thought, especially Buddhist yoga, the existence of such a *saṁskāra* does not depend on an external metaphysical entity, such as a creator-god to cause or support its appearance. The *saṁskāra* is simply the result of the habitual repetition of a common thought or behavior pattern until it becomes deeply rooted in the psyche. While to the West this may be seen as result of heredity, Eastern yoga interprets this as evidence for reincarnation. Jung's assessment of *The Tibetan Book of the Dead* was that it is nothing more than the sum total of the *saṁskāras* or archetypal contents of the collective unconscious. The purpose for which this book was written by the Tibetan lamas was to teach that behind these *saṁskāras* lie no physical or metaphysical realities, rather the *saṁskāras* are simply the outcome of human psychic history and so should be regarded as such. The significance of this Eastern teaching was clear: "The world of gods and spirits is truly 'nothing but' the collective unconscious inside me." [64] This is an interpretation that frequently reappears in Jung's analysis of religious experience and occult phenomena.

Yet another aspect of the collective unconscious which developed under a strong influence from Eastern thought was Jung's notion of synchronicity. In Jung's early discussion of the Hindu concept of *ṛta,* he had already hinted towards some kind of principle or path by which the libido or psychic energy of the unconscious would be controlled according to a predetermined cosmic pattern.[65] The term synchronicity is first used to describe this idea in Jung's memorial address for Richard Wilhelm in May 1930.[66] It is based on the Chinese text the *I Ching* which Wilhelm had translated and introduced to Jung. To begin with, Jung points out that the *I Ching* is not dependent on the causal thinking which is so fundamental to modern Western science. Rather, it stresses the acausal simultaneity of events. Jung says, "My researches into the psychology of unconscious processes long ago compelled me to look around for another principle of explanation, since the causality principle seemed to me insufficient to explain certain remarkable manifestations of the unconscious." [67] Working under the impetus of his personal experiences with the *I Ching*,[68] Jung became convinced that there are psychic parallelisms in the collective unconscious which cannot be related to each other casually. Their connection seemed to lie in the relative simultaneity of events, hence Jung's choice of the term synchronicity. Although it is a most difficult concept to capture in words—modern Western words, at least—Jung attempts to define synchronicity as follows: "It seems as though time, far from being an abstraction, is a concrete continuum which possesses qualities or basic conditions capable of manifesting themselves simultaneously in different places by means of an acausal parallelism, such as we find, for instance, in the simultaneous occurrence of identical thoughts, symbols, or psychic states." [69] Jung felt that astrology could be an example of synchronicity on a cosmic scale, and his attempt to test this hypothesis is reported in Chapter Two of his 1952 book entitled *Synchronicity: An Acausal Connecting Principle.*[70] Astrology, it should be remembered, was also highly regarded in the Indian, Tibetan, and Chinese cultures.

In his Foreword to the 1950 English edition of Wilhelm's German translation of the *I Ching,* Jung refers to a causal connection as merely a statistical truth and therefore not absolute—it is a working hypothesis as to how events evolve out of one another. By contrast, says Jung, "synchronicity takes the coincidence of events in space and time as meaning something more than mere chance, namely a peculiar interdependence of objective events among themselves as well as with the subjective (psychic) states of the observer or observers." [71] This ancient Chinese way of viewing the cosmos, in which the pattern formed by the coins or bundle of yarrow-stalks forms a pattern (or microcosm) characteristic of a particular moment in time, struck Jung as being comparable to the approach of the modern physicist, who also creates a miniature theoretical model of the whole. It is of interest to note here that in a letter dated February 1953, Jung states that it was a very early (c. 1912) lecture given by the Western physicist, Albert Einstein, which first started him thinking about the possible relativity of time and space and their psychic conditionality.[72] But although Einstein may have started the process, the notion of synchronicity did not seem to crystallize for Jung until his encounter with Eastern yoga.

With the quality of synchronicity added to Jung's notion of the collective unconscious, it is evident that the breadth and complexity of the lowest levels of Jung's "psychic house" have begun seriously to strain the ability of discursive words to convey the concept. Here again Jung's situation finds its Eastern parallel and support. Just as the yogi maintains that the *buddhitattva* can only be known through one's personal experience of it, so also Jung would say the collective unconscious must be individuated to be understood.

IV. *Hun* and *Animus, P'o* and *Anima*

Yet another aspect of the collective unconscious in Jung's thinking is what he calls the "soul-image." In Jung's writing, *anima* is the technical term used to refer to the "soul-image" or feminine component in a man, and *animus* refers to the "soul-image" or masculine component in a woman.[73] These two concepts follow Jung's representation of psychic functioning between the conscious and unconscious levels of the psyche in terms of complementary pairs of opposites. Eastern thought, of course, displays a strong tendency to think of the totality of psychic experience in terms of complementing and yet opposing pairs of opposites. In Hindu thought, for example, there is the representation of Brahman as an opposing pair of god and goddess, namely, *Siva-Sákti.* But what influenced Jung even more strongly were the Taoist opposites of *yang* and *yin.* In everything both *yang* and *yin* will always be present. Therefore, although a man is predominately *yang,* he will have a complementary or balancing *yin* aspect in his unconscious psyche. Chinese yoga calls the *yin* or feminine aspect of a male unconscious *p'o,* and the *yang* or masculine aspect of a female unconscious *hun.*[74] In his Commentary on *The Secret of the Golden Flower,* Jung finds that "*hun* means 'cloud-spirit,' a higher breath-soul belonging to the *yang* principle and therefore masculine." [75] Jung argues that although Wilhelm's use of *animus* as a translation for *hun* is acceptable, it is really better to think of the *hun* as *logos* because of its function of rising upward at death to become divine spirit. As *animus,* the *hun* or creative spirit is in the unconscious of the feminine psyche and expresses itself as a kind of inferior *logos* characterized by poor judgments and prejudiced opinion.[76]

The Chinese characters *p'o* stand for "white-spirit" which is of course the opposite of the "cloud spirit." The "white-spirit" is the earthbound, bodily aspect of the unconscious belonging to the *yin* principle. It is characterized by affect or sensuous emotion and at death it sinks downward and becomes a ghost. When in the unconscious psyche of a man *p'o,* as *anima,* represents inferior emotion or unstable feeling.[77] In the cases of both the *animus* and the *anima,* Jung sees them as manifesting in the unconscious all those human qualities which the conscious attitude lacks.[78]

When a person is unaware of the inner existence of the *animus/anima,* the latter can function as an autonomous part of the personality manifesting all the characteristics of the collective unconscious. But, says Jung, if by means of yoga (for the Easterner) or analysis (for the Westerner), the conscious ego has been successfully separated from the unconscious, the *anima/animus* will gradually cease to act as an autonomous personality and will become a function of the relationship between the conscious and the unconscious.[79] With the loss of its unconscious, autonomous character, the *anima/animus* ceases its distorting and disturbing influences and, resuming its rightful archetypal role, functions to the advantage of the individual. This beneficial psychic functioning is described by Jung in terms of markedly Eastern images.

> Interposed between the ego and the world, it acts like an ever-changing Shakti, who weaves the veil of Maya and dances the illusion of existence. But, functioning between the ego and the unconscious, the anima becomes the matrix of all the divine and semi-divine figures, from the pagan goddess to the Virgin, from the messenger of the Holy Grail to the saint.[80]

In his autobiography Jung has left a very vivid account of how the *anima* (or *animus* in the case of a woman) can function in both negative and positive ways.[81] In many ways this description reminds one of the two-sided function of *citta* in Patañjali's *Yoga Sūtras.* In her[82] negative aspect, *citta* deludes one by "dancing the illusion of existence," [83] as Jung poetically puts it in the above quotation. *Citta,* for example, in the attitude of *avidyā* or ignorance leads one to wrongly identify with the blind urges of the unconscious and so be led astray.[84] However, in her positive function, *citta,* like Jung's *anima,* reveals knowledge of one's true self. For the *Yoga Sūtras* the process involves the clear *(sattvic)* perception of *puruṣa* as the true self,[85] whereas, for Jung, it is simply a clear communication of the images of the unconscious to the conscious mind.

V. *Guru* and "Thought-Beings"

Jung's conception of the positive function of the *anima/animus* as a mediator of the unconscious to the conscious is in some sense similar to the traditional Eastern role of the *guru.* The *guru* functions not to feed in otherwise unknown external knowledge, but to help the devotee discover the knowledge that is already present within. To begin with one may be so caught up in the deluding actions of the unconscious (the negative function of the *anima/animus*) that the *guru* must first start by helping the student to see the deluding process for what it is. Thus in the Upaniṣads the approach adopted by the *ṛsis* to their students is often what the West calls the *via negativa*—the systematic negating of the wrong or deluded perceptions until the positive perceptions, which have been there all the time, are given the opportunity to arise. The technical designation for this technique in Indian thought is *neti, neti* (not this, not that)—the Upaniṣadic words the *guru* uses to reject the student's deluded perception as to the nature of his true self.[86] What is particularly negated is the fixation on sensory perception of the external world or the rational knowledge of discursive thought. By negating both of these, the *guru* leads the student to discover his intuitive processes and the inner self-knowledge which such intuition makes available. Then, of course, all the rigor of the sharpest empirical perception and rational analysis is used to test the new intuitive perception. The *guru's* function therefore is to use his intuitive, perceptual, and rational powers to help the student test his newly won insights, and to ensure that the ever-present danger of the deluding power of unconscious urges (negative *kleśas*) does not reassert itself. Eventually the time arrives when the student has sufficiently purged himself of the "twisting" and deluding forces within his own unconscious so that the assistance of a *guru* is no longer needed. Having mastered his own unconscious, he is then capable of helping others come to grips with theirs. Here one is reminded of the statement Jung makes later in his life, that he no longer has conversations with the *anima* because he has learned to accept the contents of the unconscious and to understand them. Freed from distorting emotions he no longer needs a mediator to help him communicate with the images of his unconscious.[87] Such is the psychological integration that the *guru* must have achieved if he is to help and not hinder. And, in Western terms, such is the psychological state a psychotherapist or teacher should have achieved before practicing his profession.

Jung was strongly attracted by the Indian *guru*-student relationship and the tradition of personal teaching. His letter to an American student is most revealing.

> In India since ancient times they have the custom that practically everybody of a certain education, at least, has a *guru*, a spiritual leader who teaches you and you alone what you ought to know. Not everybody needs to know the same thing and this kind of knowledge can never be taught in the same way. That is a thing which is utterly lacking in our universities: the relation of master and disciple. . . .
> Anybody whose calling it is to guide souls should have his own soul guided first, so that he knows what it means to deal with the human soul. Knowing your own darkness is the best method for dealing with the darkness of other people.[88]

As to psychological processes at work in such a relationship, Jung technically termed it "transference." "Always the more unconscious person gets spiritually fecundated by the more conscious one. Hence the *guru* in India." [89] In agreement with the traditional Eastern view, Jung felt that the optimum time for this spiritual development to take place was in the second half of one's life.[90] Joseph Henderson observes that later in life the dream images of the hero myth, with its drive for power, is replaced by the archetype of initiation. "Symbolically the ego, as hero-figure, dies and is replaced by the adept who becomes the model for the individuating person." [91] In the second half of life the *guru* replaces the external goals of material goods and personal power and becomes both the model for and the means to individuation or, as Eastern yoga calls it, self-realization.

Although Jung concluded that modern Westerners were in great need of such models and guides in their struggle towards individuation. Jung cautioned against the uncritical adoption of Eastern *gurus.* In the first place the complete unquestioning commitment and devotion required by the yogi or Zen master is virtually impossible for the Westerner. Only one born into and nurtured in the ways of the oriental spirit would have such respect for the "greater personality" as to place himself completely and without reservation in the hands of a superior Master. Even if one could bring himself to that point of complete personal surrender, Jung is not sure that it should be done, for who in the West would dare to take upon himself the responsibility of receiving such a complete surrender—except a man who was little to be trusted, one who, maybe for pathological reasons, has too much to say for himself.[92] And again there is the difficulty of the Western man's "softness," his inability to make the hard sacrifice that tasks set by the *guru* will demand. Yet in spite of all these obstacles the need of the Westerner for a model and guide towards the goal of individuation remains, and Jung felt that this role of the *guru* was one that modern psychotherapy should fill for the West.[93]

Even though Jung often evidenced a certain skepticism toward Eastern *gurus,*[94] one aspect of the *guru* tradition which he warmly embraced was the notion of "spirit *gurus,*" or as Jung called them, "thought beings." [95] Just as Western man is ready and willing to give his whole being in surrender to an external spiritual model, namely, Christ, so Eastern man readily surrenders to a *guru* which may appear entirely in the realm of thought or inner psychic experience. In his autobiography Jung reports meeting a highly educated elderly Indian who claimed to have the medieval Indian philosopher, Sankaracharya as his spirit *guru.* Jung says that this information was both illuminating and reassuring.[96] Reassuring in that Jung had had his own personal experience of a spirit guide in the form of Philemon. The Eastern parallel confirmed that this experience with Philemon was not an otherworldly fantasy, but part of reality. It was also illuminating in that it led Jung to the insight that, psychologically speaking, all meditational experiences of personified forms of God are "thought beings" placed before man by his own mind in order to aid the process of individuation or spiritual development. Nor does this make such "thought beings" any less real. Just as Eastern man, through his identity with *Ātman,* the world creator, can create thought beings of definite reality, so also Western man has the Holy Spirit within him, the *imago dei,* and therefore also has a certain ability to place thought beings before himself.[97] In Jung's view ikons and crucifixion or cross images in Western churches are the external symbols of such thought beings. In the East, says Jung, such images are called *maṇḍalas* and are used as psychic tools *(yantras)* to help in man's spiritual realization.[98]

VI. *Maṇḍala* and Circumambulation

Maṇḍala is a Sanskrit word meaning circle. In terms of Eastern yoga, a *maṇḍala* is a circular image which is drawn, painted, danced, or enacted for the purpose of assisting meditation or concentration. Frequently the inner design of the circular *maṇḍala* makes use of the number four ("quaternity" as Jung calls it) in the form of a square, a star, an octagon, etc. Meditation on the *maṇḍala* seems to help overcome the tension produced when a personality experiences psychic disorder due to an imbalance between the pairs of opposites, between the conscious and unconscious processes. The circular form of the *maṇḍala* and its focus on a central point aids in the ordering and integrating of otherwise disordered elements of the psyche. Jung concludes, "This is evidently an *attempt at self-healing* on the part of Nature, which does not spring from conscious reflection, but from an instinctive impulse." [99] Jung supports this contention with the evidence of his own drawings during his years (1918–1920) of psychological disturbance,[100] the developmental sequences of *maṇḍala* drawings by his patients[101], primitive art, Eastern religions, and finally Western medieval alchemy.[102] Although in his later years it was the study of Western alchemy that commanded Jung's attention, his basic understanding as to how to interpret *maṇḍalas* was first gained from Eastern yoga.[103] From his study of the East, and in particular of Taoist yoga, Jung came to understand that the drawing, dancing, or enacting of *maṇḍalas*

> . . . are nothing but projections of psychic events, which then exert a counter-influence on the psyche and put a kind of spell upon the personality. Through ritual action, attention and interest are led back to the inner sacred precinct, which is the source and goal of the psyche and contains the unity of life and consciousness.[104]

On the basis of his Eastern studies, Jung came to understand the *maṇḍala* to be a uniting symbol[105] or an archetype of wholeness.[106] As an archetype of wholeness the *maṇḍala* symbolizes Jung's notion of the self. The function or goal of the *maṇḍala* is to unite states of psychic dissociation so that the focal point of the personality is shifted from the conscious ego to the self. Unlike the ego, the self has for its point of reference not just the conscious ego but the totality of the psyche. Thus, with the self as the focus, both the conscious and the unconscious are brought into harmony and balance. The finished *maṇḍala* depicts just such a psychic state, and in its making (drawing, dancing, enacting) the process of healing or integration is revealed. Jung's favorite word for describing the nature of this healing process is "circumambulation." It is a term which first seems to appear in Jung's Commentary on *The Secret of the Golden Flower,* where he defines it as a "psychological circulation" or "movement in a circle around oneself" so that all sides of the personality become involved.[107] It is nothing less than self-knowledge by means of self-brooding or *tapas.* As in the Taoist *wu-wei,* it is a state in which everything peripheral is subordinated to the command of the center.[108] In less abstract terms Jung recounts the process of circumambulation as he personally experienced it.[109] During his turbulent years he had taken to drawing *maṇḍalas,* a great many of them. While engaged in drawing them Jung found himself repeatedly questioning what he was doing. Why this wasting of time on childish drawings rather than getting on with his unfinished book on "Myths and Symbols"? One of the first insights Jung reports was that he could no longer presume to choose his own goal—it was necessary that he abandon the idea of the superior position of the conscious ego and instead simply "let himself go." However the *maṇḍalas* he was drawing increasingly began to reveal to him that all the paths he had been following were leading back to a single point—the self, the center of the *maṇḍala.*

> There is no linear evolution; there is only a circumambulation of the self. Uniform development exists, at most, only at the beginning; later, everything points toward the center. This insight gave me stability, and gradually my inner peace returned. I knew that in finding the *maṇḍala* as an expression of the self I had attained what was for me the ultimate.[110]

For Jung, the fact that he was able to find the same *maṇḍala* circumambulation process at work in the spontaneous drawings of his patients—many of whom were completely unacquainted with the East—provided strong evidence that there is a fundamental drive towards order and self-healing in terms of a balancing of conflicting tendencies and events at the focal point of the psychic center, that is, the self. Since this drive towards wholeness can be observed in independently produced *maṇḍalas* found in all parts of the world and therefore cannot be attributed to a particular culture or tradition, Jung concluded that it must be "a transconscious disposition in every individual which is able to produce the same or very similar symbols at all times and in all places."[111] Since this process is centered, to begin with at least, in the unconscious, and is common to all, Jung postulated the existence of a self archetype in the collective unconscious as its cause.

Although it was yoga that introduced him to the secrets of the *maṇḍala* and its process of circumambulation, Jung never became a slavish imitator of Eastern technique. While it is undoubtedly true that his study of Eastern *maṇḍala* symbolism and ritual had an important influence in the formulation of his concepts of individuation and the self, Jung's own psychological interpretations are uniquely his own. His way of incorporating

Eastern influence is perhaps best captured in the advice he gave to his pupils: "Learn as much as you can about symbolism; then forget it all when you are analyzing a dream." [112]

VII. *Ātman* and the Self

Joseph Henderson points out that although Jung's initial definition of the self comes from his empirical study of the unconscious, it acknowledged his debt to Indian thought.[113] In his *Psychological Types* Jung speaks of the self as a primordial image having the configuration of ideas found in the *Ātman-Brahman* teachings of the *Upaniṣads.*[114] This Indian concept, says Jung, teaches liberation from the opposites by the withdrawal of libido from all external objects and internal ideas through the practice of yoga, until a state of complete detachment from all psychic contents is achieved. "As a result of the complete detachment of all affective ties to the object, there is necessarily formed in the inner self an equivalent of objective reality, or a complete identity of inside and outside, which is technically described as *tat tvam asi* (that thou art)." [115] Perhaps the meaning of Jung's sentence is more clearly conveyed in the *Upaniṣads* themselves. The state reached after cancelling out of attachment to the objects or contents of the various pairs of opposites is conveyed poetically in the *Īśa Upaniṣad.*

> [The *Ātman*] is unmoving, one, swifter than the mind. The senses do not reach It as It is ever ahead of them. Though Itself standing still It outstrips those who run. In It the all pervading air supports the activities of beings.
> It moves and It moves not; It is far and It is near; It is within all this and It is also outside all this.[116]

The *Ātman,* in this context, is described in poetic metaphors as the absolute which transcends and yet at the same time incorporates within itself all the paradoxes—the pairs of opposites of ordinary experience. The uniting aspect of *Ātman,* the *tat tvam asi* aspect, which enables one to identify external and internal experiences within a larger whole, is conveyed in a second passage, this time from the *Chāndogya Upaniṣad.* It is a conversation between father, the *guru,* and son, the student:

> 'Bring hither a fig from there.'
> 'Here it is, sir.'
> 'Divide it.'
> 'It is divided, sir.'
> 'What do you see there?'
> 'These rather fine seeds, sir.'
> 'Of these, please divide one.'
> 'It is divided, sir.'
> 'What do you see there?'
> 'Nothing at all, sir.'
> Then he said to him: 'Verily, my dear, that finest essence which you do not perceive—verily, my dear, from that finest essence this great Nyagrodha [sacred fig] tree thus arises.'
> 'Believe me, my dear,' said he, 'that which is the finest essence—this whole world has that as its self. That is reality. That is *Ātman* [self]. That thou art *[tat tvam asi]*. . . .'[117]

The traditional Hindu interpretation of this teaching by the Upaniṣadic *guru* runs as follows. That *Brahman* (Divine Spirit) which you see manifested in the external world all around you is the same spirit that you think of as your true self within *(Ātman).* Although a person in ignorance *(avidyā)* at first takes one's true inner self to be the conscious ego, the deeper insight induced by the Upaniṣadic teaching is that one's true self is not the self-conscious ego at all. Instead, it is much larger, so much larger that it cannot really be described or defined but only pointed to in metaphors. At the moment of highest insight, the true inner self, that *Ātman,* is seen to be identical with the life essence of all the external universe *(Brahman).* It is this uniting of the internal and external in the *Ātman-Brahman* symbol that becomes a model for Jung's concept of the self.

In explaining his concept of self, Jung points to the Upaniṣadic teaching that it is not the individual ego which speaks, thinks, and acts, but rather the universal *Brahman,* which speaks through the individual and so uses the individual as a means of expression. The Divine, the Absolute Spirit, says Jung, speaks through me.

> Not through me alone, but through all; for it is not only the individual *Ātman* but *Ātman-Purusha (Ātman Brahman),* the universal *Ātman,* the pneuma, who breathes through all. We use the word "self" for this, contrasting it with the little ego. From what I have said it will be clear that this self is not just a rather more conscious or intensified ego, as the words "self-conscious," "self-satisfied," etc. might lead one to suppose. What is meant by the self is not only in me but in all beings, like the *Ātman,* like *Tao.* It is psychic totality.[118]

Jung sees that the above formulation of the self, based as it is on Hindu religion with its stress on immanence, opens him to the theological criticism of having created an "immanent God" or a "God-substitute." His response is that this self, though it could be a vessel for divine grace, need not take the place of God.[119] Jung also anticipates the criticism that this self is merely a philosophical speculation and therefore has no status in reality. In answer, Jung admits that his notion of the self is only a working hypothesis; nevertheless, it is a hypothesis which is grounded in a study of empirical symbols such as the *maṇḍalas.*[120] As Jung puts it in *Mysterium Coniunctionis,* "The *maṇḍala* symbolizes, by its central point, the ultimate unity of all archetypes as well as of the multiplicity of the phenomenal world, and is therefore the empirical equivalent of the metaphysical concept of a *unus mundus* (the Self)." [121] Jung also admits that although following Eastern yoga he defines the self as the totality of the conscious and unconscious psyche, this totality is not completely open to empirical examination. It is open to empirical survey only in those of its parts which are contents of consciousness. It is Jung's view (one with which yoga may be found to disagree) that it is impossible for us to expand the conscious aspect of an individual psyche to include the whole of the unconscious, and consequently the limits of the self would always remain open and, to a large extent, unknown.[122] Thus the complexity of Jung's concept. The self is at once ego-aware and unconscious, individual and collective. The self is not only the center of the psyche but the self is also its circumference which includes consciousness and unconsciousness. "It is the center of this totality like the ego is the center of consciousness." [123]

In answer to the question as to why Jung found it necessary to formulate his notion of the self on Eastern rather than on his own European ground, Henderson makes the following observation. Jung was aware that already in medieval literature something close to his formulation of the self existed—as, for example, in St. Bonaventure's saying, "God is an intelligible sphere whose center is everywhere and the circumference nowhere. . . ." [124] Why then did Jung not stay within his own culture and use literature such as the Western medieval study of the image of God in man as his basis? Henderson argues that Jung answers this question and shows why he found the Eastern concepts preferable in a passage from *Psychological Types:*

> The relativity of God in medieval mysticism is a regression to a primitive condition. In contrast, the related Eastern conceptions of the *Ātman* are not so much a regression to the primitive as a continuous development out of the typically Eastern way that still manages to preserve the efficacy of the primitive principle. . . . This reversion to the primitive. . . . or, as in India, the uninterrupted connection with it, keeps man in touch with Mother Earth, the prime source of all power. Seen from the heights of a differentiated point of view, whether rational or ethical, these instinctive forces are "impure." But life itself flows from springs both clear and muddy. Hence all excessive "purity lacks vitality. . . ." Every renewal of life needs the muddy as well as the clear.[125]

Notes and References

1. C.G. Jung, "Richard Wilhelm: In Memoriam," *C.W.* 15, pp. 53–62.
2. Ibid., p. 55.

3. Ibid., p. 58.
4. "On The Tibetan Book of the Dead," *C.W.* 11, p. 515.
5. "On The Secret of the Golden Flower," *C.W.* 13, pp. 11–12.
6. See, for example, the conception of *citta* presented in Patañjali's *Yoga Sūtras,* (note 1, chapter 1, p. 000). See also E.T.H. Lectures, (note 3, chapter 1, p. 000), p. 118.
7. "On the Secret of the Golden Flower," *C.W.* 13, p. 51.
8. *Memories, Dreams, Reflections,* op. cit., Cp. VI.
9. *Psychological Types, C.W.* 6, p. 463.
10. Jung includes within the psyche "personality or soul," "persona," and "anima" as functional complexes "Psychological Types," *C.W.* 6; pp. 463–470); whereas in yoga, *prakṛti* as *citta* evolves into *buddhi, ahaṁkāra, manas, jñānendriya, karmendriya, tan-mātra,* etc. (See *Sāṅkhya Kārikā of Iśvara Krishṇa,* trans. by J. Davies [Calcutta: Susil Gupta, 2nd ed., 1947]).
11. *Memories, Dreams, Reflections,* op. cit., p. 167.
12. C.G. Jung, 'The Concept of Libido,' in "Symbols of Transformation," *C.W.* 5, p. 139.
13. Ibid., p. 141.
14. Ibid., pp. 121–131; 147–152 & 160–170.
15. Ibid., p. 131.
16. See E.T.H. Lectures IV to VII, Summer Semester 1939, op. cit. Although Jung's interpretation of the *Yoga Sūtra* text is generally faithful, one mistake which he makes is to equate *citta* with conscious awareness only (p. 140). As I have pointed out, Pantañjali defines *citta* as including both the conscious and the unconscious levels—in other words the total of what Jung calls the psyche. Of course there are variations within Indian thought itself. Śaṅkara, for example, in his Advaita Vedānta reinterpretation of Patañjali's Yoga restricts *citta* to the unconscious level only.
17. *Yoga Sūtras,* op. cit., II: 18 *bhāṣya.*
18. E.T.H. Lectures, op. cit., p. 144.
19. "Psychological Types," *C.W.* 6, pp. 199–201.
20. Ibid., p. 201.
21. Ibid., p. 202.
22. Ibid.
23. *Yoga Sūtras,* op. cit., II:2.
24. C.G. Jung, "Psychological Commentary on Kundalini Yoga," in *Spring,* 1975, p. 2.
25. *Yoga Sūtras,* op. cit., II:3.
26. "Psychological Commentary on Kundalini Yoga," op. cit., p. 2.
27. "Psychological Types," *C.W.* 6, pp. 202–204.
28. Jung adopted this term from the anthropologist Lucien Lévy-Brühl. See "Psychological Types," *C.W.* 6, pp. 10, 82, 131, 417n, & 418n.
29. *Yoga Sūtras,* op. cit., II:1, *bhāṣya.*
30. "Psychological Types," *C.W.* 6, p. 118.
31. Ibid., p. 202.
32. "Symbols of Transformation," *C.W.* 5, p. 380.

33. See the various kinds of *samprajñata samādhi*, yoga focused on an object or image, in *Yoga Sūtras* I: 43–47. In Patañjali's system this is contrasted with the more advanced yogic achievement of objectless or *asamprajñata samādhi* described in *Yoga Sūtras* I: 50–51. Evidently Jung rejects this latter category of *samādhi* as a figment of the overly intuitive nature of the Indian mind.
34. C.G. Jung, 'The Relations Between the Ego and the Unconscious,' in "Two Essays in Analytical Psychology," *C.W.* 7, pp. 219–221.
35. Ibid., p. 220.
36. C.G. Jung, *Analytical Psychology: Its Theory and Practice* (New York: Random House, 1968), pp. 190–192.
37. Ibid., p. 191.
38. See, for example, "On The Secret of the Golden Flower," *C.W.* 13, pp. 16–17.
39. Ibid.
40. Ibid.
41. Ibid., see section titled "Phenomena of the Way," p. 29f.
42. "Approaching the Unconscious," in *Man and His Symbols*, edited by Carl Jung. (N.Y.: Dell Pub. Co., 1976), pp. 24–25.
43. *Memories, Dreams, Reflections*, pp. 158–163.
44. Ibid., pp. 158–159.
45. Ibid., p. 160.
46. Ibid.
47. Ibid., pp. 162–169.
48. *Approaching the Unconscious*, op. cit., p. 40.
49. *Analytical Psychology: Its Theory and Practice*, op. cit., p. 41.
50. Ibid., p. 44.
51. Jung cites Lévy-Brühl very frequently. See, for example: "Symbols of Transformation," *C.W.* 5, pp. 141 & 327; *Analytical Psychology*, op. cit., p. 46; and *Approaching the Unconscious*, op. cit., pp. 6–7.
52. *Analytical Psychology: Its Theory and Practice*, op. cit., p. 46.
53. *Commentary on Kundalini Yoga*, op. cit., p. 3.
54. Kahil Gibran, *The Prophet* (New York: Alfred A. Knopf, 1958), pp. 15–16.
55. *The Thirteen Principal Upaniṣads*, trans. by R.E. Hume (London: Oxford University Press, 1931); *Bṛhadāranyaka Upaniṣad* 1.4, "The Creation of the Manifold World from the Unitary Soul," pp. 81–86.
56. "The Psychology of Eastern Meditation," *C.W.* 11, pp. 572–573.
57. Ryukyo Fujimoto, *An Outline of the Triple Sutra of Shin Buddhism*, Vol. II (Kyoto: Hyyaka-en Press, 1960), p. 149.
58. "On The Tibetan Book of the Great Liberation," *C.W.* 11, p. 490.
59. "The Psychology of Eastern Meditation," *C.W.* 11, p. 573.
60. "On The Secret of the Golden Flower," *C.W.* 13, pp. 11–12.
61. *C.G. Jung: Letters*, op. cit., Vol. I, p. 87.
62. *Psychological Commentary on Kundalini Yoga*, op. cit., p. 20. In the same article Jung points out that notions such as archetype and collective unconscious were present in ancient Western thought. The term archetype itself Jung takes from St. Augustine who used it in a Platonic sense. (pp. 5–6).

63. Ibid., p. 8.
64. "On The Tibetan Book of the Dead," *C.W.* 11, p. 525.
65. "Psychological Types," *C.W.* 6, p. 212.
66. "Richard Wilhelm: In Memoriam," *C.W.* 15, pp. 55–56.
67. Ibid., p. 66.
68. Aniela Jaffé tells us that in the early twenties Jung experimented with the *I Ching* for a whole summer. Then some years later he had further personal experience of the *I Ching* under the guidance of Richard Wilhelm. *The Life and Work of C.G. Jung,* op. cit., pp. 25–28.
69. "Richard Wilhelm: In Memoriam," *C.W.* 15, p. 56.
70. "Synchronicity: An Acausal Connecting Principle," *C.W.* 8, pp. 459–484.
71. "Foreword to the 'I Ching'," *C.W.* 11, p. 592.
72. C.G. Jung: Letters, Vol. II, op. cit., p. 109.
73. "Psychological Types," *C.W.* 6, pp. 467–472.
74. "On The Secret of the Golden Flower," *C.W.* 13, pp. 38–39.
75. Ibid., p. 39.
76. Ibid., pp. 40–41.
77. Ibid.
78. "Psychological Types," *C.W.* 6, p. 468.
79. "Psychology of the Transference," *C.W.* 16, p. 293.
80. Ibid.
81. *Memories, Dreams, Reflections,* op. cit., pp. 186–188.
82. It is of interest to note that *citta,* as an evolute of *prakṛti,* is personified as feminine, just as is Jung's *anima* concept.
83. See *Yoga Sūtras,* op. cit., I:5 for an analysis of the *kliṣṭa* or deluded states of *citta.*
84. *Yoga Sūtras,* op. cit., II:5. *Avidyā* is also described in II:4 as the root cause of all the other *kleśas* or negative functions of *citta.*
85. *Yoga Sūtras,* op. cit., I:48–51. Of course the end goal of a self or *purusa* which is freed or released from all contact with *citta* is quite different from what Jung sees as the end result of the positive function of the *anima* or *animus.*
86. See, for example, the *guru's* teaching in the *Bṛhadāranyaka Upaniṣad* 4.5.15, op. cit.
87. *Memories, Dreams, Reflections,* op. cit., p. 188.
88. *C.G. Jung: Letters,* op. cit., Vol. I, p. 237.
89. Ibid., p. 172.
90. In the Indian tradition the stages of life include those of: student (seven or eight years of age until the time of marriage), householder (from point of marriage until children are settled with their own families), forest dweller (one withdraws from family and community life and studies with a *guru*), and finally the hermit or holy man (one no longer needs a *guru* but continues spiritual development on one's own, and acts as a teacher to others). A good description may be found in H. Zimmer's *Philosophies of India.* (Princeton: Princeton University Press, 1971), pp. 151–160.
91. Joseph L. Henderson, "The Self and Individuation," in *International Encyclopedia of Neurology, Psychiatry, Psychoanalysis, and Psychology,* ed. by J.B. Wheelwright, Vol. I, 1975, p. 116.

92. *"Forword to 'Introduction to Zen Buddhism',"* C.W. 11, p. 553.
93. Ibid., pp. 553–554.
94. This is shown in *The Holy Men of India* where Jung says that while in India he did not visit the *guru* Ramana, even though Heinrich Zimmer had urged him to do so, because "the fact is, I doubt his uniqueness; he is of a type which always was and will be . . . I saw him all over India." (*C.W.* 11, p. 577). The *guru* or holy man Jung does report meeting was one who was a devotee of the Maharshi Ramana, and had a modest, kindly, devout, and childlike spirit. (Ibid., p. 578). This "childlike" innocence seemed to be, for Jung, the essence of the Indian *guru,* and, when it came to the antics of the Zen master, Jung seems to have simply thought them to be incredible.
95. *E.T.H. Lectures,* op. cit., Winter 1939, pp. 106–107.
96. *Memories, Dreams, Reflections,* op. cit., p. 184.
97. *E.T.H. Lectures,* op. cit., Winter 1939, p. 107.
98. Ibid. See also "Concerning Mandala Symbolism," *C.W.* 9, pt. 1, pp. 383–384.
99. "Maṇḍalas," *C.W.* 9, pt. 1, "Appendix," p. 388.
100. *Memories, Dreams, Reflections,* op. cit., p. 196.
101. See "A Study in the Process of Individuation," *C.W.* 9, pt. 1, pp. 290–354; and "Concerning Maṇḍala Symbolism," *C.W.* 9, pt. 1, pp. 355–384.
102. See Volumes 12–14 of *C.W.*
103. *Memories, Dreams, Reflections,* op. cit., p. 204.
104. "On The Secret of the Golden Flower," *C.W.* 13, pp. 24–25.
105. "Psychology and Religion," *C.W.* 11, p. 79.
106. "Maṇḍalas," *C.W.* 9, pt. 1, "Appendix," p. 388.
107. "On The Secret of the Golden Flower," *C.W.* 13, p. 25.
108. Ibid., pp. 25–26.
109. *Memories, Dreams, Reflections,* op. cit., pp. 196–197.
110. Ibid.
111. "Concerning Maṇḍala Symbolism," *C.W.* 9, pt. 1, p. 384.
112. *Approaching the Unconscious,* op. cit., p. 42.
113. *The Self and Individuation,* op. cit., p. 110.
114. *Psychological Types, C.W.* 6, p. 118.
115. Ibid.
116. "Isa Upaniṣad" 4–5, as translated by S.Radhakrishnan, *The Principal Upaniṣads* (London: Allen & Unwin, 1953).
117. "Chāndogya Upaniṣad" 6.12.1–3, as translated by R.E. Hume, *The Thirteen Principal Upaniṣads,* op. cit.
118. "Good and Evil in Analytical Psychology," *C.W.* 10, p. 463.
119. Ibid.
120. "Psychological Types," *C.W.* 6, p. 461.
121. "Mysterium Coniunctionis," *C.W.* 14, p. 463.
122. "Individual Dream Symbolism in Relation to Alchemy," *C.W.* 12, pp. 172–174.
123. Ibid., p. 41.
124. *The Self and Individuation,* op. cit., p. 113.
125. "Psychological Types," *C.W.* 6, pp. 244–245.

III. Where Jung Draws the Line in His Acceptance of Yoga

In the formation of his psychological theory Carl Jung was for a time strongly influenced by the yoga psychology of the East—especially by Patañjali, the fourth century Indian systematizer of the Sāṅkhya-Yoga school of thought.[1] The period of influence was mainly in the 1920s, but by the end of the 1930s Jung's main attention turned back to Western thought.[2] This is especially evident if the cognitive aspects of his psychology (for example, the processes of memory, perception, thinking, etc.) are analyzed in relation to the corresponding concepts found in Patañjali's *Yoga Sūtras.* Such an analysis shows that at least one of the reasons Jung could not completely identify with Patañjali's yoga was the lack of distinction between philosophy and psychology that seems to typify much Eastern thought. In line with other modern Western thinkers Jung claimed to follow the scientific method of keeping a clear distinction between the description of cognitive processes and truth claims attesting to the objective reality of such cognitions. Any reductionistic collapsing of philosophy into psychology or *vice versa* is the cause of what Jung critically calls Eastern intuition over-reaching itself. For Jung, this 'over-reaching' of yoga is especially evident in the widespread Eastern notion that the individual ego can be completely transcended and some form of universal consciousness achieved.[3] In Jung's eyes, this was nothing more than the psychological projection of an idea which had no foundation in human experience.

Jung viewed the East as making such errors because it had not yet reached the high level of self-awareness achieved in the modern Western development of scientific thought. The Indian, says Jung, is still pre-Kantian. In India, therefore, "there is no psychology in our sense of the word. India is 'pre-psychological.'"[4] In a 1958 letter Jung wrote, "There is no psychology worthy of this name in East Asia, but instead a philosophy consisting entirely of what we would call psychology."[5] In Jung's view Eastern psychology was nothing more than a kind of scholastic description of psychic processes with no necessary connection to empirical facts. Because of this lack of empirical method, Eastern thought, said Jung, suffers "a curious detachment from the world of concrete particulars we call reality."[6] As evidence for this contention Jung reported that Easterners, while gifted in seeing things in their totality, had great difficulty in perceiving the whole in terms of its empirical parts. For example, of his conversation with the Chinese scholar Hu Shih, Jung said, ". . . it was as though I had asked him to bring me a blade of grass and each time he had dragged along a whole meadow for me. . . . Each time I had to extract the detail for him from an irreducible totality."[7] The East, said Jung, still views reality metaphysically in terms of the whole, and describes the whole in cognitive projections which often have little to do with the nominalistic concepts of the empiricist. In a 1955 letter to a theological student, Jung makes clear that whereas modern psychology (including Freud's psychoanalysis and Jung's own analytical psychology) has an empirical foundation, the older psychologies of the East and the medieval West are founded on metaphysical concepts which often have little relation to empirical facts. It is clear that Jung views his own work as scientific while that of the older psychologies is of a quite different order—"opinion rather than fact."[8]

As a champion of modern scientific psychology Jung was not unaware of its hazards. Because of its focus on the minutia of empirical evidence, modern psychology often lost sight of the larger whole. Emphasis upon the holistic or collective nature of the unconscious was seen by Jung as one of his major contributions in helping to restore the balance between the part and the whole in modern Western thought. Jung's main empirical evidence in this regard was the dreams and drawings produced by himself and his patients. He appealed to the Eastern stress on the wholeness or collective nature of reality as providing, not additional empirical evidence, but rather historical and literary parallels to his scientific discoveries.

It is evident in the above discussion that the underlying distinction which determines where Jung draws the line in his acceptance of Eastern thought comes from his holding firmly to modern Western scientific method.[9] The essential basis of the modern scientific approach is that it carefully avoids any reductionism between psychology and philosophy or any confusion between the two. One of the more recent general statements of the domain and method of modern psychology is offered by the philosopher Gilbert Ryle.[10] Ryle argues that psychology is that science which provides explanations for the kinds of behavior of which we can ordinarily give no explanation. Ryle offers the following examples: "I do not know why I was so tongue-tied in the presence of a certain acquaintance; why I dreamed a certain dream last night; why I suddenly saw in my mind's eye an uninteresting street corner of a town that I hardly know; why I chatter more rapidly after the air-raid siren is heard; or how I came to address a friend by the wrong Christian name." [11] In addition there are the cases of perceptual illusion such as why a straight line cutting through certain cross-hatchings looks bent, which we cannot explain from our own knowledge. Psychology has also devised its own particular methods for measuring both ordinary and unusual sorts of behavior. The hallmark of this method is that it is empirical in nature. Ryle effectively argues against "the false notion that psychology is the sole empirical study of people's mental powers, propensities, and performances, together with its implied false corollary that 'the mind' is what is properly describable only in the technical terms proprietary to psychological research." [12] To illustrate his argument Ryle offers the analogy that England cannot be described solely in seismological terms. With this contention Jung would agree. But Jung's additional plea is that the psychological enterprise must be carried on with the larger perspective of the other empirical disciplines in view. A complete knowledge of England requires geographical, historical, botanical, etc., along with the seismological enterprise. Empirical psychology must be aware of the scientific achievements of physiology, anthropology, physics, history, philosophy, religion, and so on. The difference between the East and the West is that although the East includes all of life in its domain of knowledge, it achieves this holistic view by an uncritical lumping together of all knowledge. This has had the result of confusion and reductionism between disciplines and, in Jung's view, is at least part of the reason for Eastern thought losing contact with reality and indulging in "cognitive projection" rather than empirical observation. Let us test out Jung's contention in this regard by comparing his analysis of memory, perception, and knowing with the descriptions found in the *Yoga Sūtras* of Patañjali.

I. Memory and the Unconscious

The unique aspect of Jung's view of memory is that it functions at the level of the unconscious as well as at the level of the conscious psyche. Indeed for Jung, real memory necessarily first resides in the collective unconscious in a subliminal form. Only after such psychic contents are raised or individuated beyond a certain threshold level of psychic energy is consciousness of the memory achieved. For Jung's psychology, memory along with other cognitive functions such as perception, intuition, imagination, thinking, and feeling all exist in subliminal form in the unconscious. The main difference between the occurrence of these functions in the unconscious as opposed to the conscious is that in the former they possess less psychic energy or intensity and thus remain below the threshold of awareness.[13]

The way we ordinarily think of memory—as, for example, when we memorize something for an examination—is called by Jung "an artificial acquisition consisting mostly of printed paper." [14] Here Jung is referring to our usual functioning at the level of consciousness only. At the conscious level if we are asked to learn something of our past we go to a history book and 'memorize' it. For Jung this is not real memory, but merely an artificial acquisition. Real memory involves raising to consciousness the ancestral traces or archetypes which are inherent in the collective unconscious of each human being. Real memory, then, is knowing our past from within rather than from books. Jung realized that the contents of the unconscious could be divided into two kinds. The first, the contents of the collective unconscious, Jung suggested, are composed of the psychic heritage or history passed on to us by our animal ancestors, primitive human ancestors, ethnic group, nation, tribe, and family.[15] Although these collective memories determine our psychic life to a high degree, Jung described them as being 'neutral' and becoming filled with content only when they come into contact with consciousness. As Gerhard Adler notes,

> In his later writings Jung expanded and developed the concept of the archetype considerably. He distinguished sharply between the irrepresentable, transcendental archetype *per se* and its visible manifestation in consciousness as the archetypal image or symbol. Moreover the archetype *per se* appears to be an *a priori* conditioning factor in the human psyche, comparable to the biological "pattern of behavior," "a 'disposition' which starts functioning at a given moment in the development of the human mind and arranges the material of consciousness into definite patterns." [16]

Jung admitted that direct evidence for these inherited memory complexes was not available, but he argued that psychic manifestations such as the complexes, images, and symbols that we encounter in dreams, fantasies, and visions are indirect empirical evidence.[17] The second kind of content found in the unconscious are past experiences of the individual's own lifetime that have been either forgotten or repressed. These Jung calls the memories of the personal unconscious.[18] Empirical evidence for their existence is demonstrated when they can be recalled during hypnosis or certain drug states and yet remain unknowable during ordinary consciousness. It is the making present of these two types of psychic contents from the unconscious that Jung views as real memory, as opposed to the artificial memory of something memorized from a book.

In Patañjali's *Yoga Sūtras,* memory and the unconscious are both accounted for in terms of *saṁskāra.* A *saṁskāra* is defined in *Yoga Sūtras* III:9 as follows. When a particular mental state *(citta vṛtti)* passes away into another, it does not totally disappear but is preserved within consciousness as a latent form or memory trace. Such *saṁskāras* are always tending to manifest themselves anew, and therefore are also referred to as *bija* or seed states. In yoga psychology the unconscious is nothing more than the stored up *saṁskāras* left behind as memory traces of past thoughts or actions. Like the forgotten or repressed contents of Jung's personal unconscious, some of the *saṁskāras* will be the memory traces of thoughts or actions undertaken during this lifetime. But where yoga differs from Jung is that the vast majority of the *saṁskāras* making up the unconscious come not from the collective history of mankind but rather from the individual history of that particular person's past lives. For yoga the vast majority of the *saṁskāras* stored in the unconscious are not the forgotten materials from this life but memory traces from the actions and thoughts in the innumerable past lives of the individual. Whereas Jung is willing to give sympathetic consideration to this notion of *saṁskāras* from the past if it is understood as a kind of collective psychic heredity, he usually rejects the idea of reincarnation of the individual soul (although late in his life, Jung appeared to change his mind and accept the idea of rebirth—See Chapter 5). In Jung's view, this is one of these cognitive projections which yoga has fallen into because it is not firmly grounded in the empirical approach of modern scientific psychology. As Jung puts it, "Neither our scientific knowledge nor our reason can keep step with this idea." [19] For Jung then "there is no inheritance of individual prenatal or pre-uterine memories, but there are undoubtedly inherited archetypes." [20] These archetypes are "the universal dispositions of the mind, and they are to be understood as analogous to Plato's forms *(eidola),* in accordance with which the mind organizes its contents." [21]

The other major difference between Jung and yoga has to do with their differing assessments as to the degree to which the memory (and unconscious) can be known. For the Easterner yogic meditation is a psychological process whereby the *saṁskāras* or memory traces of past actions or thoughts are purged from the 'storehouse' unconscious. As these memories of the past are brought up from the unconscious their contents momentarily pass through our conscious awareness. It is in this way, says yoga psychology, that we come to know all forgotten actions and thoughts from this life as well as all actions and thoughts composing our past lives. Thus the claim of the great yogis, such as Gautama Buddha, that through intense meditation all *saṁskāras* are brought up to the level of awareness and exhaustive knowledge of one's past lives is achieved. This yogic accomplishment not only does away with memory, since everything is now present knowledge, but also with the unconscious since it was nothing but the sum total of the *saṁskāras* or memory traces of the past. A perfected yogi such as the Buddha, therefore, is said to be totally present—a mind uncluttered by the *saṁskāras* of an unconscious psyche. As the Zen master Eido Roshi put it, meditation is the removal of unnecessary mental defilements. Yoga is like a mental vacuum cleaner that removes from our minds all the *saṁskāras* collected during this and previous lives.[22] Patañjali defines yoga as the removal or destruction of all *saṁskāras* from previous lives until a completely clear and discriminating mind is achieved.[23] For Patañjali's yoga, *saṁskāras* or memory traces function as obstacles to true knowledge of reality and their removal by yogic meditation results in omniscience.[24]

Jung was well acquainted with these teachings of Patañjali. In his 1939 Summer Semester Lectures at the Eidgenössische Technische Hochschule, Zürich, Jung wrote his own commentary on the claims of the *Yoga Sūtras.*[25] Jung agreed that there were psychological techniques such as yoga that would enable us to get to know the unconscious and its memory contents. While he allowed that Patañjali's yogic meditation may be an appropriate technique for the Easterner, Jung argued that his process of active imagination was more suitable for the Westerner.[26] Jung's reasoning here was that a rigorously disciplined yogic practice such as Patañjali's would only aggravate the already chronic Western ailment—namely, overdevelopment of the will and the conscious control of the psyche. Jung felt that the better way for Western man to overcome his encapsulation within the conscious level and get to know the contents of the unconscious was through the process of fantasizing or active imagination—a technique which Jung had developed in his own psychological practice.[27]

Aside from this difference as to the best technique to use in getting to know and control the unconscious, Jung saw that the yoga viewpoint led to a complete dissolution of ego and individuality, and this he felt to be nothing more than fanciful speculation. Jung could agree that yoga, for the Easterner, or active imagination, for the Westerner, would help an individual to recover knowledge of thoughts or actions of this life which had been forgotten or repressed. He would also allow that the same technique could put one in touch with the archetypes or psychic heredity of the collective unconscious. But here Jung's cognitive theory diverges from Patañjali's yoga in three ways. The first difference is that, for Jung, one cannot usually speak in terms of individual *saṁskāras* of previous lives but only of collective predispositions (archetypes) passed on by a person's ancestors. A second difference is that whereas for yoga the *saṁskāras* are obstructions which must be removed for the achievement of knowledge, for Jung it is through the shaping of the materials of consciousness by the archetypal 'memories' that knowledge of reality results. For yoga, however, knowledge of reality is a given inherently present in the consciousness of each individual and requiring only the removal of obstructing and distorting memory traces *(saṁskāras)* for its full and complete revelation. In Jung's view, such a claim is one-sidely subjective. It does not take seriously the experiential fact that the subjective categories of the mind do not possess knowledge themselves, but merely shape external stimuli so that perceptual knowledge results. The one-sided yoga theory, therefore, is to be dismissed as unwarranted metaphysical speculation. In Jung's eyes this is one example of how yoga psychology is really mostly speculative philosophy[28] and lacks the critical rigor of modern Western psychology. The yoga claim that omniscience is realized once the obstructing *saṁskāras* are removed is, says Jung, a good example of the kind of error produced by such an uncritical approach.

A third difference arises directly from the different value given memory by the two approaches, and from the yoga claim that all *saṁskāras,* all memory, can be removed. Jung agrees with the yoga contention that ego or 'I-ness' results from the continuity of memory.[29] But Jung flatly rejects the yoga notion that since the ego-sense that memories produce is composed of nothing but obstructing *saṁskāras,* true knowledge requires that ego-sense be removed. In a 1939 letter to W.Y. Evans-Wentz, Jung speaks strongly against the notion of 'egoless knowing' prevalent in both Hindu and Buddhist yoga:

> No matter how far an *ekstasis* [religious ecstasy] goes or how far consciousness can be extended, there is still the continuity

> of the apperceiving ego which is essential to all forms of consciousness. . . . Thus it is absolutely impossible to know what I would experience when that "I" which could experience didn't exist any more. . . . You can expand your consciousness so that you even cover a field that had been unconscious to you before, but then it is your ego that is conscious of this new acquisition, and there is absolutely no reason to believe then that there is not a million times more unconscious material beyond that little bit of a new acquisition.[30]

Thus with regard to the yoga claims of realizing egolessness, Jung concludes that such a state is both a philosophical and a psychological impossibility. The yoga claim of omniscience must also be rejected, for there will always be more of the unconscious to be explored. "Agnosticism," says Jung, "is my duty as a scientist." [31]

II. Perception

The idea of an egoless state of consciousness has had a considerable influence on the yoga view of perception. Patañjali taught that on the removal of the ego producing and obstructing *saṁskāras,* a supernormal level of perception *(pratibhā)* is experienced.[32] *Pratibhā* or intuition is held to give noumenal knowledge of the object upon which the yogi is meditating. For yoga, the ordinary psychic state which is dominated by ego-consciousness, produces only everyday phenomenal knowledge of the object. For Patañjali, therefore, and for most Hindu and Buddhist schools of thought, there are two levels of perception.[33] On the lower level the ego and its *saṁskāras* so obstruct the perception that only a distorted view of the whole object is seen. According to Patañjali's analysis the distortion is caused when the perception of the object is mixed together in consciousness with the word which we use in language to name the object and the meaning or idea which this name evokes. It is the perception of the object itself which is the true perception. The perceptions of the word-label and word-meaning are legacies of convention or past usage and as such are distorting *saṁskāras.* Once these two distorting memories are purged from consciousness so that the direct experience of the object alone remains, *pratibhā* or the higher level of perception has been achieved.[34] The yoga description for *pratibhā* perception suggests a consciousness so purged of all filtering or distorting *saṁskāras* that the object shines in it as in a perfectly pure pane of glass. It is as if the cognizing consciousness becomes completely void of its own nature and takes on the nature of the object itself.[35] The object in all its aspects and qualities stands fully revealed as in a single flash.[36]

Jung's critique of this concept of *pratibhā* or higher perception is based upon his philosophic presupposition that it is impossible to have a knowing experience without the presence of a knower in consciousness. In the yoga example of consciousness taking on the nature of the object, Jung argues "There must always be somebody or something left over to experience the realization, to say, 'I know at-one-ment, I know there is no distinction.' "[37] It is simply impossible to completely dispense with the knowing ego.

> Even when I say "I know myself," an infinitesimal ego—the knowing "I"—is still distinct from "myself." In this as it were atomic ego, which is completely ignored by the essentially non-dualistic standpoint of the East, there nevertheless lies hidden the whole unabolished pluralistic universe and its unconquered reality.
> The experience of "at-one-ment" is one example of those "quick-knowing" realizations of the East, an intuition of what it would be like if one could exist and not exist at the same time.[38]

Jung's judgment as to what is really happening when the yogis think they are in a *pratibhā* state is found in his 1934 letter to the physicist Wolfgang Pauli. After suggesting that if you look long enough into a dark hole you perceive what is looking in, Jung argues that something like this is happening to the yogis. After looking at the object long enough (or at nothing as in many yogic practices), the yogi becomes aware of his own psyche. Yoga, says Jung, is simply a special technique for introspection.[39]

Jung's own analysis of perception also results in what seems to be a two-level theory. At the conscious level there are the sense perceptions of ordinary experience, and then there is what Jung calls the process of intuition which occurs mostly at the unconscious level. Whereas in yoga one goes from ordinary sense experience to the higher level of *pratibhā* or supersensuous perception, Jung starts with ordinary sense experience and then goes inward to the lower level of the unconscious.[40]

Ordinary sense perceptions, says Jung, are a result of the stimuli that stream into us from the outside world. We see, hear, taste, smell, and touch the world, and so are conscious of it. The bare sense perceptions simply tell us that something is, but not what it is. To know what something is, says Jung, involves the more complicated analysis and evaluation of the sense perception by the cognitive processes of thinking and feeling. This second order analysis of the bare sense perceptions Jung calls apperception.[41] For example, a noise which is heard on analysis strikes us as 'peculiar' (an evaluation supplied by the feeling function) and is also recognized as the noise air-bubbles make rising in the pipes of the heating system (an explanation provided by the thinking process).

Intuition is described by Jung as one of the basic functions of the psyche. He defines intuition as "perception of the possibilities inherent in a situation," [42] often described as a 'hunch' in ordinary life. Whereas sense perception is the sense of reality, the perceiving of things as they are, intuition also 'perceives,' but less through the conscious apparatus of the senses and more through its capacity for an unconscious 'inner perception' of the inherent potentialities of things. In viewing a mountain landscape, for example, the person who functions mainly at the level of sense perceptions will note every detail: the flowers, the colors of the rocks, the trees, the waterfall, etc., while the intuitive type will simply register the general atmosphere and color.[43] Then again there are those situations encountered in life where everything appears quite normal at the level of conscious sense perceptions yet the small inner voice of intuition tells us to 'look out' for things are not as they should be. In such instances, suggests Jung, we have many subliminal perceptions and from these, at the unconscious level, our 'hunches' arise. This is perception by way of the unconscious.[44] Jung says that the wisdom intuition offers us, especially when we find ourselves thrust into primitive situations, comes from the archetypes or memory traces of the unconscious. While the archetypes of the collective unconscious make available to us in outline form the ways our ancestors have reacted in key situations, it is the function of intuition to bring this wisdom forward to the level of consciousness, and to make it relevant by shaping and interpreting the sense impressions being received from the external environment. It is the function of the ego to receive such creations of the intuitive process once the level of consciousness is reached.[45]

In contrast to the yoga view of the highest level of consciousness as *pratibhā* or unlimited omniscience, Jung sees consciousness as a world full of restrictions.

> No consciousness can harbor more than a very small number of simultaneous perceptions. All else must be in shadow, withdrawn from sight. Any increase in the simultaneous contents immediately produces a dimming of consciousness, if not confusion to the point of disorientation. Consciousness not only requires, but is of its very nature strictly limited to, the few and hence the distinct.[46]

What the yogi imagines himself to be perceiving in the state of *pratibhā* would include the simultaneous sumtotal of all available sense perceptions plus all the subliminal contents of the unconscious. Jung calls this Eastern claim 'a most audacious fantasy' and argues that the very maximum consciousness can achieve is to single out for perception a small part of the external sensory input and the vast store of subliminal psychic potentials in the unconscious. In Zen meditation, says Jung, what happens is that consciousness is emptied as far as possible of its perceived contents which then 'fall back' into the unconscious. The contents that 'break through' into consciousness as the *satori* or enlightenment experience are far from random. They represent the natural healing and integrating tendency inherent in the archetypes of the collective unconscious. The allowing of new contents to come forward and be integrated at the level of the conscious ego is the Zen parallel to the therapeutic function of modern Western psychological techniques such as Jung's notion of active imagination. In Jung's view it is the unconscious and its contents that is Zen's 'original man.' [47]

Yet another perspective on Jung's understanding of perception is found in an explanation he writes to A.M. Hubbard regarding Hubbard's experiments with the psychodeletic drug mescalin. Jung describes the action of mescalin as paralysing the normal selective and integrative functions of apperception. The bare sense perceptions are added to by the myriad of emotions, associations, meanings, etc., that the sense perceptions evoke from the vast store of subliminal possibilities contained in the unconscious psyche. "These additions, if unchecked, would dissolve into or cover up the objective image by an infinite variety, a real 'fantasia' or symphony of shades and nuances both of qualities as well as of meanings." [48] Unlike the normal process of cognition where the ego and its apperceptive processes produce a 'correct' representation of the object by excluding inappropriate subliminal perceptional variants, the anaesthetic action of mescalin upon the ego consciousness opens the door to the riotous world of the unconscious. In Jung's view it is better that this doorway to the unconscious be opened by the technique of active imagination, which leaves the integrative processes of the ego-consciousness functional, and thereby enables therapeutic gains to be made.[49]

The concept of intuitive perception is used by Jung to account for cases of extra-sensory-perception (ESP). ESP is simply seen as perception by way of the unconscious, and therefore should be thought of as a special case of intuition. In a 1945 letter Jung says that he is entirely convinced of the existence of ESP and has left a place for ESP in his definition of intuition. What is needed now, he contends, is that physiology should follow his lead and leave room for paraphysiology.[50]

III. Knowledge

All Eastern schools of philosophy that adopt a two-level theory of perception also maintain that there are two levels of knowledge. Lower knowledge results when the sense organs come into contact with some object. This knowledge is limited by the factors of time (the object is known in the present but not in the past or future), space (the object is known in the present location but not in other locations), the efficiency of the sense organ, and the distortions imposed by *saṁskāras* of past usage of word-label and meaning which attach themselves to the direct perception of the object. Because of these limitations it is referred to as lower knowledge and is thought to be quite useful in everyday practical affairs, but of little use if one is searching for true or absolute knowledge of the object.[51] Such higher knowledge can be realized only through the special yogic *pratibhā* or supersensuous intuition of the object. The Sanskrit word *pratibhā,* which literally means a flash of light, is suggestive of the kind of cognition involved. Patañjali describes it as immediate and intensely clear. It is free from time and space limitations and from the distorting *saṁskāras* of word-labels, previously ascribed discursive meanings and ego-consciousness. It relies on neither the sense organs nor the rational intellect. The Sanskrit word most commonly employed in Eastern thought to refer to this higher knowledge is *prajñā.*[52]

Although *prajñā* is mentioned several times by Patañjali, it is perhaps best defined in *Yoga Sūtras* I:47 and 48. *Prajñā* is knowledge of the truth, the essence. In it there is not even a trace of false knowledge.[53] Through the constant training of yoga the mind is gradually freed from the distorting effects of conceptual thinking and from the *saṁskāras* or memory traces of the past. Finally the mind *(citta)* becomes so pure *(sattva)* that it merges with any object which may be presented to it. "No matter what this object may be it is then fully illumined and its real nature perfectly brought out." [54]

While Eastern scholars claim that the above description of *prajñā* is based directly on the actual experiences of yogis and is therefore empirical evidence, Jung argues that it is nothing more than a fanciful projection. If the cognitive structures of ego-consciousness, conceptual thinking, and sense perception are not functioning in *prajñā* (as the yogis claim), then the trance they achieve can be nothing more than unconsciousness. If the yogi is unconscious he can hardly be realizing absolute knowledge of the object. One cannot be fully aware and unconscious at the same time. For Jung this internal contradiction within Eastern thought is totally unacceptable.[55] The fact that this conflict does not seem to trouble Eastern scholars leads him to conclude that the Eastern intellect is underdeveloped when compared with the Western intellect.[56]

Jung's theory of knowledge also seems to have two levels. The lowest level results from the ordinary reception of sense perceptions and the apperception of these in a routine mechanical fashion, almost totally without reference to the unconscious realm. The analysis of artificial memory cited above (Section I), is a good example of what Jung means here. Although this may provide useful technical knowledge, it leaves man cut off from his intuitive processes and from the deeper wisdom of the ages. Higher knowledge results when the intuitive processes engage the external sense perceptions with the *a priori* forms of the archetypes so that a newly created and truly meaningful symbol is given birth in consciousness.[57] This is Jung's process of individuation by which the ego through the cognitive processes of sensing, intuiting, thinking, and feeling employs the formal structures of the archetypes to appropriate selected sense apperceptions from the multitude of environmental stimuli. In this way both the inner archetypes and the external environment, becomes known. As this integration of archetypes with external sense perceptions proceeds, a 'self' is gradually individuated or separated out as the person's own particular uniqueness. For Jung the highest knowledge is knowledge of the self. This is achieved when the self becomes sufficiently integrated for the ego to recognize it as a unified whole.[58] It is through the integrating structure of the self, which extends outward from the ego in ever-expanding concentric circles embracing both the conscious and the unconscious psyche, that the wisdom of the world is known. As Jung puts it, "Individuation does not shut one out from the world, but gathers the world to oneself."[59] For Jung it is the circular *maṇḍala* that best symbolizes the archetype of the self and helps to integrate the personality until the state of self-knowledge is finally realized. But regardless of how much we may integrate and make ourselves conscious through this process, "there will always exist an indeterminate and indeterminable amount of unconscious material which belongs to the totality of the self."[60] Given the necessity of the ego for conscious awareness, the limits of higher knowledge, for Jung, are much more restricted than the wide-open *prajñā* of the yogis. According to Jungian psychology, total knowledge of the self can never be achieved.

Notes and References

1. Patañjali's *Yoga Sūtras,* trans. Rāma Prasāda (Allahabad: Bhuvaneswari Asrama, 1924).
2. See Jung's biography *Memories, Dreams, Reflections* edited by Aniela Jaffé (New York: Vintage Books, 1965). For a systematic presentation of Jung's psychological theory in a single volume see *The Psychology of C.G. Jung* by Jolande Jacobi (New Haven: Yale University Press, 1973).
3. C.G. Jung, *Collected Works,* vol. II (Princeton: Princeton University Press, 1969), p. 505. (Hereafter referred to as *C.W.*)
4. C.G. Jung, "The Holy Men of India," *C.W.* 11, 580.
5. *C.G. Jung: Letters,* vol. II, ed. by Gerhard Adler (Princeton: Princeton University Press, 1974), p. 438.
6. Ibid. Within Western psychology Jung is criticized as falling into the same trap and neglecting the body, the psycho-physiological reality, in his psychology. See Edward Whitmont, "Prefatory Remarks to Jung's 'Reply to Buber' ", *Spring,* 1973, p. 193.
7. Ibid.
8. Ibid., pp. 234–235.
9. *Memories, Dreams, Reflections,* op. cit., pp. 200–223. See also *C.G. Jung: Letters,* vol. I, pp. 261–264.
10. Gilbert Ryle, *The Concept of Mind* (New York: Penguin, 1963), pp. 301–311.
11. Ibid., p. 307.
12. Ibid., p. 308.
13. C.G. Jung, "On the Nature of the Psyche," *C.W.* 8, pp. 171–173. Here Jung seems to echo William James' notion of a flimsy threshold separating the differing energy levels of the conscious and the unconscious. See James' *Varieties of Religious Experience* (New York: Mentor, 1958).
14. Ibid., p. 349
15. Jolande Jacobi, *The Psychology of C.G. Jung,* op. cit., p. 34.
16. *C.G. Jung: Letters,* vol. I, op. cit., p. 226n. In this note Adler is quoting from Jung's "A Psychological Approach to the Dogma of the Trinity," *C.W.* 11, para. 222.
17. Ibid., pp. 35–36. See also Jung's *C.W.* 11, pp. 518–519.
18. Ibid., pp. 30–33.
19. C.G. Jung, "On the Tibetan Book of the Dead," *C.W.* 11, p. 517.
20. Ibid., p. 519.
21. Ibid., p. 517.
22. Eido Roshi, "Zen Mystical Practice," in *Mystics and Scholars* ed. by Harold Coward and Terence Penelhum (Waterloo: Wilfrid Laurier University Press, 1977), pp. 27–29.
23. *Yoga Sūtras,* op. cit., III:9 and IV:27.
24. *Yoga Sūtras,* op. cit., IV:28 & 29.
25. "The Process of Individuation: Notes on Lectures given at the Eidgenössische Technische Hochschule, Zürich by Prof. C.G. Jung, October

1938-June 1939." E.T.H. Lectures recorded by Barbara Hannah. Unpublished manuscript.
26. Ibid., pp. 1–10 & p. 42.
27. C.G. Jung, "On the Secret of the Golden Flower," *C.W.* 13, p. 14.
28. E.T.H. Lectures, op. cit., p. 11.
29. C.G. Jung, "The Structure and Dynamics of the Psyche," *C.W.* 8, p. 390.
30. *C.G. Jung: Letters,* vol. I, op. cit., pp. 262–264.
31. Ibid., p. 264.
32. *Yoga Sūtras,* op. cit., III:34 & 35.
33. Jadunath Sinha, *Indian Psychology: Cognition* (Calcutta: Sinha Publishing House, 1958), p. 334. Of the schools of Indian philosophy only the materialist Cārvāka, the Mīmāṁsaka, and the Viśiṣṭādvaita Vedānta reject the two-level theory of perception and accept only ordinary sense-perception as a valid source of knowledge. The Sāṁkhya-Yoga, Nyāya-Vaiśeṣika, Advaita Vedānta, Grammarian, Buddhist, and Jaina schools all accept supersensuous perceptions *(pratibhā),* although they give different accounts of them. For an excellent account of these various views of *pratibhā* see Gopinath Kaviraj, "The Doctrine of Pratibhā in Indian Philosophy," *Annals of the Bhandarkar Oriental Research Institute,* 1924, pp. 1–18 & 113–132.
34. *Yoga Sūtras,* op. cit., I:43.
35. Ibid., I:44.
36. Ibid., III:32.
37. C.G. Jung, "On the Tibetan Book of the Great Liberation," *C.W.* 11, p. 504.
38. Ibid., p. 505.
39. *C.G. Jung: Letters,* vol. I, op. cit., p. 175.
40. C.G. Jung, "The Archetypes and the Collective Unconscious," *C.W.* 9, pt. 1, p. 282.
41. C.G. Jung, "The Structure and Dynamics of the Psyche," *C.W.* 8, pp. 140–141.
42. Ibid., p. 141.
43. *The Psychology of C.G. Jung,* op. cit., p. 12.
44. Richard Evans, *Conversations with Carl Jung* (New York: Van Nostrand, 1964), p. 74.
45. *The Psychology of C.G. Jung,* op. cit., pp. 32–33.
46. C.C. Jung, Foreword to "Introduction to Zen Buddhism," *C.W.* 11, p. 550.
47. Ibid., pp. 551–557.
48. *C.G. Jung: Letters,* vol. II, op. cit., p. 223.
49. Ibid.
50. *C.G. Jung: Letters,* vol. I, op. cit., pp. 389–390.
51. *Indian Psychology: Cognition,* op. cit., p. 339.
52. "The Doctrine of Pratibhā in Indian Philosophy," op. cit., p. 2.
53. *Yoga Sūtras,* op. cit., I:48.
54. "The Doctrine of Pratibhā in Indian Philosophy," op. cit., p. 9.
55. E.T.H. Lectures, op. cit., p. 136.
56. "On the Secret of the Golden Flower," *C.W.* 13, p. 8.
57. *Memories, Dreams, Reflections,* op. cit., p. 393.

58. C.G. Jung, 'Conscious, Unconscious and Individuation,' in "The Archetypes and the Collective Unconscious," *C.W.* 9, pt. 1, pp. 275f.
59. "The Structure and Dynamics of the Psyche," *C.W.* 8, p. 226.
60. "Two Essays on Analytical Psychology," *C.W.* 7, para. 274. See also 'The Psychology of Transference,' in "The Practice of Psychotherapy," *C.W.* 16, para. 536.

IV. Jung's Criticism of Yoga Spirituality

At times, C.G. Jung reluctantly bestowed careful and guarded advice on his fellow Europeans practicing yoga; at other times, he was expressly antagonistic towards the "pitiable imitator" of alien spiritual techniques. His assailings against what he considered to be a rage for the foreign and exotic are interspersed throughout his writings, and they come first as a shock to the Jung enthusiast.

No other individual in recent times has contributed more towards an understanding of the psychology of religious experience than Jung. Without his complexes and archetypes the study of religious symbolism would be deficient. His analysis of psychic data in terms of process and energy and the development of the uniquely Jungian 'individuation' process, which is a self-integration of the total psyche, have been significant in fathoming the depths of human interiority.

This same individual who coined such terms as complex, introversion, extraversion, collective unconscious, active imagination, and others became a close friend of Heinrich Zimmer, a noted Indologist, and wrote an introduction for one of his books. He contributed forewords to books by D.T. Suzuki and Richard Wilhelm, and for the latter he penned a memorial essay. He produced commentaries on *The Tibetan Book of the Great Liberation, The Tibetan Book of the Dead,* and *The Secret of the Golden Flower.* This same Jung, who was so sensitive to other cultures, was harsh on those who tried to cross over cultural boundaries:

> . . . if anyone should succeed in giving up Europe from every point of view, and could actually *be* nothing but a yogi and sit in the lotus position with all the practical and ethical consequences that this entails, evaporating on a gazelle-skin under a dusty banyan tree and ending his days in nameless non-being, then I should have to admit that such a person understood yoga in the Indian manner. But anyone who cannot do this should not behave as if he did.[1]

Remarks such as these have never been fully explained. Once some reasons for Jung's pronouncements are made clear, then the more serious work of evaluating his discoveries as adding to our knowledge of yoga can commence. The implications of this study are far-reaching, in particular, because Jung's major contribution, the discovery of the archetypes, can aid us in understanding one of the subtlest doctrines of yoga.

Jung offers his views on the practice of yoga by Europeans under a variety of circumstances, but his remarks illustrate, reflect, or support six different themes in his writings. These are as follows: 1) the observation that some people will do anything to avoid facing themselves; 2) the rebuttal to those critics who charged him with exotic therapeutic techniques; 3) his own theory of the natural course of religious development; 4) the analysis of yoga experience in his own terminology; 5) his view on East-West religious differences; and 6) his belief that the West should develop its own spiritual method for reaching the same goal as yoga. There is no single, overriding reason why Jung criticized the adoption of yoga by Europeans even though the bulk of his remarks are confined to his writings on East-West religious differences. All six themes should be taken collectively when giving an account of Jung's position.

I. An Observation About People

The popularity of imported religious practices as well as the syncretistic character of spiritual vocabulary today is even more striking than it was during Jung's lifetime. Still, over the long haul, there has been a conspicuous few who have not been fanatical simply for a newly found persuasion but who have been reactionary to anything thoroughly and traditionally European or American. Their displeasure with personal heritage, Jung believed, was symptomatic of a chronic rejection of themselves, and his remarks of thirty years ago would apply today:

> People will do anything, no matter how absurd, in order to avoid facing their own souls. They will practice yoga and all its exercises, observe a strict regimen of diet, learn theosophy by heart, or mechanically repeat mystic texts from the literature of the whole world—all because they cannot get on with themselves and have not the slightest faith that anything useful could ever come out of their own souls.[2]

Any spiritual method involves the directing of one's attention to the depths of the soul, and over the past four millenia yogis developed highly successful techniques for the inward regression of psychic energy. For any experience or set of experiences to be "spiritual" there must be some connection, no matter how slight, with what is interior. In modern psychological terms, this entails a plunge into the unconscious and the bringing to awareness of all sorts of fearful and painful contents. The first material actually re-appears to the person because it includes those feelings and thoughts which were successfully suppressed in the past. If this dark side of the individual is not faced, then depth experience, whether it be considered spiritual or not, is impossible. Jung's own profession involved the making known to people what is painful and pathological about themselves, and he knew all too well that only those who face their dark side can make further progress. He was therefore in principle against "the uncritical appropriation of yoga practices by Europeans."[3] Jung believed that such practices could be a distraction from looking seriously in the dark corners of the psyche, and certainly such running away from personal problems is not absent from the contemporary spiritual scene in the modern West.

II. A Rebuttal to Critics

Dream analysis, active imagination, and other therapeutic methods are familiar to the readers of Jung. His interpretations of the dreams, the fantasy and the artistic images, and other productions of his patients and clients often sent him afield into the literature and the art of world religions to discover more satisfying meanings for this material. His extensive essays on the major archetypal symbols have become source material for students of religion. While Jung's first hesitation with yoga practice was the simple recognition that many people were using it to run away from themselves, a second reason for him not endorsing its use was a curious result of his own diligent work. He wanted to draw criticism away from his own procedures:

> I have no wish to disturb such people at their pet pursuits, but when anybody who expects to be taken seriously is deluded enough to think that I use yoga methods and yoga doctrines or that I get my patients, whenever possible, to draw mandalas for the purpose of bringing them to the "right point"—then I really must protest and tax these people with having read my writings with the most horrible inattention.[4]

I suspect that Jung's ire with those practicing yoga received some of its force from his reaction to the criticism levelled at him. He wanted to be as scientific as possible and to maintain the respect of his colleagues. Curiously enough, such a charge today would be considered a fine compliment in many circles.

III. The Natural Course of Religious Development

For Jung, the history of religious development is a record of humanity coming to know the archetypes. Indeed all of Jung's thought is traceable to his theory of the archetypes for they are what ultimately constitute the human person. The archetypes are tendencies or potentialities for action and thought inherent in the very structure of the psyche. They are instinctual and are manifested primordially as physiological urges; furthermore, as inherited modes of psychic functioning, they are centers of psychic energy becoming manifest in symbolic thinking. Indeed, the archetypes are the structural conditions of all human processes. In a recent book entitled *Re-visioning Psychology,* James Hillman observes that even though many have identified Jung's theory of the archetypes as his major achievement, "perhaps his main contribution lies not so much in these ideas as in his radical personified formulation of them." [5]

The development of religion involves the interaction of these unconscious structures with consciousness. In the beginning the gods, who live in mysterious, fearful, and faraway places, are but the projections of these powers into the external environment. Another way of indicating this is to note that in primitive religions there is no distinction between the human and the external and the internal environments. In a second stage of religious development, the powers and forces of the various gods are drawn together into the one god or the divine couple. Both religious beliefs correlate with the principle archetype which Jung called the 'self' and signify the single unified and personified psyche. The real connection between the human, the psychic, and the divine is made in a third and higher phase based on the god incarnate. The divine or archetypal becomes humanized and vice versa. Finally, the potentialities of the human psyche are realized fully in a stage which is expressed as a religion of ideas.[6] As Jung saw it, yoga is a highly sophisticated religion of ideas which crowns the long and replete history of Indian religions. Recently, historians of religions have taken a contrary position because their findings indicate that yoga is as ancient as any religious factor of Indian religions.[7]

In letters written in 1923, long before he outlined precisely his ideas on the progression of religions, Jung employed the view that religions develop naturally as an argument against the practice of yoga. To Oskar Schmitz, author of *Psychoanalyse und Yoga,* Jung described how the Germanic race was in its initial state of polydemonism developing into polytheism when Christianity was thrust upon it. A highly developed Mediterranean religion to the god incarnate was a shock to the northern European peoples. The archetypes were repressed as the sacred oaks were severed from their roots. What is most natural for Germans, therefore, is to allow the polytheistic barbarian to emerge so that their religious development can continue. Identifying the "rage for the foreign and far-distant as morbid" and warning against the movement from the cultural state of the day without strength from primitive roots, Jung stated his case:

> For what has issued from the Eastern spirit is based upon the peculiar history of that mentality, which is most fundamentally different from ours. Those peoples have experienced an unbroken development from the primitive condition of natural polydaemonism to polytheism in grandest unfoldment and then beyond that to the religion of ideas, within which the original magical practice was able to develop into a method of self-improvement. These assumptions are not applicable to us.[8]

Hence, for a third reason, the people in Jung's part of the world are simply not prepared for yoga. Furthermore, if they do eventually assimilate the practices and techniques of other religions, they should do so firmly rooted in their own religious heritage. The growing familiarity with the religions of India and China was a sign that Europeans were slowly beginning to know or to recognize these same elements within themselves. To deny their own religious background or to suppress it would have the same effect as running away from themselves. This would not be the authentic assimilation of yoga.

IV. An Analysis of Yoga

As early as 1920, Jung was offering this explanation of yoga: "Yoga is the method by which the libido is systematically 'introverted' and liberated from the bondage of opposites."[9] Indeed, withdrawal of attention away from the external world is one of the eight stages of yoga listed by the famous systematizer, Patanjali, in his *Yoga Sūtras* 2.29. Withdrawal is in fact the pivotal stage between the external exercises for relaxing the body and the mind and the interior phases of concentration on images and processes of knowing. Attention is then focused on a single item of knowing, and withdrawal is also effected from interior psychic states. The lowering of consciousness activates the contents of the unconscious and attention is shifted away from the personal ego complex towards the dark backdrop of the unconscious.

This analysis of the ultimate state of yoga, the eighth and final stage of Patanjali's yoga, absorption *(samādhi)*, led Jung to state a fourth reason for doubting the possibility of Europeans enjoying the fullness of yoga:

> There is no doubt that the higher forms of yoga, in so far as they strive to reach *samādhi*, seek a mental condition in which the ego is practically dissolved. Consciousness in our sense of the word is rated a definitely inferior condition, the state of *avidyā* (ignorance), whereas what we call the "dark background of consciousness" is understood to be a "higher" consciousness.[10]

This passage appears in any essay written in 1939. Much of what it suggests needs clarification, not the least of which is the notion that normal awareness in the yoga theory of knowledge is inferior because it is a state of ignorance. Everyday common sense awareness is consciousness complicated by a flux of objectivity, forgetfulness, cravings, distractions, and so forth. We are ordinarily ignorant of the pure consciousness at the core of our mind, and yoga directs us to an experience of this "higher" consciousness. As the great commentator on the *Yoga Sūtras*, Vyāsa, tells us: "Yoga is *samādhi*, the quality of the mind pervading all of its states, which are fickle, dull, distracted, one-pointed, and restrained."[11]

Knowledge or experience can be broken down into four constituents according to the yoga tradition: 1) awareness; 2) a dynamic agent; 3) an activity; and 4) an object of the activity. The object is simply what is known while the activity is the means of knowing. There are various kinds of activities, and through yoga one learns to control and to suppress them in progressive stages of interiority. The agent is the ego while the pure awareness is identical with the spirit. Yoga leads to an experience of spirit apart from the remaining factors of knowing.

Absorption or *samādhi* is the condition for the experience of the pure consciousness of spirit. While yogins have for centuries considered this a state of pure consciousness, Jung identified it as a trancelike or unconscious state. He believed that it is an absorption into the collective unconscious, the deepest layer of the psyche and the realm of the archetypes. The central archetype, being the focal point of the total psyche, is the self. Jung's concept of the collective unconscious does correspond to the instinctive principle of yoga which is also fully unconscious, since it is the opposite of pure spirit, and which is the abode of withdrawal. In yoga the absorption into the unconscious origin of ego consciousness isolates spirit and produces an enlivening insight into the spirit's pure consciousness. Jung identified a problem of perspective for those Europeans practicing yoga:

> "Universal consciousness" is logically identical with unconsciousness. It is nevertheless true that a correct application . . . induces a remarkable extension of consciousness. But, with increasing extension, the contents of consciousness lose in clarity of detail. In the end, consciousness becomes all-embracing, but nebulous . . . a state in which subject and object are almost completely identical. This is all very beautiful, but scarcely to be recommended anywhere north of the Tropic of Cancer.[12]

Jung believed that his own process of individuation reaches the same goal as yoga, namely, the shifting of the center of the personality away from the ego and towards the self. Individuation is an individual's journey within to the spiritual core of the psyche. The logical question as to whether Jung's self and the spirit of yoga are really the same can be addressed when the other themes are examined in this study, but it is interesting to note that Jung recommended yoga merely as an example of another way for reaching essentially the same experience. The full practice of it, he further cautioned, was only for specialists.

Jung's appreciation for other religions was fostered by the symbolic material which he found in them and which was useful in deciphering the archetypal imagery he encountered in his work. For Jung, consciousness was unthinkable apart from its constituents: ego, categories, and objects. He believed that there was a fundamental bias among Europeans for the symbolic, and consequently he interpreted yoga's uplifting, translucent, and isolating experience of spirit as an unconscious state. This experience is ultimately nonsymbolic and incomprehensible to most Europeans.

V. East-West Religious Differences

Jung recognized that all psychic activity is composed of reactions, functions, and compensations of energy processes. He tended to see opposition and harmony all around him as necessary even though the height of opposition which the yogi reaches in the isolation of spirit from everything else is unattainable for most of us. One of the major categorical dualities which has plagued religious studies for too long is a superficial division between Eastern and Western religions. The underlying assumption is that the various Eastern religions have so much in common that as a whole they are opposed in type to Western religions. Jung keyed into this opposition between East and West:

> In the West, there is the mania for "objectivity," the asceticism of the scientist or of the stockbroker, who throw away the beauty and universality of life for the sake of the ideal, and not so ideal, goal. In the East, there is the wisdom, peace, detachment, and inertia of a psyche that has returned to its dim origins, having left behind all the sorrow and joy of existence as it is and, presumably, ought to be.[13]

Hence, the East offers a typically introverted point of view while the West offers the opposite extraverted point of view. We are object oriented in the West while Orientals are easily given over to introspection. The empirical bias since Kant is the predominant trend in European philosophy and science according to Jung, and Europeans are extraverted in their thinking, relegating mind to a subsidiary role in the knowing process. Spirit in the yoga scheme of things is cosmic principle for which the physical and psychic aspects of the world exist. This led Jung to postulate an introverted bias in Eastern philosophy because spirit is a cosmic factor discovered through interiorizing exercises.

Since the appearance of critical philosophy, which gave birth to modern psychology in Jung's opinion, mind has come to signify a psychic function instead of a soul entity. When the European, prejudiced as one is toward objective reality, is moved by the interior experience which yoga and other spiritualities can yield, a dilemma is created. The extravert either rejects one's own tradition altogether because everything worthwhile must come from outside according to the objective bias, or the Western, critical, scientific modality of viewing reality is embraced more fervantly in an attempt to explain away yoga states as sheer fantasy.

The very idea that the extraverted type encompasses the whole Western world and that it is opposed to an introverted attitude type covering all kinds of Eastern religions is to perpetuate the stereotype of an incense-shrouded Eastern world. Jung used such a viewpoint to discourage Europeans from practicing yoga. He even suggested something positive for those seeking an interior life:

> Instead of learning the spiritual techniques of the East by heart and imitating them in a Christian way—*imitatio Christi!*—with a correspondingly forced attitude, it would be far more to the point to find out whether there exists in the unconscious an introverted tendency similar to that which has become the guiding spiritual principle of the East. We should then be in a position to build on our own ground with our own methods.[14]

In every individual the conscious attitude is compensated by its opposite in the unconscious. The impasse of East-West religious differences is based on the model of the total psyche balanced by unconscious and conscious attitudes and is further supported by Jung's idea of the natural development of religion. The real lesson to be learned from the contemporary encounter of world religions is that the total psyche possesses all capabilities and specifically an introverted tendency which has been neglected in the European and American developments in science.

VI. A "Western" Equivalent of Yoga

For those who feel a lack of interior experience Jung suggested that they should not simply mimic alien spiritual techniques but that they should build on the recent progress in science:

> Therefore it is sad indeed when the European departs from his own nature and imitates the East or "affects" it in any way. The possibilities open to him would be so much greater if he would remain true to himself and evolve out of his own nature all that the East has brought forth in the course of millenia.[15]

According to yoga teaching, the psyche has the power of self-liberation, and that same goal is the purpose for Jung's process of individuation. The contemporary American scene seems to validate the possibility of several spiritualities from various cultures existing along side one another without loss of their essential doctrines and practices. When Jung urged that "we must get at Eastern values from within and not from without,"[16] he was denying to some extent what has come to pass in more recent times. He was also failing to recognize that every spirituality is part of the total human tradition and thereby is accessible to every human being. The enormous expansion of global awareness is breaking down the impenetrable bastion of culture. Every person in the modern West today is confronted with a great variety of spiritual methods, and many have responded wholeheartedly to one or another of these ways. Even though in the popular understanding of religion and religious methods these various spiritualities may lose their individuality and be lumped together, some people are learning yoga from *gurus,* others are learning Zen from *roshis,* and so forth. Even Jung seemed to contradict himself on this possibility when he wrote:

> But since there is *one* earth and *one* mankind, East and West cannot rend humanity into two different halves. Psychic reality still exists in its original oneness, and awaits man's advance to a level of consciousness where he no longer

> believes in the one part and denies the other, but he recognizes both as constituents of one psyche.[17]

Many critics of Jung believe that he sacrificed the original unity of the psyche with his emphasis on opposition, compensation, and the realm of the collective unconscious. Jung and his followers insist that never was the unity and equilibrium of the total psyche abandoned especially with the discussion of *the* unconscious as if it were a separate entity. By the same judgment and counter-argument the Jungian view of East-West religious differences can be argued or criticized. It seems that Jung emphasized these differences more than the possibilities open to all people for all kinds of religious experiences.

Perhaps Jung simply did not anticipate the immediate situation, or his negative attitude toward the practice of yoga may have been inversely related to his overwhelming interest in symbolism. Jung was fascinated with the imagery irrupting from the unconscious which indicated the way to self-integration while yoga presses the individual past imagery and focal points to trance experience and the isolation of pure awareness. Two kinds of experiences, one symbolic and the other nonsymbolic, are the special goals of individuation and yoga respectively. Jung seemed to recognize that his conception of the self was based on its symbolic representation and was quite different from the yoga notion of pure awareness:

> I say to whomsoever I can: "Study yoga—you will learn an infinite amount from it—but do not try to apply it, for we Europeans are not so constituted that we apply these methods correctly, just like that. An Indian guru can explain everything and you can imitate everything. But do you know *who* is applying the yoga? In other words, do you know who you are and how you are constituted?" [18]

Representative passages have been cited which demonstrate that there was no single reason or simple attitude inciting Jung to write discouragingly about the practice of yoga by Europeans. One can find numerous other passages, but they do not seem to contain anything different from the six themes identified here. First of all, Jung knew all too well that people would pursue any course to run away from facing the dark side of their personalities. Secondly, this pioneer in psychotherapy was most uncomfortable with the mystique which surrounded him. Some believed that he was a wizard while others presumed that he employed yoga and other borrowed methods in his work. Jung's well defined and highly documented theory of the natural course of the development of religion represented still a third reason for the reaction to yoga as an unnatural grafting on European culture. The very nature of yoga and the terminology and the presuppositions inherent in its methods form a fourth reason for stating a radical incompatibility between the European world and the practice of yoga. Fifthly, Jung had recourse to a position on the complementarity of opposites, and so he divided East and West along religious lines. Finally, for a sixth reason, Jung believed that yoga was just another method for self-awareness, and so the emphasis should not be on it specifically but on its purpose for being. A Western form of yoga should then be developed.

Notes and References

1. C.G. Jung, "The Psychology of Eastern Meditation," Psychology and Religion: West and East, *C.W.* 11, p. 568.
2. C.G. Jung, "Psychology and Alchemy," *C.W.* 12, pp. 99–101.
3. C.G. Jung, "The Psychology of Eastern Meditation," *C.W.* 11, p. 571.
4. C.G. Jung, "Psychology and Alchemy," *C.W.* 12, 101–102.
5. J. Hillman, *Re-visioning Psychology* (New York: Harper & Row, 1975), p. 20.
6. For Jung's theory on the development of religion see: "Psychology and Religion," "Psychology and Religion: West and East, *C.W.* 11, pp. 84–88.
7. For example see: Mircea Eliade, *Yoga Immortality and Freedom,* Bollingen Series, 56 (Princeton: Princeton University Press, 1969), pp. 101ff.
8. C.G. Jung, "Letters" in, *Psychological Perspectives, 6,* 1975, p. 81.
9. C.G. Jung, "Schuller's Ideas of the Type Problem," "Psychological Types," *C.W.* 6, p. 119.
10. C.G. Jung, "The Psychological Commentary on The Tibetan Book of the Great Liberation," *C.W.* 11, p. 485.
11. Rāma Prasāda (trans.), *Patanjali's Yoga Sūtras with the Commentary of Vyāsa and the Gloss of Vāchaspati Misra* Sacred Books of the Hindus,

vol. 4. (Allahabad: Apurva Krishna Bose, 1912; reprint ed., New York: AMS Press, 1974), p. 1. This text includes the Sanskrit of Patanjali's *Sūtras* as well as Vyāsa's commentary. All translations from Sanskrit cited in this study are my own.

12. C.G. Jung, "Conscious, Unconscious, and Individuation," The Archetypes and the Collective Unconscious, *C.W.* 9:1, pp. 287–88.
13. C.G. Jung, "The Psychological Commentary on The Tibetan Book of the Great Liberation," *C.W.* 11, p. 493.
14. Ibid., p. 483.
15. C.G. Jung, "Commentary on The Secret of the Golden Flower," "Alchemical Studies," *C.W.* 13, pp. 9–10.
16. C.G. Jung, "The Psychological Commentary on The Tibetan Book of the Great Liberation," *C.W.* 11, p. 484.
17. C.G. Jung, "Basic Postulates of Analytical Psychology," "The Structure and Dynamics of the Psyche," *C.W.* 8, p. 354.
18. C.G. Jung, "Yoga and the West," "Pyschology and Religion: West and East," *C.W.* 11, p. 534.

PART II

Jung and Indian Thought: Conceptual Comparisons

V. Jung and Karma*

Early in this century Western writers often pictured *karma* and rebirth as resulting in a callous fatalism. J. N. Farquhar, in his widely read, *The Crown of Hinduism,* portrayed the Indian experience of *karma* as follows:

> Since the sufferings of these people were the justly measured requital of their past sins, no power on earth could save them from any part of their misery. Their *karma* was working itself out and would inevitably do so. Thus, Hindus not only shared the common conviction of the ancient world, that degraded tribes were like animals and could not be civilized. Their highest moral doctrine taught them that it was useless to attempt to help them in the slightest; for nothing could prevent their *karma* from bringing upon them their full tale of misery.[1]

It is not surprising then that *karma* and rebirth have often been understood in very negative and inhumane terms in Western thought. While it is possible to find *karma* equated with fate in Indian sources (e.g., in some Purānic materials), in other instances (e.g., the Mahābhārata) the forces of time and fate appear as non-karmic elements.[2] In Patañjali's *Yoga Sūtras* 2:12–14 and 4:7–9, *karma,* rather than being fatalistic or mechanistic, is understood as a memory trace or disposition from

* First published in *The Journal of Analytical Psychology,* vol. 28, 1983.

previous thought or action—an impulse which can either be acted upon and reinforced or negated by the exercise of free choice.[3] Wendy Doniger O'Flaherty has outlined the great variety of competing and contrasting understandings of *karma* within the Indian sources themselves.[4] Thus, it is clear that Farquhar's early presentation of *karma* and rebirth to the West is unfairly one-sided. More recently the view of *karma* as a mental disposition which may carry over from one birth to the next has been picked up and given further development by Carl Jung.

The aim of this Chapter is to examine the way in which *karma* and rebirth have been understood by Carl Jung and to identify the contribution these Indian concepts have made to his psychological theory. Although many Hindu and Buddhist concepts fascinated him, the idea of *karma* and rebirth continued to play a central role in the development of Jung's thinking to the end of his life.[5]

Jung's encounter with Eastern thought is complex, and in some respects can be described as a love/hate relationship. After his break with Freud in 1910, and his 1912–1918 confrontation with the unconscious, one of the major sources Jung turned to for support and new insight was Eastern religion.[6] During the period 1920–1940, for example, the Upanisadic notion of *ātman* played a major role in the development of Jung's 'self' concept.[7] After 1940, and especially after his trip to India, Jung tended to turn his back on the East and adopt Western alchemy as his major source of inspiration. But the Eastern concept of *karma* and rebirth continued to reappear in Jung's thinking. In fact, careful analysis demonstrates that his attitude to *karma* and rebirth changed dramatically over the years. Throughout the last years his thinking came very close to the Indian perspective. For Jung the study of the Eastern ideas of *karma* and rebirth suggested that consciousness was wider than the typical modern Western fixation on the scientific intellect. As we shall see, these Indian ideas played a major role in the formation of Jung's 'archetype' concept, and they continued to provoke Jung's thinking even after he had left other Eastern notions such as yogic meditation far behind.

The main basis of Jung's understanding of *karma* probably came from his depth study of Patanjali's *Yoga Sūtras.* Evidence of this comes from notes taken by Barbara Hannah at Jung's lectures given at the Eidenössische Technische Hochschule, Zürich, October 1938-June 1939. During this period Jung gave a detailed commentary on the *Yoga Sūtras* including a thorough discussion of *karma* in terms of *klesás,* (mental obstructions), previous lives, and unconscious potentiality for this life.[8]

Although Jung was acquainted with the more fatalistic interpretations of *karma,* it was the yoga analysis of Patañjali and Vyāsa that strongly influenced his thinking.

I. *Karma* as Archetype

Although the archetype came to be Jung's most significant psychological postulate, it was an idea that evolved slowly in his mind, interacting constantly with the Indian notion of *karma.* In his list of definitions attached to his 1921 publication, *Psychological Types,* "archetype" is not listed indicating that the concept was not yet formed.[9] Direct influence from Indian thought is evidenced in Jung's 1932 lectures on Kuṇḍalinī Yoga. In Lecture One Jung states, "There is a rich world of archetypal images in the unconscious mind, and the archetypes are conditions, laws, or categories of creative fantasy, and therefore might be called the psychological equivalent of the saṁskāra [memory traces]".[10] And at the end of the Lecture Four, in answer to the question, "Are the saṁskāras archetypes?" Jung replies, "Yes, the first form of our existence is a life in archetypes."[11] Three years later in his *Psychological Commentary on "The Tibetan Book of the Dead,"* Jung is more explicit in his formulation of archetype in terms of *karma* theory:

> According to the Eastern view, *karma* implies a sort of psychic theory of heredity based on the hypothesis of reincarnation. . . . We may cautiously accept the idea of *karma* only if we understand it as *psychic heredity* in the very widest sense of the word. Psychic heredity does exist—that is to say, there is inheritance of psychic characteristics, such as predisposition to disease, traits of character, special gifts, and so forth.[12]

By 1942 Jung, in writing his definitive work, *The Psychology of the Unconscious,* admits to a deliberate extension of the archetype notion by means of karmic theory. *Karma,* he says, is essential to a deeper understanding of the nature of the archetype.[13] The influence of *karma* theory of the *Yoga Sūtra* type is especially evident in the way Jung here describes archetypes as at first latent (*bija* or seed states) which later filled out or actualized (*saṁskāras* or "seed" memory traces which have "sprouted and flowered").

> . . . the unconscious contains, as it were, two layers: the personal and the collective. The personal layer ends at the earliest memories of infancy, but the collective layer comprises the pre-infantile period, that is, the residues of ancestral life. Whereas the memory-images of the personal unconscious are, as it were, filled out, because they are images personally experienced by the individual, the archetypes of the collective unconscious are not filled out because they are forms not personally experienced. On the other hand, when psychic energy regresses, going even beyond the period of early infancy, and breaks into the legacy of ancestral life, then mythological images are awakened: these are the archetypes. An interior spiritual world whose existence we never suspected opens out and displays contents which seem to stand in sharpest contrast to all our former ideas.[14]

Although Jung himself clearly credits *karma* theory with the filling in of his notion of archetypes, it is interesting to note that little recognition is given to this major Eastern influence by either Jacobi, Jung's systematizer, or Jungian scholars. Instead Jacobi credits Plato's 'idea' and Bergson's *les eternals increées* as sources of Jung's thought. Jacobi also cites analogies with Gestalt psychology and acknowledges Augustine as the source of the term 'archetype,' but nowhere is mention made of *karma.*[15] This apparent attempt to hide or ignore the Eastern content in Jung's archetype may be an example of Western bias, or of a fear among the Jungians that such an admission would make their already suspect psychology even less acceptable to the mainstream of Western psychology. Whatever the reason, the obscuring of Jung's considerable debt to *karma* theory—a debt which he himself openly acknowledged—has veiled a significant impact that Eastern thought has had upon the modern West. For it is precisely the archetypal notions in Jung's psychology that have proven productive in the applications of Analytical Psychology to Western art, literature, and religion.[16]

II. Personal *Karma,* Collective *Karma* and Rebirth

Just as there are a variety of views in Indian thought as to the personal or collective nature of *karma,*[17] so also there is uncertainty over the matter in Jung's thinking. Jung seems to have been acquainted with only the Indian doctrine of personal *karma,* which, in his earlier writings he tended to distinguish from his own position of collective *karma* in the collective unconscious. For example, in a 1937 letter to Swami Devatmananda, Jung describes and rejects the Indian doctrine of *karma* as teaching retribution for each individual action and thus determining an individual's fate in his next life.[18] In a 1946 letter to Eleanor Bertine, Jung notes that our life is not made entirely by ourselves.

> The main bulk of it is brought into existence out of sources that are hidden to us. Even complexes can start a century or more before a man is born. There is something like *karma.*[19]

A 1940 lecture entitled "Concerning Rebirth," cites the Buddha's experience of a long sequence of rebirths but then goes on to say, "it is by no means certain whether continuity of personality is guaranteed or not: there may only be a continuity of *karma.*" [20]

The main statement of Jung's earlier position favoring collective rather than personal *karma* comes in his 1936 "Psychological Commentary on The Tibetan Book of the Dead." After characterizing the *Sidpa Bardo* as the fierce wind of *karma* which whirls the dead man along until he comes to the "womb-door," and the *Chonyid Bardo* as a state of karmic illusions resulting from the psychic residue of previous existences, Jung observes that neither scientific knowledge nor reason can accept the hypothesis of reincarnation assumed in the Tibetan Buddhist understanding of Bardo *karma.* But he allows that we may accept the idea of *karma* if we understand it as the psychic heredity of broad psychic characteristics such as traits of character, special gifts, and so forth. Just as we have inherited characteristics like eye and hair color on the physical level, so on the psychic level there are the universal dispositions of the mind—the archetypes. These archetypes are "eternally inherited forms and ideas which have at first no specific content. Their specific content only appears in the course of an individual's life, when personal existence is taken up in precisely these forms." [21] The source of the content of these inherited archetypes comes not from one's personal *karma* but from the collective *karma* of one's ancestors.[22] In a letter to E. L. Grant Watson (February 1956), Jung clearly distinguishes his understanding of the personal experience of inherited *karma* from what he takes to be the Indian view.

> Inasmuch as *karma* means either a personal or at least individual inherited determinant of character and fate, it represents the individually differentiated manifestation of the instinctual behavior pattern, i.e., the general archetypal disposition. *Karma* would express the individually modified archetypal inheritance represented by the collective unconscious in each individual. I avoid the term of *karma* because it includes metaphysical assumptions for which I have no evidence, i.e., that *karma* is a fate I have acquired in a previous existence . . .[23]

In Jung's early thinking, therefore, there is no personal inherited *karma* as such, there is only the collective inherited *karma* of one's ancestors, the archetypes, which one creatively individuates in one's own personality development. A recent Jungian, Edward Edinger, proposes the Catholic image of a "treasury of merits" as helpful in understanding Jung's thinking, ". . . the psychological accomplishments of the individual leave some permanent spiritual residue that augments the cumulative collective treasury, a sort of positive collective *karma*." [24]

In a letter dated shortly before his death in 1961, Jung says that his continued wrestlings with the question of *karma* and rebirth has renewed his interest in the East, especially in Buddha.[25] During the last years prior to his death, Jung seemed to soften his earlier rejection of the notion of personal *karma* and its psychological function in rebirth. The best insight into Jung's thought during this later period is found in the Chapter titled, "On Life After Death" in his autobiography, *Memories, Dreams, Reflections.* Jung notes that the problem of *karma* and personal rebirth has remained obscure to him due to the lack of empirical evidence. But then he goes on to say,

> Recently, however, I observed in myself a series of dreams which would seem to describe the process of reincarnation with somewhat different eyes, though without being in a position to assert a definite opinion.[26]

The above quotation suggests that Jung is willing to count dream experiences as empirical evidence, and that this particular series of dreams could be evidence for reincarnation. Jung adds however that the occurrence of similar dreams in other persons would be required before the evidence could be judged as more than a unique and therefore non-conclusive occurrence. Since Jung has no confirming evidence from the experience of others, he takes his own dream as a suggestive lead only, but one that has opened his mind to the possibility that reincarnation does occur.

Jung does not give any detailed analysis of the psychological processes which would be involved in personal reincarnation. However, he does offer a general speculation which brings him very close to traditional Indian thought.

> I could well imagine that I might have lived in former centuries and there encountered questions I was not yet able to answer; that I had to be born again because I had not fulfilled the task given to me. When I die, my deeds will follow along with me—that is how I imagine it. I will bring with me what I have done.[27]

III. *Karma* as Motivation In This Life and The Next

In his later thought Jung sees *karma* and rebirth in terms of a "motivation toward knowledge" which may be personal or impersonal in nature. Jung asks, "Is the *karma* I live the outcome of my past lives, or is the achievement of my ancestors whose heritage comes together in me?"[28] He answers the question in terms of a psychological motivation toward knowledge. Jung perceives the meaning of his existence in terms of a question which life has addressed to him—a question which perhaps preoccupied he and/or his ancestors in a previous life, and which they could not answer. He admits that this question from the past could be the result of the collective *karma* of his ancestors or the result of his own *karma* acquired in a previous life. Either way it could be experienced today, suggests Jung, as "an impersonal archetype which presses hard on everyone and has taken particular hold on me—an archetype such as, for example, the development over the centuries of the divine triad and its confrontation with the feminine principle, or the still-pending answer to the Gnostic question as to the origin of evil, or to put it another way, the incompleteness of the Christian God-image."[29] Should Jung's way of posing the question or his answer prove unsatisfactory, then "someone who has my *karma*—or myself—would have to be reborn in order to give a more complete answer."[30] Thus the karmic motivation toward knowledge is the explanation for this life and the cause of the next.

Jung even goes so far as to entertain the Indian concept of release from *karma-samsara* via the path of knowledge. He says:

> It might happen that I would not be reborn again so long as the world needed no [more complete] answer, and that I would be entitled to several hundred years of peace until someone was once more needed who took an interest in these matters and could profitably tackle the task anew.[31]

Thus for Jung motivation for knowledge is the *karma* which leads from past lives into this life and on into future lives.

The notion of "an earned otherworldly peaceful pause" and the idea of "a determinant or motivation for rebirth" are both consistent with Indian theories of *karma* and rebirth. Jung even goes so far as to suggest that once a completeness of understanding was achieved, there would then no longer be a need for rebirth. The karmic goal of motivation for knowledge would have been realized.

> The the soul would vanish from the three-dimensional world and attain what the Buddhists call *nirvāna.* But if a *karma* still remains to be disposed of, then the soul relapses again into desires and returns to life once more, perhaps even doing so out of a realization that something remains to be completed.[32]

As to the exact motivation involved, Jung says that in his own case it must have been "a passionate urge toward understanding which brought about my birth." [33] He suggests that the psychological processes resulting in psychic dissociation illness (e.g., Schizophrenia) may provide an analogy for the understanding of life after death. Just as in a disturbed person a split-off complex can manifest itself as a projected personification, so rebirth might be conceived as a psychic projection. As evidence Jung offers one of his own dreams:

> I was walking along a little road through a hilly landscape; the sun was sinking and I had a wide view in all directions. Then I came to a small wayside chapel. The door was ajar, and I went in. To my surprise, there was no image of the Virgin on the altar, and no crucifix either, but only a wonderful flower arrangement. But then I saw that on the floor sat a yogi—in lotus posture, in deep meditation. When I looked at him more closely, I realized that he had my face. I started in profound fright and awoke with the thought: "Aha, so he is the one who is meditating me. He has a dream, and I am it." I knew that when he awakened I would no longer be.[34]

In terms of analytical psychology, the meditating yogi represents Jung's unconscious prenatal wholeness. The yogi's meditation projects Jung's unified self, like a magic lantern projects an image upon a screen. Jung understands this dream as drawing attention to the fact that our ultimate reality is not located at the level of everyday ego-centered experience, as we usually take it to be, but at the deeper level of the unconscious and its archetypes. ". . . our unconscious existence is the real one, and our conscious world a kind of illusion, an apparent reality constructed for a specific purpose, like a dream which seems a reality as long as we are in it.[35] Thus, the empirical world is merely the projected karmic illusion and is characterized by an ego-conscious focus. The decisive question for man, says Jung, is: "Is he related to something infinite or not?" [36] The problem with the modern world is that its *karma* is too ego-centered. What is needed is a shift of the karmic center of gravity from the ego to self, from the conscious toward the unconscious. For Jung this is the essence of transcendence in religious experience. In psychological terms it requires the successful individuation of the self or God archetype.

III. Empirical Evidence for *Karma* and Rebirth

Throughout his life Jung admitted his strong attraction to Indian *karma* and reincarnation theory, but its lack of empirical verification was the obstacle to its full acceptance. Most often he would classify the doctrine of reincarnation as a belief which, like the belief in God, did not admit of scientific proof.[37] Although he searched Western experience broadly, he could find only testimonies to personal experiences which could not be scientifically tested. One wonders how Jung would respond to the current studies of reincarnation by Ian Stevenson.[38] Stevenson has collected evidence in India regarding reincarnation in the form of memories of experiences from previous lives reported often by children which can be verified by going to the location where the previous life was supposed to have taken place (usually a distant village) and verifying the details reported—details which, it would seem, could only have been known by the person having lived in the distant village previously. Stevenson is also collecting and verifying similar reports from other cultures, and thus might well end up providing the kind of cross-cultural confirmation Jung desired.

Jung does seem to have given some kind of empirical status to dream materials. In *Memories, Dreams, Reflections* he states, to me dreams are a part of nature that we may perceive more or less correctly just as our eyes see things more or less correctly.[39] Thus, for Jung, the data or stimuli of our perceptions, be they sights, sounds or dreams, are real. Later in life Jung's dreams gave him evidence pointing to his own reincarnation. It was the evidence of his own dreams, plus those of a close acquaintance, which led to a very positive assessment of Indian *karma* and rebirth theory in the last years before his death. To Jung the Indian understanding seemed a great advance on the common Western view that a person's character is the particular admixture of blessings or curses which fate or the gods bestowed on the child at birth—the Western version of prenatal *karma.*[40]

IV. Summary

In Indian thinking, *karma* and rebirth is understood sometimes as mechanistic fate but more often as an individually created memory trace or disposition which can either be acted upon and reinforced or negated by the exercise of free choice. This latter notion of *karma* from Patañjali's *Yoga Sūtras* played a major role in the formation of Jung's 'archetype' concept, and continued to provoke Jung's thinking to the end.

In writing his *Psychology of the Unconscious,* Jung uses the idea of *karma* as seed states pregnant with potential to develop his description of the archetypes as latent seed states which are later actualized. Although Jung himself credits *karma* theory with the filling in of this notion of archetypes, little recognition is given to this Indian contribution by Jungian scholars.

In his own thinking Jung vacillated between viewing *karma* as individual or collective. In Jung's early thinking, there is no personally inherited *karma* (as the *Yoga Sūtras* suggest), there is only the collective inherited *karma* of one's ancestors, the archetypes, which one creatively individuates in one's own personality development. However in his last years Jung comes close to accepting the *Yoga Sūtra* notion of personal *karma* and its psychological function in rebirth. This *karma* he saw as a "motivation toward knowledge" which could be either personal or collective in nature. He thought of his particular *karma* as the need to incorporate evil into the Christian concept of God. Should the solutions offered in his Analytical Psychology not solve this problem, then his *karma* might cause him to be reborn in order to provide a more complete answer. Release or rest from the cycle of *karma-samsāra* might not occur until he had found a satisfactory answer. Thus in Jung's last thoughts, *karma* is the motivation for knowledge which leads from past lives into this life and perhaps on into future lives.

Jung notes that throughout his life the problem of *karma* and rebirth remained obscure due to lack of empirical evidence. However, in his last years, his own dreams, and those of a friend, began to provide for him evidence pointing to his own reincarnation. This led Jung to a very positive assessment of the Indian *karma* and rebirth theory before his death.

Notes and References

1. J. N. Farquhar, *The Crown of Hinduism* (New Delhi: Oriental Publishers Reprint Corporation, 1971), p. 142. (Originally published in 1913).
2. *Karma and Rebirth in Classical Indian Traditions* ed. by Wendy Doniger O'Flaherty (Berkeley: University of California Press, 1980), p. xxiii.
3. See *The Yoga System of Patanjali* translated by J. H. Woods, Harvard Oriental Series, vol. 17 (Delhi: Motilal Banarsidass, 1966).
4. *Karma and Rebirth in Classical Indian Traditions,* op. cit., pp. ix-xxv.
5. C.G. Jung, *Memories, Dreams, Reflections,* ed. by A. Jaffe (New York: Vintage Books, 1965), pp. 317–326.
6. *Memories, Dreams, Reflections,* op cit., Cps. V, VI & VII.
7. See Chapter 2, section on "Atman and Self."
8. Barbara Hannah, "The Process of Individuation: Notes on Lectures given at the Eidenössische Technische Hochoschule, Zurich, by C.G. Jung", October, 1938–June, 1939, unpublished.
9. C.G. Jung, "Psychological Types," *C.W.* 6, 1975.
10. C.G. Jung, "Psychological Commentary on Kundalini Yoga," *Spring,* 1975, p. 8.
11. Ibid., p. 30.
12. C.G. Jung, "The Psychological Commentary on The Tibetan Book of the Dead," *C.W.* 11, p. 517.
13. C.G. Jung, "The Psychology of the Unconscious," *C.W.* 7, 1942, p. 76.
14. Ibid.
15. Jolande Jacobi, *The Psychology of C.G. Jung* (New Haven: Yale University Press, 1973). See also her *Complex, Archetype and Symbol in the Psychology of C.G. Jung* (New York: Bollingen, 1959).
16. See, for example, the writings of Robertson Davies, Northrop Frye, Paul Tillich.
17. See Wendy O'Flaherty's summary of the various Indian views in her "Introduction" to *Karma and Rebirth in Classical Indian Traditions,* op. cit., pp. ix-xxv.
18. *C.G. Jung: Letters,* op. cit., vol. I., p. 226–227.
19. Ibid., p. 436.

20. C.G. Jung, "Concerning Rebirth," *C.W.*, 9, Pt. 1, p. 113.
21. C.G. Jung, "Psychological Commentary on The Tibetan Book of the Dead," *C.W.* 11, p. 518.
22. C.G. Jung, *Memories, Dreams, Reflections,* op. cit., p. 317.
23. *C.G. Jung: Letters,* op. cit., vol. 2, p. 289.
24. Edward F. Edinger, *Ego and Archetype* (Baltimore: Penguin Books, 1973), p. 220.
25. *C.G. Jung: Letters,* op. cit., vol. 2, p. 548.
26. *Memories, Dreams, Reflections,* op. cit., p. 319.
27. Ibid., p. 318.
28. Ibid., p. 317.
29. Ibid., p. 318.
30. Ibid., p. 319.
31. Ibid.
32. Ibid., pp. 321–322.
33. Ibid., p. 322.
34. Ibid., p. 323.
35. Ibid., p. 324.
36. Ibid., p. 325.
37. *Memories, Dreams, Reflections,* op. cit., p. 319.
38. Ian Stevenson, "The Explanatory Value of the Idea of Reincarnation" in *The Journal of Nervous and Mental Disease,* 164, pp. 305–326.
39. *Memories, Dreams, Reflections,* op. cit., pp. 161–162.
40. C.G. Jung, "Mysterium Coniunctionis," *C.W.* 14, p. 225.

VI. Jung and Kuṇḍalinī

References to Kuṇḍalinī Yoga appear sporatically throughout Jung's writings.[1] The occasion which prompted his set of four lectures devoted specifically to Kuṇḍalinī is reported by Barbara Hannah, one of Jung's students, as follows:

> It was in the autumn of 1932 that the Indologue, J. W. Hauer, at that time professor for his subject at Tübingen, came to Zürich to give us a seminar on Kundalini Yoga. This was a thrilling, interesting parallel to the process of individuation, but, as always happens when a perfected Indian philosophy is placed before a European audience, we all got terribly out of ourselves and confused. We were used to the unconscious taking us into this process very gradually, every dream revealing a little more of the process, but the East has been working at such meditation techniques for many centuries and has therefore collected far more symbols than we were able to digest. Moreover, the East is too far above everyday reality for us, aiming at Nirvana instead of at our present, three-dimensional life. Jung was confronted with a very disoriented group who had greatly appreciated but had been unable to digest Hauer's brilliant exposition of Kundalini Yoga.[2]

To cure his students of their "intellectual indigestion," Jung devoted his next few lectures to an interpretation of Kuṇḍalinī Yoga so that his students would be able to integrate with their study of Jungian psychology. Jung's aim in these lectures was not to present a descriptive analysis of Kuṇḍalinī Yoga in its own terms, but rather to help his students to see resonances within its Indian thought forms to the Jungian process of individuation. Thus Jung's method was to briefly examine the symbolic nature of each of the seven *chakras* of Kuṇḍalinī Yoga, and then to offer a psychological interpretation in terms of his own psychology. In this way he was able to bring his students back to a focus on the process of individuation, with Kuṇḍalinī Yoga being seen as providing interesting parallel evidence from another culture.

I. Kuṇḍalinī Yoga In Its Tantric Context

Kuṇḍalinī Yoga takes its rise in the Hindu and Buddhist Tantric sects of the Middle Ages.[3] In contrast to the approach of the Sankhya-Yoga system of Patañjali, in which the aim is to circumvent and crush the passions within, the Tantric hero *(vīra)* goes directly *through* the sphere of the passions to the spiritual goal. This is accomplished not by indulging in the passions, as one might be led to think, but rather by shifting attention from the object of passion to the inner energy of passion—without trying either to prolong or suppress the energy. Rather than being puritanically avoided, the passions themselves are used as the very means *(sādhana)* by which self-realization may be achieved. The goal of the Tantric hero is "to incorporate the excluded forces as well as those accepted generally, and experience by this means the essential nonexistence of the antagonistic polarity—its vanishing away, its *nirvāṇa;* that is, the intrinsic purity and innocence of the seemingly dark and dangerous sphere."[4] Rather than attempting to repress their personal biological impulses through the ascetic rigors of classical Jain, Hindu and Buddhist yoga, the Tantric approach was world-affirmative. Instead of championing *sattva* (mental purity) over *rajas* (passion), as do Patañjali's *Yoga Sūtras,* for Tantra it is the person endowed with the vigor and action of *rajas* that wins through to victory. The Tantric hero triumphs by way of the passions themselves, riding them the way a cowboy rides a wild bronco to obedience. Heinrich Zimmer states the philosophy clearly:

> It is an essential principle of the Tantric idea that man, in general, must rise through and by means of nature, not by the rejection of nature. "As one falls to the ground," the *Kularnava Tantra* states, "so one must lift oneself by the aid of the ground." . . . The creature of passion has only to wash away his sense of ego, and then the same act that formerly was an obstruction becomes the tide that bears him to the realization of the absolute as bliss *(ānanda)*. Moreover, this tide of passion itself may become the baptizing water by which the taint of ego-consciousness is washed away. Following the Tantric method, the hero *(vīra)* floats beyond himself on the roused but canalized current.[5]

Many of these Tantric ideas resonate with Jung's psychology, so it is easy to understand their attractiveness for Jung's students. The positive evaluation of nature, the need to integrate the dark forces of the psyche, the necessity of going beyond ego-consciousness, are Tantric themes directly paralleling Jung's own thinking. But, as was the case with Patañjali's *Yoga Sūtras,* we shall see that Jung worries that his students will be seduced by aspects of Tantric Kuṇḍalinī Yoga which he maintains must be rejected by modern Westerners.

An aspect of Tantra Yoga which would appeal to students of Jung is its approach of experimenting with one's own mind in appropriating worldly experience.[6] Just as Jung taught that a senior analyst could be a helpful guide for the beginner, so Tantra stressed the need for a senior *guru.* Especially if the meditation involved the "five forbidden things" (i.e., wine, meat, fish, parched grain and sexual intercourse) the supervision of a *guru* was essential to ensure a spiritual result and to guard against deterioration into either libertinism or revolution. The experimental nature of the method also parallels Jung's approach in that it does not confer ontological status to the objects of its meditations—gods, goddesses, etc., are important only in their function as constructs of mental experience. Their existential reality is not a concern. It is their ability to function as devices for discovering what is inside the mind that is stressed.[7] The focus on goddesses as well as gods, the importance of the feminine power *(śakti),* which was largely absent from the classical yogas such as that of Patañjali, also resonates strongly with Jung's emphasis on the importance of the *anima* or the feminine aspect of the psyche.

According to Tantric theory, the subtle body of the human being is made up of a certain number of *nāḍīs* ("conduits" such as blood vessels and nerves) and of *chakras* ("circles" usually translated "centers"). The vital energy in the form of "breaths" is said to circulate through the *nāḍīs* while cosmic energy exists in a latent state in the *chakras.*[8] The seven major *chakras* may be briefly described as follows. (1) The *mūlādhāra* (*mūla* meaning "root") is located at the base of the spine between the anus and the genitals. It is symbolized as a red lotus of four petals with a yellow square in the middle (earth). In the center of the square is a triangle with its apex downward *(yoni).* At the center of the triangle is the *linga* with the Kuṇḍalinī (translated, "serpent") coiled eight times around it and blocking the opening of the *linga* with its mouth. Thus Kuṇḍalinī blocks the awakening and manifestation of the "root-power" of the *mūlādhāra chakra.* (2) The next higher *chakra* is called the *svādhiṣṭhāna* which is situated at the level of the genitals and is pictured as a vermillion lotus of six petals. In the middle of the lotus is a white half-moon upon which is written a seed *(bija) mantra* or sound. (3) The *maṇipūra chakra* is at the level of the navel and is pictured as a blue-black lotus of ten petals in the middle of which is a red triangle upon which a god and goddess sit mounted on a bull. These first three *chakras* or levels are said to govern the lives of most people. The last four *chakras* represent the higher modes of consciousness. (4) *Anāhata,* the fourth *chakra,* is found at the level of the heart. It is colored red with a twelve-petaled golden lotus in the middle of which are two intersecting triangles. In this center spiritual awakening is said to occur as the Lord reaches down to awaken the devotee by sound (OM) or touch. (5) The *viśuddha chakra* is centered in the throat and is symbolized by a lotus of sixteen petals of smoky purple hue. In the middle is a white circle containing an elephant. It is the level of complete purity. (6) At the point between the eyebrows, the *ājñā chakra* is described as the lotus of command. It is pictured as a white lotus of two petals in the middle of which is a white triangle *(yoni)* pointing downward and containing a white *linga.* It is said to be the locus of the cognitive faculties *(buddhi, ahaṃkāra, manas* and the *indriyas)* but purified and so completely free of the normal pollutions and limitations. There, one is said to experience a direct intuition of the essence of reality (e.g., as the *Ṛsis* "seeing" of the Vedas, or the devotee's vision of the Lord). (7) *Sahasrāra,* the final *chakra,* is described as beyond all duality and located at the top of the head. It is represented as a many-colored thousand-petaled lotus, facing downward. The petals bear all the possible articulations of the Sanskrit alphabet. In the center of the lotus is the full moon enclosing a triangle. It is here, says Eliade, that the final union of Śiva and Śakti, male and female powers, is realized.[9] Here the Kuṇḍalinī (the *śakti* or female power) ends its journey after having ascended through the various *chakras* and, in passing, awakening each lotus to full blossom. In the union of the serpent power *(Śakti)* with the Lord *(Śiva),* the level of the body and of worldly experience is said to be completely transcended. Thus, this final *chakra* is simultaneously a complete union of all the opposites of experience and an ultimate transcending of them.

According to Eliade, the process of "raising the Kuṇḍalinī" is begun when the sleeping goddess is awakened through the grace and guidance of a *guru.* This awakening apparently arouses an intense heat and its upward progress through the *chakras* is manifested by the lower part of the body becoming as inert and cold as a corpse, while the part through which the Kuṇḍalinī is passing is burning hot.[10] The identification of the power of Kuṇḍalinī with heat reminds one of the role played by *tapas* or psychic heat in Patañjali's yoga. The actual awakening of the Kuṇḍalinī and its journey through the *chakras* is accomplished through special spiritual disciplines including the arresting of respiration *(kumbhaka)* and special postures *(āsana).* These are purifying practices which remove blockages to the free flow of energy through the subtle body, and to eventual union with the universal or Śiva aspect. For present purposes it is not necessary to describe these rather complex and esoteric practices in detail. The interested reader is referred to the helpful summary offered by Mircea Eliade, *Yoga: Immortality and Freedom* (Cp. VI. "Yoga and Tantrism"). With this overview of Kuṇḍalinī Yoga in mind, let us now turn to the interpretation offered by Carl Jung in his four 1932 lectures on the subject.[11]

II. Jung's Interpretation of Kuṇḍalinī Yoga

In his interpretation Jung's general approach was to comment on the symbolism of the *chakra* and then to offer an interpretation using his own psychological theory. Rather than focusing on the Kuṇḍalinī theory of the process of spiritual unfolding, and the obvious parallels with the individuation process, Jung stressed instead the symbolic meanings of the *chakras.* In Lectures I and II he began with the lowest *chakra* and worked his way through the first four *chakras.* The final three *chakras* are covered in Lectures III and IV. Since the symbolism of each *chakra* plays a role in Jung's interpretation, it is useful to outline his understanding of symbols.

Chakras as Symbols. The *chakras* are symbols, says Jung, in that they bring together, in image form, a complex and manifold group of ideas which can be understood from three aspects: *sthūla* or things as we ordinarily see them; *sūkṣma,* the level of theoretical understanding, abstraction or wisdom; and *para,* the transcendent level beyond sense experience and mental theory (the Eastern goal about which Jung has grave doubts). The symbolism of each *chakra* evokes and incorporates all of these aspects. In modern terminology a symbol may be thought of as a *Gestalt.* "A symbol, then, is a living *Gestalt,* or form, the sum total of a highly complex set of facts which our intellect cannot master conceptually, and which therefore cannot be expressed in any other way than by the use of an image." [12] *Chakras* are symbols in that they embody highly complex psychic facts which can only be expressed in images. Thus, says Jung, the *chakras* are of great value to us in that they represent a real effort to give a symbolic theory of the psyche. It is because the psyche is so complicated, so vast and so rich in elements unknown to us that we have no choice but to turn to symbols to express what we know about it. Particular theories lose sight of the essential totality of the psyche. It is this totality which symbols as *Gestalts* can safeguard. The Kuṇḍalinī *chakras* are valuable to modern Westerners, because it is an Eastern attempt to understand the psyche as a whole.

> . . . the East, and India especially, has always tried to understand the psyche as a whole. It has an intuition of the Self, and therefore it sees the ego and consciousness as only more or less inessential parts of the Self. All of this seems very strange to us. It appears to us as though India were fascinated by the background of consciousness, because we ourselves are entirely identified with our foreground, with the conscious. But now among us too, the background, or hinterland of the psyche has come to life, and since it is so obscure, and so difficult of access, we are at first forced to represent it symbolically.[13]

The *sthūla* is the personal aspect of a symbol—we are immersed in it and identified with it. It is when we reach a standpoint which is supra-personal, which allows us to transcend and analyze our own personal experiences, that the *sūkṣma* aspect is reached. The creation of a culture, a religion, a philosophic viewpoint, takes us beyond ourselves and allows us to begin to see the *sūkṣma* aspect of our experience. The Kuṇḍalinī *chakra* system is one such culture or viewpoint, reached in India, which has allowed *sūkṣma* understanding, supra-personal understanding to develop. Just as in the West Platonic thought has helped us to recognize that things have both an outer form (the *sthūla* aspect) and an inner idea (the *sūkṣma* aspect), so for the East the Kuṇḍalinī *chakras* have fulfilled a parallel function. Jung suggests a major difference between Eastern and Western experience is that for the East the *sūkṣma* aspect, the inner essence, is real, is substantial (though subtle in nature); for the West, however, the *sūkṣma* is more often a mere hypothesis or theory which must be confirmed by empirical facts.[14] Because of this difference, Western scientific psychology is anchored to the *sthūla* or empirical aspect as its touchstone. Kuṇḍalinī Yoga, which wants to transcend the empirical or the *sthūla* and places more reality in the *sūkṣma,* can easily slide off into the *para* or completely other-worldly (as is claimed to occur at the highest or *sahasrāra chakra*). It is exactly at such points of claimed total transcendence of the empirical or *sthūla* aspect of experience that Jung draws the line in his appreciation of Kuṇḍalinī Yoga.

The Mūlādhāra Chakra.[15] For Jung the *mūlādhāra,* as is each *chakra,* is a whole world. It characterizes one kind of mental state—our ordinary world in which the self is asleep and the ego is awake. The *mūlādhāra* is our daily routine conscious world where we are victims of impulses, instincts, the unconscious. We are as helplessly entangled in our biological roots as the sea serpent which has no control over the forces of its dark ocean environment. In the *mūlādhāra,* in the relentless routine of daily life, we are like fishes in the sea with little consciousness or control. This is symbolized in the color of the *chakra* which is dark red—the color of passion.[16] Once in a while, however, in rare moments of psychological quiet, we may get an inkling of the next *chakra.* It may be an unusual urge to go to church, to the mountains or into nature, where there is the faint stirring of another kind of emotion. Some strange urge within (the rousing of the Kuṇḍalinī) forces us out of the normal routine. Jung summarizes it this way.

> So we may assume that the place where the Self, the psychological non-ego, is asleep, is the most banal place in the world—a railway station, a theatre, the family, the professional situation—there the Gods are sleeping, there we are just as reasonable, or as unreasonable as unconscious animals. And this is *mūlādhāra.*[17]

The urge of awakening in the *mūlādhāra* moves us to the next higher *chakra* in Kuṇḍalinī Yoga, but in Jungian theory from routine ego-consciousness to the first glimmerings of the unconscious.

The Svādhiṣṭhāna Chakra. While Kuṇḍalinī symbolism begins deep down and gradually works up, Jung starts on the surface of "unaware ego-consciousness" and then dives into the unconscious as the process of individuation, of self-discovery, begins. These forays down into the unconscious are evidenced in our dreams, says Jung. Just as the symbolism of the second *chakra* is related to water, so our dreams and myths of individuation lead us to water, to the baptismal font. The way up to greater self-awareness leads first down into the water where the monsters of the deep are faced, and from which rebirth may take place.

> So the symbolism in the *svādhiṣṭhāna chakra* is the world-wide idea of baptism by water with all its dangers of being drowned or devoured by the *makara*. Today, instead of the sea or the leviathan, it is [psychological] analysis which is equally dangerous. One goes under the water, makes the acquaintance of the leviathan there, and that is either the source of regeneration or destruction.[18]

With the beginning of the individuation process, the possibilities for the first glimmers of self-awareness are symbolized in the lighter red (vermillion) coloring of the lotus petals. Both Kuṇḍalinī and Jung stress the dangers involved in this psychic awakening and thus the need for careful guidance from a *guru* (in Kuṇḍalinī Yoga) or an analyst (in Jungian Psychology). Progress into the *svādhiṣṭhāna chakra* or into the beginnings of individuation is only possible, says Jung, if you have aroused the Kuṇḍalinī, the sleeping serpent of the unconscious.

Before going into Jung's interpretation of the rousing of the Kuṇḍalinī, let us take note of the stress he puts on the way in which his interpretation of the first two *chakras* differs from the Eastern understanding of Kuṇḍalinī Yoga. Jung repeatedly states that in approaching an Eastern theory such as Kuṇḍalinī Yoga, the Western mind must assimilate Eastern thinking to the Western mentality, or be poisoned by the alien thinking. Although the Eastern ideas are very attractive to the Western mind ". . . they are a foreign body in our system—*corpus alienum*—and they inhibit the natural growth and development of our own psychology. . . . Therefore one has to make really heroic attempts to stand up against these symbols, in order to deprive them of their influence." [19] Jung's great concern for his students who were in the midst of their own processes of individuation, and thus very susceptible to the allure of Kuṇḍalinī Yoga as presented by Professor Hauer, is seen in his repeated stressing of the need for them to seek to understand these Eastern symbols from the secure base of their own Western thinking. Thus Jung's brilliant and shocking turning of the Kuṇḍalinī symbols on their head, by insisting that from our

Western experience the *mūlādhāra* must be seen as above and ego-conscious, whereas the *svādhiṣṭhāna* must be understood as below and unconscious. Of course, this Jungian interpretation is just the reverse of Kuṇḍalinī Yoga, but it succeeded in rescuing his students onto the solid Western footing of Jungian psychology. As Jung puts it, in Western thinking "we begin in our conscious world, so our *mūlādhāra* might be, not down below in the belly, but up in the head." [20] Of course that seems to put everything upside down, but in Jung's view it is necessary if we are to assimilate Kuṇḍalinī thinking.

> In the East the unconscious is above, while with us it is below, so we can reverse the whole thing, as if we were coming down from the *mūlādhāra,* as if that were the highest centre . . . We can only understand their picture of the world in as much as we try to understand it in our own terms. . . . We must realize, or take into consideration at least, that the *mūlādhāra* is here, the life of this earth, and here the God is asleep. And then we go to the *Krater*—to use that old quotation from Zosimus—or to the unconscious, and that is understood to be a higher condition than before, because there we approach another kind of life. And we move there only through the Kuṇḍalinī that has been aroused.[21]

Thus Jung's interpretation radically changes the assumptions of Kuṇḍalinī Yoga, by seeing the *ājñā* or second highest center as unconscious rather than super-conscious, and by placing the second *chakra,* the *svādhiṣṭhāna,* below the *mūlādhāra.* All this Jung does under the rubric of understanding Eastern thought in the terms of his own psychology.

For Jung, the key requirement for the awakening of Kuṇḍalinī is the right psychological attitude. To approach the unconscious one must have a purified mind and a guiding grace which pushes one onward. That guiding grace or inner spark is the Kuṇḍalinī. It may appear in strange guises such as fear or neurosis or an overpowering interest, but it must be superior to one's ego-will. Otherwise one gives up and turns back when the first obstacle in the unconscious is encountered. Once the Kuṇḍalinī is aroused, says Jung, it provides the urge that will not let one turn back. And for Jung the Kuṇḍalinī is none other than the *anima.*[22]

In our ordinary consciousness in which man alone seems to be the only active power, the Gods, the Kuṇḍalinī, the *anima* seems asleep. Yet it is there as potential always waiting to provide the spark that would lead to the beginning of new growth, of individuation, of a new kind of consciousness.

The essential characteristic of this new kind of consciousness, which typifies the *svādhiṣṭhāna* world, is its sense of eternity, of separation from ordinary ego-consciousness. It has about it an impersonal quality which appears to be an illusion when viewed from the rational ego-centered perspective of the *mūlādhāra* world. Psychologically this is very dangerous for us, says Jung, for we naturally want to identify with this new discovery of the unconscious. Its impersonality, the existence of powers separate from our ego-consciousness, make us uneasy. Yet to quickly identify leads to neurotic inflation, foolishness, and even schizophrenia. "You must not identify with the unconscious. You must keep outside, detached, and observe objectively what happens." [23] It is here that the role of the analyst or *guru* is to assist one in keeping from being overbalanced by this shattering first experience of the Kuṇḍalinī. Shattering though it may be, this first experience of the Kuṇḍalinī is essential, "otherwise you cannot realize the self, and the purpose of this world has been missed." [24] In Jung's view the majority of modern Westerners have not experienced the awakening of the Kuṇḍalinī. They are like people who have not yet been born. They go through the motions of life without any awareness of the spark of the inner self. At the end of their lives they are returned to the pleroma from whence they came, as if they never had been.

The Maṇipūra Chakra. Having awakened and become aware of the existence of the Kuṇḍalinī in the *svādhiṣṭhāna,* in the *maṇipūra* one begins to realize that it is the fire within that is one's true self. Thus the *maṇipūra* part of one is no longer in time and space but seems to be immortal. Its symbolism of "fire" fits well with the symbols of the divine found worldwide in the ancient religions. The fire represents the experience of divine as well as our inner passions. Psychologically, says Jung, after our baptism into the passions hidden in the deep waters of the unconscious, the *maṇipūra* is the experience of these emotions flaming up—after baptism comes temptation and hell. It is difficult and painful, as in the primitive initiation ceremonies. It is the fire which the Buddha speaks of—ourselves and our world as being on fire with desires which can never be satisfied. Yet only with the facing of one's own flames of desire can one move through them to reach another world.[25]

The Anāhata Chakra. After the passions of the belly, the next higher center is located at the level of the heart and the lungs. At the level of the *anāhata* we find ourselves lifted up from the passions of earthly experience. After having been immersed in the whirlpool of one's passions and instincts comes the great leap from *maṇipūra* to *anāhata* experience—a leap which most people never make. Psychologically, says Jung, it means that we no longer identify with our desires but reach a plane of impersonal experience.[26] Since most people never reach this level it is hard to talk about. How is one lifted out of one's worldly passions to this higher level? It begins when one discovers and identifies a new thing within, namely, the first glimmers of the self. In the *chakra* symbolism this is seen as the Lord reaching down and touching the devotee, and in the mystical sound of OM. In *anāhata* one experiences the possibility of rising above the womb of nature, above the world of emotions, and of looking at them reflectively. As one withdraws and distances oneself from one's emotions, significant progress is made in the discovery of the self.

> In *anāhata* individuation begins. But here again you are likely to get an inflation. Individuation is not that you become an ego; you would then be an individualist. An individualist is a man who did not succeed in individuating; he is a philosophically distilled egotist. Whilst individuation is becoming that thing which is not the ego, and that is very strange. No body understands what the Self is, because the Self is just what you are not—it is not the ego. The ego discovers itself as a mere appendix of the Self in a sort of loose connection. The ego is always far down in the *mūlādhāra* and suddenly becomes aware of something up in the fourth story, above, in *anāhata,* and that is the Self.[27]

For Jung, therefore, *anāhata* is psychologically interpreted as the discovery of the self. It is a world characterized by impersonality and objectivity in their best sense. Jung exemplifies by quoting St. Paul, " 'It is not I that lives, it is Christ that liveth in me,' meaning that his life had become an objective life, not his own life but the life of a greater one . . ." [28] But in *anāhata* the withdrawal from the emotions is only begun, thus frequent erruptions of *maṇipūra* psychology are to be expected.

The Viśuddha Chakra. Jung interprets the *viśuddha* purification of all worldly obstruction *(kleśas)* as the experience at the level of psychic abstraction or mental concepts. In *anāhata* we have begun to distance ourselves from the physical world and in *viśuddha* that process is completed. "*Viśuddha* means," says Jung, "a full recognition of the psychical essences or substances as the fundamental essences of the world, and not by virtue of speculation but by virtue of fact, as *experience*." [29] It is the world of the psychologist, like Jung, who has come to know the reality of such psychic entities as ego, archetypes and self, not from someone else, but in his own experience. To experience the self has required that one's center of gravity be shifted from ego (and the emotions) to the more impersonal awareness of the self. Rather than thought and feeling being identical with objects, as they tend to be in *anāhatta,* in *viśuddha* the bond between external objects and internal thoughts and feelings is dissolved. This opens the way to seeing reality only as the psychical world, and the external world as a mere reflection of the psyche. In Jung's view such a move is dangerous, a kind of yogic mental inflation which the modern Westerner with his scientific grounding in empirical reality cannot accept. But the value of the *viśuddha,* for modern Westerners, is in its teaching that in the case of purely psychical things, for which there is no physical evidence (e.g., the concept of God), such psychical concepts, when personally experienced, are realities.[30] Thus in *viśuddha* the sustaining data of experience may be more psychical than physical in nature.

In his discussion of the *viśuddha chakra* we see Jung beginning to draw lines as to what of Kuṇḍalinī Yoga can be assimilated into Western experience. As we move on to the last two *chakras*

Jung suggests that we are, as it were, completely beyond our Western reach. Yet he continues to examine the *chakra* symbolism in the hope that we can at least say something theoretical about it. But it is clear that as far as Jung is concerned the psychological interpretation of Kuṇḍalinī Yoga useful to Westerners has been completed.[31]

The Ājñā Chakra. Jung's interpretation of *ājñā* symbolism is that it suggests a world in which the psychic realities of the *viśuddha* are no longer experienced. The *ājñā chakra,* says Jung, consists of nothing we can experience; it is fully divine and so beyond our human ken. The God, which was dormant in the *mūlādhāra* and then felt as an arousing spark, is now fully awake and the dominant reality. Whereas in *viśuddha* the physical reality was still felt as opposed to the psychical reality, in the *ājñā* world there is nothing but psychic reality—and that in union with the divine (with Śiva). The ego is said to disappear (something which Jung believes to be psychologically impossible), as one dissolves completely into the self. "The psychical is no longer a content in us, but we become contents of it."[32] We have returned to our origin, the divine.

The Sahasrāra Chakra. The possibility of a *chakra* that is beyond even the incipient mental duality of the *ājñā* is so unimaginable to Jung that he can barely bring himself to comment. Whereas the *ājñā* seems to retain at least the mystic sense of a momentary psychic separation before the union of the self with God, in the *sahasrāra* there is no God or self. There is not even the smallest seed sense of something other. Thus there can be no psychic experience for all is one—Brahman without a second. For Jung such conjecture is simply an example of Eastern intuition overreaching itself. It is better that the Westerner should not even think about such speculations least he be led astray. Jung concludes that the *sahasrāra* is an entirely philosophical concept with no substance whatever for Westerners. Since it is beyond any possible experience, it is without any practical value for us.[33]

III. Conclusion

Jung's reinterpretation of Kuṇḍalinī Yoga in terms of his own psychological theory is an exceptional tour de force. In all likelihood, it cured the intellectual indigestion being experienced by the majority of his 1932 students. However with today's much better knowledge of Eastern thought, it is doubtful that Jung's "rope trick" of standing Kuṇḍalinī Yoga on its head and then lopping off the last two *chakras* as "superfluous speculations with no practical value" would be accepted. What Jung's "Commentary" accomplished then, and still does today, is to provide added insight into *his* understanding of the *process of individuation,* not an accurate description of Kuṇḍalinī. The conceptual structure of Kuṇḍalinī Yoga provided a colorful, if at times confusing, backdrop against which Jung could develop his own thinking about the ego, the emotions and the self. For modern students of comparative psychology or religion Jung's "Commentary" is also useful in suggesting some key points of similarity and difference between Eastern and Western thought.

Notes and References

1. See the following paragraphs in Jung's *Collected Works*—9, pt I: 142, 632, 641, 648, 661, 667, 674, 679; 10: 169; 11: 847, 875; 12: 122, 184, 199; 13: 35, 334; 16: 380, 540–564 (an extended discussion where Jung connects Kuṇḍalinī *chakras* with psychogenic disturbances); 18: 17, 263, 1225.
2. Barbara Hannah, *Jung: His Life and Work—A Biographical Memoir* (New York: G.P. Putnam, 1976), p. 206.
3. A.L. Basham, *The Wonder That was India* (New York: Grove Press, 1959), p. 178, p. 280, p. 337.
4. Heinrich Zimmer, *Philosophies of India,* edited by Joseph Campbell (Princeton: Princeton University Press, 1971), p. 579.
5. Ibid., pp. 576–577.
6. Agehananda Bharati, *The Tantric Tradition* (New York: Anchor Books, 1970), p. 20.
7. Ibid., pp. 20–21.

8. Mircea Eliade, *Yoga: Immortality and Freedom,* translated by Willard Trask (Princeton: Princeton University Press, 1971), pp. 236–237. The following description of the seven *chakras* is based on Eliade, pp. 241–245, and on Heinrich Zimmer, *Philosophies of India,* op. cit., pp. 583–588.
9. Mircea Eliade, op. cit., p. 243.
10. Ibid., pp. 245–246.
11. C.G. Jung, "Psychological Commentary on Kuṇḍalinī Yoga" (from the Notes of Mary Foote), *Spring,* 1975 (pp. 1–32) and 1976 (pp. 1–31).
12. C.G. Jung, "Psychological Commentary on Kuṇḍalinī Yoga," *Spring,* 1976, p. 20.
13. Ibid., p. 21.
14. C.G. Jung, "Psychological Commentary on Kuṇḍalinī Yoga," *Spring,* 1975, pp. 4–6.
15. This description is taken from C.G. Jung, Ibid., pp. 9–10.
16. Ibid.
17. Ibid., p. 10.
18. Ibid., p. 11.
19. Ibid., p. 9.
20. Ibid., p. 12.
21. Ibid., pp. 12–13.
22. Ibid., p. 14.
23. Ibid., p. 19.
24. Ibid., p. 21.
25. Ibid., pp. 24–28.
26. Ibid., p. 29.
27. Ibid., p. 31.
28. Ibid.
29. C.G. Jung, "Psychological Commentary on Kuṇḍalinī Yoga," *Spring,* 1976, p. 7.
30. Ibid., p. 16.
31. Ibid.
32. Ibid., p. 17.
33. Ibid.

VII. Mysticism in the Psychology of Jung and the Yoga of Patañjali*

I. Mysticism Defined

The study of mysticism has occupied an important place in almost all of the great religious traditions. In recent years, however, the term "mysticism" has been used so loosely in *everyday language* that its traditional meaning is in danger of becoming lost. Bookstores typically link mysticism with the occult, and frequently display books on mysticism in the "occultism" section. Such psychic phenomena as visions, levitation, trances, and altered states of consciousness are frequently dubbed "mystical." Walter Principe recently reported the following newspaper item.

> Last May the *Toronto Star's* headline-writer announced: 'Scientist offers electronic way to mysticism'—this to entice readers to an article about a 'meditation machine' or revolving bed that is 'intended,' says the photo-caption, 'to help people enjoy the spiritual experiences formerly available only to religious mystics.' [1]

---

* First Published in *Philosophy East and West,* vol. 29, 1979.

With such imprecision in the use of the term mysticism abounding, it is important that any scholarly discussion begin with a precise definition of the subject.

In his book entitled *Mysticism and Philosophy,* Walter Stace points out that the very word "mysticism" is an unfortunate one. "It suggests mist, and therefore foggy, confused, or vague thinking. It also suggests mystery and miraclemongering, and therefore hocus-pocus." [2] But when an examination is made of the experiences reported by the great mystics, something which is much different emerges. Rather than being "misty" or "confused" mystical experiences are typically described as clear illuminations, having all the qualities of direct sensory perception. Stace, in fact, suggests that it is helpful to think of mystical experience as in some respects parallel to ordinary sense experience, that is, as a perception of a spiritual presence which is greater than man. Defining it as a perception, says Stace, allows one to avoid Russell's error of describing mysticism as only an emotion, and therefore as simply subjective.[3] The question raised is this: Does mystical experience, like sense experience, point to any objective reality, or is it a merely subjective psychological phenomenon? This question is, of course, one which is formulated by a philosopher for philosophical reasons, but it is a question which necessarily raises psychological issues. Is the psychological process of the mystical experience in some way analogous to sense perception? Or is it as Rudolf Otto (following Immanuel Kant) suggests something that begins amid all the sensory data of the natural world, and indeed cannot exist without such data, and yet does not arise *out of* them but is merely occasioned by them.[4] Otto, of course, prefers an analogy to aesthetic experience as the best way of evoking a sense of the mystical. He also seems to suggest the existence of a separate psychological faculty specially suited for the reception of numinous stimuli emanating from the wholly other (the *numen*).

Frederick Copleston recently pointed out a paradox which is characteristic of mystical experience. "In the case of mysticism a man may be conscious of the fact that the experience described transcends the range of his own experience; and yet at the same time his reading and effort of understanding may be for him the occasion of a personal awareness of God." [5] On this point virtually all scholars agree. Mysticism is characterized by the experience of an unseen reality,[6] a spiritual presence,[7] a *numen,*[8] or an absolute[9] that is transcendent in that "it is identifiable neither with the empirical world as its appears to us in everyday experience and in natural science nor with the finite self considered as such. . . ." [10] It is this very transcendent character of mystical experience that causes scholars to reject psychic phenomena such as imaginative visions, voices, ecstasies, raptures, and so on as not mystical in and of themselves. As Father Copleston puts it, "we all know that some people see things or hear voices without even a prima facie connection with the divine. And of course there are also pathological psychological states resembling ecstasy which can be accounted for by purely naturalistic explanations." [11] Mystical experience, by contrast, is transcendent of both the sensory experience of the empirical world, and any all-encompassing identification with a finite ego of the sort which typifies pathological states.

Other than a general agreement that mystical experience is transcendent in nature and must not be confused with extraordinary psychic accomplishments and certain pathological states, there seems to be little consensus about the psychological processes involved. There is Stace's suggestion that something like sense perception is the process involved. Otto, however, rejects the perception analogy as too narrow and instead, in an analogy from aesthetics, invokes a special mental faculty which would function amid the data of feeling perception and cognition, and yet somehow be independent of all of these. William James makes the very general suggestion that mystical experience of the transcendent occurs through the psychological processes of the subconscious self.[12] In the midst of this confusion and disagreement about the psychological processes involved, it may prove helpful to examine comparatively the thought of the Western psychologist Carl Jung and the yoga psychologist Patañjali in relation to mystical experience.

II. Mysticism in the Analytical Psychology of Carl Jung

Writing his "Late Thoughts," [13] Carl Jung puts down his own personal religious experience as clearly as may be found anywhere in his writings. There is no doubt that Jung's experience was highly mystical. All around himself Jung felt the forces of good and evil moving, but, in the end, the only thing that really mattered was the degree to which the individuated self could transcend these opposing forces.

It seems to have been Jung's view that as an isolated ego, a person would never succeed in reuniting the opposing forces. Those forces within the personality would simply overpower one's ego, and chaos would ensue. What saves us from this fate, said Jung, is the fact that deep within each of us is the God-image which is the psychological foundation of our psyche. The God-image or archetype is inherent in the collective unconscious as the primal stratum or foundational matrix. The experiencing of the God archetype has a unifying effect upon the whole personality. Especially noticable is the way in which the opposing tensions are brought together by the guiding influence of the God archetype over the individual ego. In Jung's view mysticism plays a large role in this whole process of uniting and balancing the opposing forces within experience. (In this context the term "mysticism" is being used, as just defined by Copleston, to mean the process of identifying with something more than the finite ego.)

Mystical experiences, Jung felt, may have a powerful effect upon a person. The forces involved arise from the unconscious and transcend the finite ego so that,

> He cannot grasp, comprehend, dominate them; nor can he free himself or escape from them, and therefore feels them as overpowering. Recognizing that they do not spring from his conscious personality, he calls them mana, daimon or God." [14]

Although these forces are nothing other than aspects of the unconscious, to call them merely "the unconscious," while empirically correct, would not be satisfactory for most people. The mythic terms "mana," "daimon," or "God," even though simply synonyms for the unconscious, prove to be especially effective in the production of mystical experience. The personification of the unconscious in such concepts enables an involvement of a wide range of emotions (for example, hate and love, fear and reverence). In this way, says Jung, the whole person is challenged and engaged.

> Only then can he become whole and only then can 'God be born', that is, enter into human reality and associate with man in the form of 'man.' By this act of incarnation man—that is, his ego—is inwardly replaced by 'God', and God becomes outwardly man, in keeping with the saying of Jesus: 'Who sees me, sees the Father.'' [15]

For Jung the basic psychic process involved in the mystical experience is clearly the replacing of the conscious ego with the more powerful, numinous, forces of the unconscious—called by the Western Christian, "God." As to the content of these overpowering forces of the unconscious—the content of this "God" concept—Jung is more explicit. The monotheism of Western religion and the all-encompassing absolute implied must be taken seriously. Within the One God must be found room for all the opposites encountered in experience, including even the opposites of good and evil. Only then, says Jung, will the unavoidable internal contradictions in the image of the Creator-God be reconciled in the unity and wholeness of the self. "In the experience of the self it is no longer the opposites "God" and "man" that are reconciled, as it was before, but rather the opposites within the God-image itself." [16] Good and evil stand encompassed, held in tension, and transcended within the one absolute.

What is of interest for this discussion of mysticism is not so much the theological argument assumed (and which Jung worked out in detail in his *Answer to Job*), but rather the psychological dynamics indicated. Jung's analysis shows mystical experience to occur when the finite, conscious ego is inwardly replaced by God, with God being understood as a personification of the numinous qualities of the unconscious. And here Jung is not making a metaphysical claim that God either exists or does not exist. Jung is simply observing that the processes involved in our experience of God are those of the unconscious. To put it simply, if we assume that God exists then the way he acts upon us in overpowering mystical experiences is through the psychological processes of the unconscious—particularly via the God archetype.

A good illustration of this process is offered by Jung in his essay *The Holy Men of India.*[17] There Jung describes mysticism as the shifting of the center of gravity from the ego to the

Self, from man to God. This, observes Jung, is the goal of *The Exercitia Spiritualia* of Ignatius Loyola—to subordinate "self-possession" (possession by an ego) as much as possible to possession by Christ.[18] Just as Christ manifests the reconciliation of the opposites within God's nature, so also does the person who surrenders his life to Christ overcome the conflict of the opposites within and achieves unity in God. As Jung puts it,

> God is the union of the opposites, the uniting of the torn asunder, the conflict is redeemed in the Cross. So Przywara says: 'God appears in the cross,' that is he manifests himself as the crucified Christ. The man who wishes to reach this unity in God, to make God real in himself, can only attain this through the Imitatio Christi, that is he must take up his cross and accept the conflict of the world and stand in the center of the opposites.[19]

For the Christian, God appears empirically in the suffering of the world, in the pain produced by the conflict between the opposites. One who would identify with God, therefore, does not seek to escape from the suffering of the world's conflicts, but rather gives up one's ego and identifies with Christ. By attempting to unite mystically with Christ, says Jung, "I enter the body of Christ through his scars, and my ego is absorbed into the body of Christ. Then like St. Paul, I no longer live but Christ lives in me."[20] Jung takes special care to ensure that the preceding statement is not to be understood in the form "I am Christ" but rather, as Paul puts it in *Galatians* 2:20, ". . . it is no longer I who live, but Christ who lives in me. . . ." In terms of psychological dynamics, the finite ego has been subordinated to the self.

A detailed description of the arising of the self in Jungian theory is rather complex and difficult. It is Jung's view that each of us share in three different levels of consciousness; the conscious level of the ego; the dreams, memories, and repressions which comprise the personal unconscious; and the predispositions to universal human reactions, the archetypes, which compose the collective unconscious. It is of course the notion of the archetypes and the collective unconscious which is the trademark of Jung's thought. And it is the idea of a "master archetype," namely, the "self" or "God" archetype that is fundamental for Jung's analysis of mysticism.

Of all the archetypes, it is the "self" or "God" archetype which has the power to encompass all aspects of life in a way that is integrated and mature. To be comprehensive, both conscious stimuli from the external environment and internal impulses from within the personal and collective unconscious must be included. If one remains fixated on the conscious ego, its limited internal and external awareness will result in only a small portion of the stimuli available from all three levels of consciousness being included. In most ordinary experience there is only experience of the conscious level of ego awareness. Being grounded in the collective experience of mankind, and being present within the unconscious of each person, the archetypes are the psychological mechanisms which enable us to get out from the too narrow encapsulation of our conscious egos.

The archetypes are constantly trying to "raise up" or "reveal" some of the basic wisdom of mankind. But this requires the action of the thinking, feeling, sensing, and intuiting functions of the psyche. First there is the encounter of some external stimuli, for example, the seeing of an ordinary wooden cross on a building in a Christian culture. Initially the cross has no mystical significance and functions only at the ego conscious level as a secular sign to designate the building as a church. But over the years as one matures, the cross image gradually acquires more significance and is carried, by the process of intuition, deeply into the psyche until the level of the collective unconscious is reached. There the God archetype, which has all the while been struggling upward to reveal itself, resonates sympathetically with the cross image and its Christian content of the crucified Christ. With the help of the other psychic functions (thinking, sensing, and feeling) the God archetype is given further individuation, using both the person's own creativity and the materials presented by a particular cultural tradition until the mystical revelation occurs.

Jung observes that initial indications often appear in dreams,[21] when the symbol being created first reaches the level of the personal subconscious. One becomes vaguely aware, perhaps for the first time, that the cross image is something much more than merely a sign to indicate that a building is a church.

Rather than the church building, the cross and the figure of Christ simply being seen as routine parts of everyday life to be manipulated by the ego for its own purposes, the cross is now sensed as being *numinous*—as having a power and meaning about it which causes the conscious ego to pale by comparison. As the cross symbol becomes more complete, and the God archetype achieves full individuation at the level of conscious awareness, there occurs what Jung describes as a shift in the center of gravity within the psyche from the ego to the self. This is the mystical moment of illumination when the ego becomes aware of the larger and deeper collective dimension of consciousness and reality. In religious terms it may be variously described as a sudden or a gradual awakening. But the key is that whereas previously things were experienced in a narrow egocentric way, now it is a sense of profound identity with the universal "self" which dominates. One is simultaneously united on the various levels within the psyche and taken out beyond the finite limitations of the ego. Thus, the mystical character of Jung's "self"-realization experience.

Although the cross and the crucified Christ are expected symbols of mystical self-realization in Christian cultures, Jung found the *maṇḍala* to be the most universal. As an image, it is the *maṇḍala's* characteristic of having an individualized center, yet expanding outward with the potential to include everything, that makes it a suitable symbol for mystical experience. Jung puts it as follows:

> The mandala's basic motif is the premonition of a center of personality, a kind of central point within the psyche, to which everything is related, by which everything is arranged, and which is itself a source of energy. . . . This center is not felt or thought of as the ego, but if one may so express it, as the *self*. Although the center is represented by an innermost point, it is surrounded by a periphery containing everything that belongs to the self—the paired opposites that make up the total personality. This totality comprises consciousness first of all, then the personal unconscious, and finally an indefinitely large segment of the collective unconscious whose archetypes are common to all mankind.[22]

Two things about the *maṇḍala* symbol impressed Jung. First, it occurred as a symbol for meditation in almost all great religions, and, in addition, it appeared independently in the dreams of his modern patients. Second the *maṇḍala* symbol wonderfully conveyed the sense of development around the center—but development that included all sides and left nothing out. For Jung the *maṇḍala* was a pictorial representation of the circumambulation process of development which he took to be basic to the personality.[23]

Even though Jung felt that there were very definite differences between the mystical experiences of Eastern and Western religions, the psychological processes involved seemed very similar. Whereas in the East the *maṇḍala* served as a symbol both to clarify the nature of the deity philosophically and to aid in the development of that divine nature within one's own personality, so also the presentation and evoking of the proper relationship between God and man in Christian religion was expressed in the symbol of Christ or the cross.[24] In both cases the senses of completeness, union and unity, were highlighted, and these were universally reported as characteristics of mystical experience. In his *Commentary on the Secret of the Golden Flower,* Jung supported this contention of the commoness of mystical experience. He analyzed a mystical experience reported by Edward Maitland, the biographer of Anna Kingsford, and found in it the same sense of symbolic unity contained in the ancient Taoist Chinese text.[25]

While both Eastern and Western mysticism bear witness to the sense of transcendent unity that such philosophers as Walter Stace have called "the core of mysticism," [26] Jung is very careful to make clear the subtle psychological differences in the way that unity is experienced.

> Between the Christian and the Buddhist mandala there is a subtle but enormous difference. The Christian during contemplation would never say, "I am Christ" but will confess with Paul, "Not I, but Christ liveth in me" [The Buddhist] sutra, however, says: "Thou wilt know that thou art the Buddha." [27]

At bottom both statements express a fundamental sense of unity, but in Jung's view, the way the unity is experienced is altogether different. The Buddhist statement "Thou art the Buddha" or the Hindu Upanisadic teaching "I am Brahman" requires complete removal of the individual ego or *ahaṃkāra.* The Western statement "Christ liveth in me" implies not a destruction of the ego but rather an invasion or possession by God so that the individual ego continues to exist only now as servant of the Lord. In mysticism, as in the other areas of psychological functioning, Jung simply would not accept the claim of Eastern thought that there could be conscious experience without a finite ego as the experiencer. As Jung saw it, the transcendent unity of the self needs the individual ego in order to be known, and the finite ego needs to be superceded by the transcendent self, if integration and enlightenment is to occur.[28] From Jung's perspective a complementary relationship between the ego and the self, between the individual and the divine is the necessary foundation for mystical experience. The mystical sense of the unity of the observer with all things requires an ego-observer as a basic prerequisite for that experience.

III. Mysticism in the Yoga Psychology of Patañjali

Patañjali's yoga psychology approaches mysticism as a case of intuition or supersensuous perception *(pratibhā)* from which distorting subjective emotions have been purged.[29] It will be recalled that the Western philosopher Stace defines mysticism in just such a perceptual way so as to avoid Russell's criticism that mystical experience is merely subjective emotion and as such has no direct touch with reality. Patañjali's claim is exactly the opposite. According to his yoga psychology, mystical experience is a case of the direct supersensuous perception of reality, with various levels of mystical impurity being caused by obscuring emotions not yet purged from the perception. It is worth noting at the outset that in yoga theory a major cause of obscuring emotion is the individual ego *(ahaṁkāra)*—the very aspect of the psyche that Jung felt to be essential.

Yoga psychology, following the Sāṅkhya theory of Indian philosophy,[30] conceives of consciousness as composed of three aspects or substantive qualities *(guṇas): sattva* (brightness, illumination, intelligence), *rajas* (emotion, movement), and *tamas* (dullness, inertia). Although each of these *guṇas* keeps its own separate identity, no individual *guṇa* ever exists independently. Rather, the three *guṇas* are always necessarily found together like three strands of a rope. However, the proportionate composition of consciousness assigned to each of the *guṇas* is constantly changing.[31] Only the predominant *guṇa* will be easily recognized in a particular thought or perception. The other two *guṇas* will be present but subordinate, and therefore their presence will have to be determined by inference. If a "psychological cross-section" were taken through an ordinary state of consciousness, there would be a dominance of *tamas* and *rajas* especially in its evolved forms of ego, sense organs, and their everyday experiences. In our routine states of consciousness there is a noticeable lack of *sattva* or pure discriminative awareness. However, in mystical experience the proportionate composition of consciousness by the *guṇas* is reversed with *sattva* becoming dominant. At its height a pure *sattva* experience would be like the direct transparent viewing of reality with no emotional *(rajas)* or bodily *(tamas)* distortion intervening. This is technically termed *nirvicārasamādhi* in Indian mysticism, and is defined as a supernormal perception that transcends the ordinary categories of time, space, causality, and has the capacity to directly "grasp" or "see" the real nature of things.[32] It is this mystical experience of pure *sattva* intuition that is given detailed psychological analysis in *sūtras* I:41–51 of Pantañjali's *Yoga Sūtras.*

Patañjali begins his analysis with a general description of the mystical state of mind, which in Sanskrit is technically termed *samādhi.* In *samādhi* the mind *(citta)* is so intensely focused upon the object of meditation that the ordinary sense of the observer being separated from the object of study is overcome. There is a sense of being one with the object. As Pantañjali puts it, it is as if the mind has become a transparent crystal that clearly reflects or transforms itself into the shape of the object being studied.[33] Vyāsa clarifies the intended meaning as follows: "As the crystal becomes colored by the color of the object placed beside it, and then shines according to the form of the object, so the mind is colored by the color of the object presented to it and then appears in the form of the object."[34] The ability of the mind to function in a crystal-like fashion requires a *sattva* dominance within consciousness.

The object referred to in this description may be any finite aspect of reality. The purpose of the object is simply to give the beginner a point of focus for his concentration, consequently it helps the process if the object exhibits a natural attractiveness to the student. One of the main tasks of the spiritual teacher or *guru* is to guide the student in selecting an object of meditation—the one that will be the most helpful. Since in Eastern thought it is generally held that the divine or absolute, whether it be conceptualized as Brahman, Buddha, Tao, or in some other form, is inherent in all of reality, therefore any aspect of reality may be suitably selected as an object for meditation. It may be some part of nature such as a flowing stream, it may be an image of Brahman such as Lord Śiva or Mother Kāli, it may be the example set by the master Yogi Īśvara, or, at the most esoteric level, it may be nothing other than the flow of consciousness itself—mind *(citta)* taking itself as the object of its own meditation.[35] The process is not unlike that proposed by Jung where some object, such as a cross, provides the starting point for the subsequent individuation of the archetype into a symbol. However, it is immediately apparent that while both Patañjali and Jung begin with an object as a point of focus, Jung never leaves the object—it simply becomes transformed in one's experience from a surface sign to a deeply meaningful and in some sense universal symbol which mediates and integrates reality. Patañjali's yoga, however, expects that the finite object, which is a limited symbol and therefore only partially able to mediate or manifest reality, must in the end be transcended. Only then can reality be fully "seen." It is this final state of unlimited congruence with reality (objectless *samādhi*) that is held by Patañjali to be the highest mystical state. And it is just such an attainment which Jung refuses to accept as possible, because it would require that the knowing ego, as one of the finite objects within consciousness, be transcended. In Jung's view this results in a mystical state with no knower to experience it, and therefore it is simply psychologically impossible. With this objection in mind let us now examine Patañajli's description of the four levels of increasingly pure object *samādhi* and the final state of objectless *samādhi* (or the direct unlimited oneness with reality).

Of the four states of object *samādhi,* the lowest or most impure is called *savitarka.* It is impure, says Patañjali in *Yoga*

Sūtra I:42, because the *sattva* "reflection" of the object is obscured by a mixing up within consciousness of the following ingredients: (1) the word *(śabda)* used in conventional speech to label that object; (2) the conceptual meaning *(artha)* of that object; and (3) the direct perception *(jñāna)* of the object itself. Vyāsa explains that this mixed-up experience of the object has a twofold cause. On the one hand there is the distortion caused by the habitual way in which word labels have been used to classify objects in this and previous lives. This has the mixing-up effect *(vikalpa)* within consciousness of causing our experience to be dominated by the conventional word labels of our language and culture (for example, saying "child," with the connotation "just another child") rather than by the perception of the object that is uniquely occurring at that moment (for example, "a brown-eyed child of a quiet, reflective mood with unfathomable beauty, dignity, and potential"). The other causes of *vikalpa* or confusion are the cognitive inferences based upon the conceptual meaning which the perception of the object evokes in our mind (for example, "a child is a gift of God to be treasured and loved" or "a child is a constant source of emotional frustration and a continuous drain upon the bank account"). Such cognitive inferences are either accepted from the traditional systems of thought of one's culture or belief (for example, a Christian view, or a materialistic view) or may be made up by one's own imaginative thinking.[36] For most of us then, even when we manage to block out external distractions and concentrate sufficiently so as to become "caught up into oneness" with the object of our meditation, the kind of *samādhi* achieved is one that is obscured by the habitual way in which we give the object in view a word label ("stereotype it") and give it a biased or slanted coloring in our thinking.

In the second half of Vyāsa's commentary on *Yoga Sūtra* I:42, the second level of object *samādhi* is defined as one in which the habitual patterns of past word usage and the biased patterns of inferential thinking are purged from the mind. Only then is the *sattva* or crystalline aspect of consciousness freed from the *rajas* or emotional obscuration so that "the object makes its appearance in the mind in its own distinct nature (unmixed up with word and meaning)." [37] The technical term for this state is *nirvitarkasamādhi* and may be translated as "distinct mystical perception." And it is this purified state of perception, says Vyāsa, that becomes the seed or basis for new verbal or inferential knowledge, namely, the truths taught by the mystics *(yogins)*—the truths they have learned from this higher form *(nirvitarka)* of perception. Vacaspati Miśra, in his gloss, points out that the *yogi* or mystic himself has no need to verbalize such truths, since he has it as a primary experience (for example, when you are hearing the greatness of the music there is no need to try to verbalize that greatness in words). But because of his compassion for others, the mystic speaks these truths, realizing however that the very speaking of them will necessarily add *rajas* or emotional distortion due to the usage of words and imagination.[38]

Whereas the two lower levels of object *samādhi* are based upon the gross or outer form of the object, the two higher levels are directed toward the inner essence—what might today be called the atomic or microcosmic structure of the object. Descriptions of such states are offered in *Yoga Sūtras* I:43 and 44, although the distinctions become so subtle as to virtually deify conceptualization. The third level is called *savicārasamādhi.* In *savicāra* experience the flow of consciousness so completely identifies with the object alone that the mind is as it were "devoid of its own nature."[39] I take Vyāsa to mean by this that there is a complete loss of ego consciousness. This does not mean one lapses into some sort of stupor. On the contrary, what is implied is that one is so "caught-up" in the object that there is no room left for a separate awareness of one's own ego as the thing that is having the experience. One has forgotten oneself. The object in all its vividness of both external characteristics and internal qualities totally commands one's attention. The only distinguishing characteristics given to the experience are provided by the object itself. In the *savicāra* state awareness of the object includes both its gross form and its microcosm or inner essence, but is limited in space and time to the present. The *yogin's* knowledge ("knowing by becoming one with") of the object is complete, but it is knowledge only as of the present moment in space and time.

Nirvicāra or the final stage of object *samādhi* differs only from *savicāra* in that in the *nirvicāra* the limitation to the present moment in space and time is overcome. Now the *yogin* is so completely one with the object that he is one with all its past states, as well as its present moment, and shares fully in the various possibilities of the future. The last limitations of space and time are transcended. According to Vyāsa a mystical state reaches the *nirvicāra* level when it is, as it were, void of its own nature and becomes the object itself. This is the highest level of knowledge of a finite object which may be reached. An example of such a *nirvicāra* state might be the knowledge that a lover of a particular person realizes when the other person is so completely known that, as we put it, "they are like an open book." In the Christian tradition, one might identify the knowledge Amos had of Israel,[40] Jesus had of the Samaritan woman at the well,[41] or St. Francis of the animals. Mystical experience of this sort is far from being "misty," "vague," or "mysterious." It is as vivid and immediate as is possible for one who habitually lives at the lower levels of awareness to imagine. Its psychological nature would seem to, as Stace suggested, approximate that of sense perception—only on a supernormal level. And from the perspective of Patañjali's yoga psychology, the two highest levels of object *samādhi* are characterized by a complete self-forgetting or egolessness. The mystic consciousness has so fully become one with the object that it no longer appears as an object of consciousness. The duality of subject and object is overcome, leaving only the steady transformation of pure *sattva* consciousness into the form of the object allowing the thing-itself *(svarūpa)* to shine forth in itself alone.[42]

The highest level of mystical realization in Patañjali's yoga is reached when even the limitation of focusing on a finite object is left behind. *Yoga Sūtras* I:50 and 51 describe the establishment of "seedless" or objectless *samādhi.* No longer does the yogin meditate on an object, not even such an exhalted object as the Lord himself. Now consciousness turns in upon itself and becomes one with its own self-luminous nature. According to both Saṅkhya theory and yoga psychology, in this state there is only pure knowing consciousness. The lower "filtering organs" of ego *(ahaṁkāra),* mind and sense organs with their component *rajas* or emotion have been dropped off or transcended. There remains only the pristine existence of reality itself which is revealed to be nothing other than the pure discriminative consciousness of the true self *(puruṣa).*[43]

In agreement with the authors previously discussed, Patañjali, although very familiar with psychic powers *(siddhis)* such as levitation,[44] warns against confusing such attainments with true mystical experiences. Special powers may be produced by drugs, by fasting or as side effects of true spiritual meditation. Consequently the *yogin* or mystic must be constantly on guard against the temptation to use such powers, as will naturally come to him, for his own fame and fortune. To do that, says Patañjali, would be tantamount to falling off a high cliff after having struggled hard to scale the heights. The distance that the fallen *yogin* would crash down would exceed the upward progress he had achieved.

IV. The Psychologies of Jung and Patañjali Compared

The preceding review of Jungian psychology and Patañjali's yoga shows both points of agreement and difference. Both authors agree with the definition of mystical experience presented by the philosophers in Section I as being characterized by a loss of the sense of finite ego and a corresponding increased identification with a transcendent spiritual reality. But there was definite disagreement about the degree of ego loss which occurs and about the kind of psychological process which is mainly responsible for the mystic's identification with the larger transcendent reality.

With regard to the degree of ego loss involved, it was Jung's view that in mystical experience there was a replacing of the conscious ego with the more powerful numinous forces of the unconscious arising from the God or self archetype. As he put it there is a shifting of the center of gravity within the personality from ego to self, from man to God. This shift of the center resulted in more of the sum total of reality being experienced and included within the personality. The mystical experience is comprehensive of both conscious stimuli from the external environment and internal impulses from within the personal and collective unconscious. This breadth of awareness means that one participates in the conflicts of the opposing forces which constitute the world. In the Christian context this is expressed as the suffering of Christ and is symbolized by the cross. The ego loss envisaged by Jung is the loss required so that one could say with Paul, "it is no longer I who live, but Christ who lives in me." The ego has not been totally lost or discarded but merely made into a servant of the Lord.

Jung correctly recognized that there was a fundamental disagreement between himself and Patañjali over the degree of ego loss involved in mystical experience. Whereas in Jung's view the mystic experience of reality required the continued existence of an ego in order to be known, for Patañjali's yoga the ego was nothing more than a limiting and distorting emotional obscuration which had to be removed if the real was to be fully known. In the two lower states of *savitarka-* and *nirvitarka-samādhi* the presence of ego and its habitually limiting ways of perceiving and thinking rendered the mystical experience impure. However in the higher states of *savicāra-* and *nirvicāra-samādhi,* the mind by virtue of being completely devoid of its own ego is able to be perfectly transparent to the object being meditated upon. Such complete and direct experience of some objective aspect of reality requires that the mystic not allow his own ego and mental processes to get in the way. Although Patañjali, with his requirement for a complete negation of ego, has already gone well beyond Jung's more limited Western point of view, the ultimate state has still to be reached according to yoga. In addition to the limiting factor of the individual ego being removed, the full mystic experience requires that reality be experienced in its completeness and not in just the limited form of a finite object as one point of meditation. For the Eastern point of view even if the object of one's meditation be an incarnation of the divine, the Lord himself, something of the fullness of reality will have been "dropped off" to enable the limited incarnation to take place. Thus, for Patañjali, it is the objectless *samādhi* in which consciousness becomes one with its own self-luminous nature, that is the highest mystical experience. It is such an experience that is indicated by phrases such as "I am Brahman" or "I am Buddha," and that differs so radically from the Christian "Christ lives in me."

With regard to the kind of psychological processes involved, Jung seems to follow the lead of Rudolf Otto and William James whereas Patañjali is much closer to the approach suggested by Walter Stace. In Jung's analysis, mystical experience, although it may begin with intuition, necessarily also involves the other psychological processes of feeling, thinking, and sensing. For Patañjali, the processes of emotion and thinking had to be purged until only pure perception remained. Jung, to a large extent, followed Otto's suggestion of an analogy to aesthetic experience. Patañjali, like Stace, appealed to the model of sense perception. Jung followed James in pointing to the unconscious as the locus of mystical experience, for yoga the opposite condition of complete consciousness is identified as the mystical.

In the face of the earlier comparative psychological study, we find ourselves left with what is perhaps a new and expanded version of Stace's question, "Does mystical experience point to an objective reality or is it merely a subjective phenomenon?" Now the psychological question must be added, "Can there be mystical experience without an individual ego?" Or put another way, "Is unlimited consciousness of the fullness of reality psychologically possible?"

Notes and References

1. Walter H. Principe, "Mysticism: Its Meaning and Varieties", in *Mystics and Scholars* edited by Harold Coward and Terence Penelhum (Waterloo: Wilfrid Laurier University Press, 1976), p. 1.
2. W. T. Stace, *Mysticism and Philosophy* (London: Macmillan, 1961), p. 15.
3. Ibid., pp. 13–18.
4. Rudolf Otto, *The Idea of the Holy* (New York: Oxford University Press, 1963), p. 113.
5. Frederick C. Copleston, *Religion and Philosophy* (Dublin: Gill and Macmillan, 1974), p. 90.
6. William James, *The Varieties of Religious Experience* (New York: Mentor, 1958), pp. 58ff.
7. Spiritual presence" is Arnold Toynbee's term which Walter Stace adopted in his *Mysticism and Philosophy*, op. cit., p. 5.
8. *The Idea of the Holy*, op. cit., p. 7.
9. "Absolute" is the term adopted by Evelyn Underhill in her *Mysticism* (New York: Meridan, 1955).
10. *Religion and Philosophy*, op. cit., p. 75.
11. Ibid.
12. *The Varieties of Religious Experience*, op. cit., pp. 385–386.

13. C. G. Jung, *Memories, Dreams, Reflections* (New York: Vintage, 1965), Cp. XII.
14. Ibid., p. 336.
15. Ibid., p. 337.
16. Ibid., p. 338.
17. C. G. Jung, "The Holy Men of India" in *C.W.* 11:576–586.
18. Ibid., p. 581.
19. C. G. Jung, "The Process of Individuation in the Exercitia spiritulia of St. Ignathus of Loyola," June 1939—March 1940, unpublished Eidgenössische Technische Hochschule Lectures, Zurich (E.T.H. Lectures), pp. 122–123.
20. Ibd., p. 123.
21. C. G. Jung, "Psychology and Religion," *C.W.* 11:23ff.
22. C. G. Jung, "Concerning Mandala Symbolism," *C.W.* 9, Pt. I:357.
23. Another image which Jung sometimes used in the same way as the *maṇḍala* was that of the tree. This is especially seen in his 1945 Festschrift article entitled "The Philosophical Tree," written in honor of Gustay Senn, Professor of Botany, University of Basel. In it Jung says, "If a mandala may be described as a symbol of the self seen in cross section, then the tree would represent a profile view of it: the self depicted as a process of growth." *C.W.* 13, p. 253.
24. C. G. Jung, "Psychology and Religion," *C.W.* 11:79–80.
25. C. G. Jung, "Commentary on The Secret of the Golden Flower," *C.W.* 13:26–28.
26. W. T. Stace, *The Teachings of the Mystics* (New York: Mentor, 1960), pp. 14–15.
27. C.G. Jung, "The Psychology of Eastern Meditation," *C.W.* 11:574–575.
28. C.G. Jung, *The Holy Men of India, C.W.* 11:584.
29. The following section is an interpretation of Patañjali's *Yoga Sūtras,* especially *sūtras* I:41–51, with the Commentary *(Bhāsya)* by Vyāsa and the Gloss *(Tika)* by Vācaspati Miśra. *Patañjali-Yogadarsanam* (Varanasi: Bhāratīya Vidhyā Prakāśana, 1963). Best English translation by Rama Prasada (Allahabad: Bhuvaneswari Asrama, 1924).
30. See *Sāṅkhya Kārikā of Īśvara Krishna,* trans. J. Davies (Calcutta: Susil Gupta, 1947).
31. *Yoga Sūtra* II:18, *bhāṣya.*
32. See Gopinath Kaviraj, "The Doctrine of Pratibhā in Indian Philosophy", *Annals of the Bhandarkar Oriental Research Institute* (1924):I–18 and 113–132.
33. *Yoga Sūtra* I:41.
34. Ibid., *bhāṣya.*
35. This is the "seedless" or "objectless" samādhi described by Patañjali in *Yoga Sūtra* I:51.
36. *Yoga Sūtra* I:42, *bhāṣya.*
37. Ibid.
38. Ibid., *tikā.*
39. *Yoga Sūtra* I:43, *bhāṣya.*
40. *Amos* 6:1–14.
41. *John* 4:1–26.

42. *Yoga Sūtra* I:43, *tikā.*
43. *Yoga Sūtra* I:51, *bhāsya.*
44. Chapter III of the *Yoga Sūtras* gives a complete list of the psychic powers and how to attain them.

VIII. Prakṛti and the Collective Unconscious: Puruṣa and Self

The aim of this chapter is to compare some aspects of the ancient yoga system of Patañjali with facets of the psychology of Jung in order to throw some new light on the meaning of Patañjali's yoga and also on Jung's interpretation of that system. At first sight these two names represent radically different approaches to the study of the activity and nature of man. Jung's approach is purely psychological: he deals with empiric psychic reality, builds up a theory of psychic reality, and evolves a method of psychic therapeutics.[1] Patañjali on the other hand, elaborates the practice of mysticism, complemented by a metaphysical theory. The difference is most striking when we look at the theoretical end-point of Jung's system: the scientific hypothesis which has no metaphysical pretensions: and at the cornerstone of yoga: its Sāṅkhya metaphysics. However, when we look at the practical aspect of yoga, culminating in *samādhi,* we are dealing with a psychic experience. And here an area of valuable comparisons opens up. In this chapter the place and function of the key concepts of *prakṛti* and *puruṣa* in the practice and metaphysics of Patañjali will be related to Jung's concepts of the "collective unconscious" and of "spirit".

I. The Theory of Psychic Reality

Both Patañjali and Jung try to circumscribe what they mean by the totality of psychic life though they give different epistomological values to their description. Jung has caused a Copernican revolution in the conception of psychic reality by doing away with the narrow opposition between a human psyche and a material cosmos which had dominated Western thought for so long. For him man is a physico-psychic being that partakes not only of a physical world, but is also part of a psychic universe infinitely wider than his ego-consciousness. The ego-consciousness in Jung's system has been compared to the tip of an iceberg, the submerged part forming the "personal unconscious," and the ocean constituting the universe of the "collective unconscious". With the collective unconscious we enter into a psychic world of cosmic dimensions, which is in direct continuity with the personal conscious and unconscious psyche. Jacobi aptly summarized it as follows:

> For the collective part of the unconscious no longer includes contents that are specific for our individual ego and result from personal acquisitions, but such as result 'from the inherited possibility of psychical functioning in general, namely from the inherited brain-structure.' This inheritance is common to all humanity, perhaps even to all the animal world, and forms the basis of every individual psyche. The unconscious is older than consciousness. It is the "primal datum" out of which consciousness ever arises afresh.[2]

Remarkable similarities appear when we look at the Sāṅkhya metaphysics on which yoga is based. It is apposite to note here that, although the doctrine is intended to represent a metaphysical statement, it is intrinsically related to practice and experience, which it endeavors to systematize. In other words, yoga metaphysics is the projection onto the ontological plane of the analysis and categorization of psychic experience. Sāṅkhya is a philosophy of dualism: total reality comprises two irreducible realms of *prakṛti* and *puruṣa*. *Puruṣa* stands for the multiplicity of individual, perfect spirits, and may be put aside for the moment. *Prakṛti* is the matrix of all physical and psychic being. When its undifferentiated *pralaya* (cosmic dissolution) state was upset at the beginning of a cosmic cycle, an evolutionary movement was set in motion. This movement successively produced out of this mass of first matter, the universal potentiality of mind *(buddhi),* and of individuality *(ahaṁkāra).* Then followed *manas,* coordinator of all senses; the senses, inner and outer; the subtle and gross elements; and hence the totality of cosmic manifestation.[3] This evolutionary process may seem arbitrary when judged as an ontological, causal explanation. However, its fundamental meaning is to be sought in another direction: as the dynamic explantion of man's physico-psychic reality. The Indian tradition offers repeated examples of analyses of two psychic phenomena; waking up out of deep sleep, and the gradual process of sinking into deep meditation. These analyses were of paramount importance in the elaboration of the evolutionary process of *prakṛti.* It is on this level that we find striking similarities to Jung's concept of psychic reality. Jung makes a strong connection between psychic life and brain-structure; yoga postulates the common essence of man's body and mind, springing from that one *prakṛti.* As Eliade says: "In fact, the difference between cosmos and man is only a difference of degree, not of essence".[4] Psychic life, for yoga, goes down beneath the ego-function, and reaches back in time through evolution. When Jung speaks of the "inherited possibility of psychical functioning in general," [5] these words seem to fit the cosmic *buddhi* and *ahaṁkāra,* thus reaching down into the primal evolutes of *prakṛti.* For Yoga, as for Jung, psychic reality reaches beyond the individual into a cosmic psychic world, not only as a result of past evolution and inheritance, but also as a matter of actual reality.[6]

The question now arises how the second member of Sāṅkhya dualism, the *puruṣa,* fits into the system. In the ontological scheme, the *puruṣa* is placed right at the beginning of the cosmic evolution which it is presumed to direct teleologically throughout. However, it is not present as an experienced entity. As far as yoga practice goes, *puruṣa* is the unknown, the undiscovered, the ultimate aim: the experienced process is from *prakṛti* to the ultimate discovery of *puruṣa.* Therefore, as the focus of the discussion is at this moment on the practice itself, *puruṣa* may be disregarded now, and reconsidered later when the final stage of *samādhi,* the revelation of *puruṣa,* is considered.

II. The Practice: Approaches and Methods

At first one is struck by an apparent opposition between the approaches of Jung and yoga. While Jung seems to aim at an enlarging of consciousness, Yoga techniques strive for a progressive narrowing of consciousness. According to Jung, modern (Western) man lives too completely within the narrow confines of his personal consciousness, and disregards to an enormous and dangerous extent the wider world of the unconscious that is part of his psyche. That is why his awareness must be in some way widened, in order to take in the forces and intentions of the realm of the unconscious. Yoga, on the other hand, sees man dissipating himself in the constant flow of physico-psychic life, spreading and losing his energies in the million directions in which the outside world, his senses, and his mind constantly draw him. Man, therefore, must close the gates of the outer world, and direct his mind to the narrow confines of his own interior life.

On closer inspection, this opposition between "widening" and "narrowing" consciousness is a superficial one, related only to figures of speech and not to reality. What both Jung and yoga in fact strive after, at least as their immediate aim,[7] is to penetrate into psychic life beyond the limits of the ego. Both are looking for just that: a consciousness which is different from "normal consciousness," a psychic reality and content that lies "beyond," or "beneath," or "within" the ego. This psychic realm beyond, beneath, within the ego, as discovered by Jung and yoga, is precisely what we want to compare. But before describing the content of his psychic beyond, we have to say a few words about the different methods of penetrating it used by the two disciplines. Jung describes his own method succinctly as follows:

> Usually, a consciousness is characterized by an intensity and narrowness that have a cramping effect, and this ought not to be emphasized still further. On the contrary, everything must be done to help the unconscious to reach the conscious mind and to free it from its rigidity. For this purpose I employ a method of active imagination, which consists in a special training for switching off consciousness, at least to a relative

> extent, thus giving the unconscious contents a chance to develop.[8]

These last words excellently describe how Jung's method is essentially indirect. It consists in the analysis of dreams, symbols, archetypes, thrown up by the unconscious when consciousness is "switched off." During this dormant state the latent forces, realities, intentions of the unconscious flow over into consciousness and appear under symbolic guise. Jung's method is the analysis, interpretation, evaluation, and synthesis of these symbols emerging at the time of the twilight of consciousness.

Yoga technique is totally different. It is essentially a concentration, a conscious directing of thought, a penetration into the beyond by the active mind. No question here of "switching off consciousness"; on the contrary, the method sharpens consciousness, which is made into the surgical knife that penetrates beyond the ego. There is a certain withdrawal, as there is in Jung, but not withdrawal from cnsciousness itself, but a withdrawal from empiric, outward-directed consciousness into the inner world. The withdrawal from the superficial world is performed in order to allow consciousness with all its vigor and luminosity to descend into the world within. Later on the question will be asked whether the end-point of this yogic withdrawal, *samādhi,* has to be equated with total unconsciousness. But as long as we consider the methods themselves, we cannot but be struck by the complete difference between Jungian and yogic methods. Whereas Jung puts consciousness to sleep so that the world within may reveal itself by symbols, yoga dams the mental stream by thought, so that thought may penetrate beyond the mental stream. This difference of approach arises from the fact that the Indian tradition accepted the existence of a large "world within," whereas, according to Jung, Western man has become so outward-directed and unaware of the inner world of the psyche, that for him an indirect method is necessary.

III. The "World Within"

The first movement of yogic penetration is withdrawal from the outer world, from "normal consciousness." After the proper moral preparation, the method starts with *āsana,* control of posture.[9] This gradually acquired control brings the yogin's body to a physical condition in which consciousness is no longer troubled by the movement and stimulation of physical restlessness, because, as Patañjali says, the "posture is steadily easy." [10] Thus the body itself becomes both a symbol and a cause of the penetration beyond the ego. Eliade remarks that "the motionless, hieratic position of the body imitates some other condition than the human; the yogin in the state of *āsana* can be homologized with a plant or a sacred statue; under no circumstances can he be homologized with man qua man, who, by definition, is mobile, agitated, unrhythmic." [11] It is interesting to note here that on the one hand a "plant-like" condition calls up an unconscious state basic to all psychic life (collective unconscious), and that the sacred statue, on the other, somehow reminds one of aspects of Jung's archetypes.

Prāṇāyāma, breath-control, in a similar but different way fosters the removal of normal ego-consciousness. Breathing is closely connected with the fluctuation of mental states, as Bhoja remarked in his commentary on the *Yoga-Sūtras.*[12] By making the breathing perfectly rhythmical and slowing down its pace, a condition is induced that is similar to that of deep, dreamless sleep. Again one is reminded of Jung, for whom sleep is a most important state wherein the wider psychic world tends to reveal itself. But there is a difference of approach. Jung wants man to give himself over to the suggestive waves of dreams, expecting they will let hints, symbols, and archetypes emerge into consciousness; in yoga the sleep-condition is deliberately induced and consciously controlled, as we read in Patañjali.[13]

Pratyāhāra, withdrawal from the senses, leads to the very threshold of discovery of the inner world. The senses, open windows through which the outer world continuously infiltrates consciousness, are neutralized and sensory activity is brought to a standstill; the mind is insulated against all outside interference, and closes itelf into its own autonomous sphere. But this "autonomy" does not result in the total suppression of mental images: even though detched from the outward stimulus, the yogin continues to comtemplate them. However, this contemplation is now a direct one, independent from the activity and influence of the senses. That is why this contemplation is able to penetrate into the very essence of its object.[14]

This brings us to the intellectual effort of penetration, called *sanyama,* which progresses through the steps of *dhāraṇā* (concentration, *dhyāna* (contemplation), and *samādhi* (trance). This contemplative effort is at first object-bound, but soon moves from the gross to the subtle aspects of the subject-matter: it penetrates into the subtle aspects of *prakṛti* and identifies itself with them. These subtle aspects of *prakṛti* are the creative matrix of all physical and psychic manifestations, not only in the sense that they lie at the beginning of a cosmic evolution, but also that they are the actual continuing underlying powers out of which psycho-physical reality constantly emerges. Therefore, withdrawal from the outer world has brought the yogin into direct contact with the very essence of nature as a whole, and not just with his own personal little internal world. "It is a real descent into the very essence of the physical world, and not only into qualified and individual phenomena." [15] As Patañjali puts it, "And the province of the subtle reaches up to the noumenal," in which the latter refers to *prakṛti.*[16] In other words, the deepest level of this penetration reaches the undifferentiated womb of *prakṛti,* essence and totality of the physico-psychic world. Withdrawal has resulted in cosmic inflation.

Inflation because this cosmic vision is a peculiar kind of vision: it is a knowledge where the subject is what it knows, where it is identified with its object. This vision is an assimilation, it brings man into a state of "cosmicization".[17] Microcosmos and macrocosmos find their identity within the "macranthropos," or in Samkhya terms, man has consciously fused his body, senses, ego, and mind with the totality of *prakṛti.* According to Patañjali, "at this point his power reaches down to the minutest, and up to the largest".[18]

This is where the *siddhis,* the occult powers as described by Patañjali in Book III, find their place and explanation. Assimilation through knowledge means possession. Assimilated to *prakṛti,* creative essence of the whole cosmos, the yogin acquires extraordinary powers. We are not concerned here with discussing in how far it is possible to acquire some of these powers in certain trances. What we are interested in is the claims that accompany the psychological stage which we are describing as cosmic inflation. These powers essentially consist of knowledge of the cosmos and man, of superhuman influence on the body, of conscious participation from within in the creative power and the luminosity of *prakṛti*. In fact, the yogin claims to have reached the "state of the gods" so that all the perfections of the gods of the celestial regions are within his grasp.[19] By coinciding with the totality of nature, he has realized within himself the coincidence of all opposites—emptiness and totality, dissolution and creation, death to the world and vital union with nature, loss of the narrow ego and gain of the "mind-at-large," subject and object. We said all opposites: but we must give special mention to the antinomy of good and evil as a very important one. "The yogin must cultivate a habit of thinking in which things would appear in their true perspectives—the attractions of the physical world, the pleasures of the body, and the pride of possessions would all disappear; even the distinction between virtue *(punya)* and vice *(papa)* would vanish, for this is true only of the phenomenal ego, and not of the transcendental self," says Professor Bhattacharya, referring to *Yoga Sūtras* II; 14, and IV; 7.[20] The disappearance of virtue and vice (before they are both overcome by the resurgent self) is exactly what is meant by the coincidence of opposites. Jung also accepts this relativity of good and evil, as he accepts that both belong to the fullness of the collective unconscious, which is essentially ambivalent. He himself connects it with yoga when he refers to the fact that the yogin seeks this freedom from good and evil, and he says that "freedom from opposites presupposes their functional equivalence."[21]

This brings us to Jung. How does the content of "the world within" discovered by the yogin compare with Jung's collective unconscious? Here is how Jung describes it:

> The shadow is a tight passage, a narrow door, whose painful constriction no one is spared who goes down to the deep well. But one must learn to know oneself in order to know who one is. For what comes after the door is, surprisingly enough, a boundless expanse full of unprecedented uncertainty, with apparently no inside and no outside, no above and no below, no here and no there, no mine and no thine, no good and no bad. It is the world of water, where all life floats in suspension; where the realm of the sympathetic system, the soul of everything living, begins;

> where I am indivisibly this and that; where I experience the other in myself and the other-than-myself experiences me.
>
> No, the collective unconscious is anything but an incapsulated personal system; it is sheer objectivity, as wide as the world and open to all the world. There I am the object of every subject, in complete reversal of my ordinary consciousness, where I am always the subject that has an object. There I am utterly alone with the world, so much a part of it that I forget all too easily who I really am. 'Lost in oneself' is a good way of describing this state. But this self is the world, if only a consciousness could see it.[22]

This passage needed to be quoted in full, because it is rare that one catches Jung in this mood of total description, and his description in this case is strikingly similar to what we called the "cosmicization" of the yogin in his interior descent. The collective unconscious is the "total world," "where the soul of everything living begins." It is the undifferentiated "world of water," where all the opposites are included, and where the subject is drowned in the "self of the whole world." All these characteristics are fundamental to *prakṛti,* in which the yogin finds the inflation of his own being. But these parallelisms need fuller consideration. First we will describe the collective unconscious objectively as a "content," and afterwards subjectively as "inflation of the ego."

The equation of *prakṛti* with "the Great Mother," totality of the collective unconscious, and primal archetype, has been proposed by Jung himself: "Samkhya philosophy has elaborated the mother archetype into the concept of *prakṛti* (matter) and assigned to it the three *guṇas* or fundamental attributes: *sattva, rajas, tamas:* goodness, passion and darkness. These are the three essential aspects of the mother: her cherishing and nourishing goodness, her orgiastic emotionality, and her Stygian depths." [23] There is no need to further insist on the equivalence of *prakṛti* to the collective unconscious, as womb and mother of all the world, but it is worth while mentioning how in the later development of Indian thought, *prakṛti* became identified with *Māyā* and *Śakti,* whose correspondence with the great archetypal figure of the Mother is even more pronounced.

Another aspect of the collective unconscious to which Jung referred in the previous quotation is its ambivalence, or the way in which it contains all the antinomies. When penetrating into the subtle aspects of nature, the yogin contemplates the essential play of opposites in the constant interaction of the complementary *gunas*. This is how Jung describes the content of the collective unconscious.

> Symbols and complexes come and go; eternally unfolding, moving, and changing, they set their stamp on the life of the psyche, only to sink back again into the primordial womb of the unconscious, returning to their archetypal forms of existence, until the time becomes ripe for them to emerge once more. In their undifferentiated state they bear within them salvation and doom, good and evil, health and sickness, and every conceivable pair of opposites.[24]

In this text one could practically replace the words "symbols and complexes" by *guṇas,* and "unconscious" by *prakṛti.* We have noted before how the opposites of good and evil are explicitly mentioned both in Jung and yoga.

Zaehner makes an interesting suggestion equating the libido-concept of Jung with *prāṇa* of Indian thought.[25] Libido, indeed, is for Jung the psychic energy, "the totality of that force which pulses through and combines one with another all the forms and activities of the psychic system." [26] And Jung himself calls *prāṇa* "both the breath and the universal dynamic of the cosmos." [27] The parallel is obvious, but we do not insist on it here, because Patañjali's classical yoga, however much it owes to the Upaniṣadic insights into *prāṇa,* does not elaborate on this more mystical and archetypal aspect of *prāṇa.* Another chapter in this volume deals with *prāṇa* and libido.

It is time now, after having considered some of the most important characteristics of the content of the "world within" of Jung and yoga, to focus on the subjective aspect: its repercussions on the subject, which could be generally described as "positive inflation." The yogin in meditation descends beyond the ego into a world of cosmic dimensions, into the essence of the cosmos itself; and the world of the collective unconscious that wells up, according to Jung, when the ego-function is dormant, has similar cosmic dimensions. It follows from this that the new consciousness is cosmically inflated. We saw how the yogin becomes the "macranthropos", god-like, and endowed with superhuman powers. We find an echo of the "macranthropos" in Jung:

> If it were possible to personify the unconscious, we might think of it as a collective human being combining the characteristics of both sexes, transcending youth and age, birth and death, and from having as its command a human experience of one or two million years, practically immortal. If such a being existed, it would be exalted above all temporal change; the present would mean neither more nor less to it than any year in the hundredth millenium before Christ, it would be a dreamer of age-old dreams and, owing to its limitless experience, an incomparable prognosticator. It would have lived countless times over again the life of the individual, the family, the tribe, and the nation, and it would possess a living sense of the rhythm of growth, flowering and decay.[28]

Is it any wonder that contact with that unconscious produces "inflation." Jung says:

> I also showed that to annex the deeper layers of the unconscious, which I have called the collective unconscious, produce an extension of the personality leading to the state of inflation. . . .[29] The fantasies and dreams which now appear assume a somewhat different aspect. An infallible sign of collective images seems to be the appearance of the "cosmic" element, i.e., the images in the dream or fantasy are connected with cosmic qualities, such as temporal and spatial infinity, enormous speed and extension of movement, "astrological" associations, telluric, lunar, and solar analogies, changes in the proportions of the body, etc. . . .[30] This inflation, says Jung "gives rise to a feeling of superiority that may well express itself in the form of 'godlikeness' . . . (the individual) will feel himself a superman, holding in his hands the scales of good and evil." [31]

These few quotations should be sufficient to show how for Jung that contact with the collective unconscious inflates the personality in a way similar to the "cosmicization" of yoga. These same subjective elements appear in both: transcendence of the ego, cosmic expansion, coincidence of opposites, sense of immortality, feeling of deification and possession of superhuman powers.

There is an important aspect of the "collective unconscious" of Jung which we have not so far explicitly treated: the "archetypes". We have kept explicit treatment of the archetypes out of this discussion because the "symbolic", archetypical aspect of yoga (mystical physiology and mythology) is only present in an embryonic stage in the classical yoga of Patañjali. A close study of Tantric and Śakta mysticism would strengthen our case considerably, but is outside the immediate ambit of this study.[32] The case for classical yoga is in fact made stronger by leaving out the archetypal, symbolic aspects, and concentrating on the general aspects of the content of the "world within," and its repercussion on the ego.

IV. Transcendence: Integration or Isolation?

Cosmicization realized in the union of conscious and unconscious, or in the plumbing of the depths of *prakṛti,* is for both Jung and yoga an intermediary, preliminary stage, which has to be transcended. How do the two systems conceive this transcendence? Jung explains it as follows:

> But once the unconscious contents break through into consciousness, filling it with their uncanny power of conviction, the question arises of how the individual will react. Will he be overpowered by these contents? Will he credulously accept them? Or will he reject them? (I am disregarding the ideal reaction, namely, critical understanding). The first case signifies paranoia or schizophrenia; the second may either become an eccentric with a taste for prophecy, or he may revert to an infantile attitude and be cut off from human society; the third signifies the regressive restoration of the persona.[33]

For the moment we are only interested in the first and second cases which denote "identification with the collective psyche. This would be equivalent to acceptance of the inflation." [34]

And Jung goes on to describe this acceptance in more archetypal language:

> Therefore all those who do not want to dismiss the great treasures that lie buried in the collective psyche will strive, in one way or another, to maintain the newly won union with the fundamental sources of life. Identification seems to be the shortest road to this, for the dissolution of the persona in the collective psyche is a direct invitation to wed oneself with the abyss and blot out all memory in that embrace. This piece of mysticism is characteristic of all better men, and is just as innate in every individual as the 'longing for the mother,' the nostalgia for the source from which we sprang. As I have shown elsewhere, there lies the root of regressive longing which Freud conceives as 'infantile fixation' or the 'incest wish' a special value and a special cogency. This is brought out in myths, where it is especially the strongest and best man among the people, the hero, who gives way to the regressive longing and deliberately exposes himself to the danger of being devoured by the monster of the maternal abyss. He is, however, a hero only because in the final reckoning he does not allow himself to be devoured, but conquers the monster, not once but many times. The victory over the collective psyche alone yields the true value, the capture of the hoard, the invincible weapon, the magic talisman, or whatever it be that the myth deems most desirable. Therefore, whoever identifies with the collective psyche—or, in terms of the myth, lets himself be devoured by the monster—and vanishes in it, is near to the treasure that the dragon guards, but he is there by extreme constraint and to his own greatest harm.[35]

This text clearly elucidates the two points we want to make: Jung conceives the psychic possibility of "fixation" in the inflation stage. This fixation, indeed is destructive and often leads to madness. And, secondly, this stage of identification with the collective psyche must be transcended. How does Jung conceive this final stage of transcendence?

The psychic "mechanism" or function that achieves this process is called the "transcendent function," "comparable in its way to a mathematical function of the same name which is a function of real and imaginary numbers. The psychological 'transcendent function' arises from the union of conscious and unconscious contents." [36] "The tendencies of the conscious and the unconscious are the two factors that together make up the 'transcendent function.' It is called 'transcendent' because it makes the transition from one attitude to the other organically possible, without loss of unconscious." [37] "Thus, in coming to terms with the unconscious, not only is the standpoint of the ego justified, but the unconscious is granted the same authority. The ego takes the lead, but the unconscious must be allowed to have a say too . . ." [38] The process that is thus set in motion is called by Jung the "process of individuation." [39] The essence of it consists in a new integration of planes, a new synthesis where conscious and unconscious are harmonized into a "new personality," to which Jung gives the names of "self" or "spirit."

Yoga, too, accepts the possibility of fixation in the state of cosmicization, and urges the yogin to press on and achieve the ultimate "transcendence." Patanjali declares that the cosmic expansion that accompanies some states of trance "is caused by Objective Existence for the *Videhas* and *Prakritilayas.*" [40] He means that for some beings, like the gods, it is a state caused by the play of *prakṛti* itself, and they do not transcend *prakṛti* but are imprisoned in it, and subject to rebirth. This type of trance is declared to be inadequate, and needs to be transcended by the real yogin. It is the preliminary stage of cosmicization where the occult powers manifest themselves. In Book III, where Patañjali describes these powers in detail, he sounds the same warning. He tells the yogin that at this stage he will be tempted by all the enjoyments and powers of the paradise of the gods, but that he needs to resist them, because his ultimate aim lies beyond this stage, in *kaivalya,* absolute freedom.[41] Eliade summarizes it all beautifully:

> To be sure, this cosmicization is only an intermediate phase, which Patanjali scarcely indicates, but it is exceptionally important in other Indian mystical schools. Obtained after 'unification,' 'cosmicization' continues the same process—that of recasting man in new, gigantic dimensions, of guaranteeing him macranthropic experiences. But this macranthropos can himself have but temporary existence. For the final goal will not be obtained until the yogin has succeeded in 'withdrawing' to his own center and completely dissociating himself

from the cosmos, thus becoming impervious to experience, unconditioned, and autonomous. This final 'withdrawal' is equivalent to a rupture of plane, to an act of real transcendence.[42]

This text is important as it uses the same words found in Jung: "transcendence," and a new "center." But there is a great difference in meaning. The transcendence of the final stage of yogic *samādhi* does not constitute the integration of two planes, but a total rupture of planes; the revelation and isolation of *puruṣa,* pure spirit, now completely freed from any connection with *prakṛti.* This new state is not a synthesis of conscious and unconscious elements into an integrated new selfhood, but a new "transconsciousness," which has no relation to either the unconscious or to ego-consciousness. Viewed from the point of view of yoga doctrine, the transcendence and reintegration Jung describes takes place within *prakṛti:* it is nothing more than the reconciliation of forces that are essentially prakritic. The transcendence of yoga, on the other hand, is said to completely sever all ties with *prakṛti,* and to bring the realization of the pure and autonomous realm of pure spirit, of *puruṣa.*

V. "Spirit" and *Puruṣa*

After having followed Jung and yoga in the processes of withdrawal and inflation, and having discovered a very useful parallel all along that line, we now seem to have struck a point where the two radically part company. However, one is tempted to look to Jung for a concept equivalent to the *puruṣa* for an experience and a reality one could fruitfully compare with the experience and reality of *puruṣa* in yoga. Jung's concept of "self" or "spirit" is worth considering in this respect. Perhaps the most important document for this comparison is Jung's article on "Spirit and Life." [43]

In the first half of this essay Jung seems to approach a concept that is surprisingly close to what yoga understands by *puruṣa:*

If we are to do justice to the essence of the thing we call spirit, we should really speak of a 'higher' consciousness

> rather than of the conscious, because the concept of spirit is such that we are bound to connect it with the idea of superiority over the ego-consciousness. The superiority of the spirit is not something attributed to it by conscious reflection, but clings to it as an essential quality . . . Psychologically, the spirit manifests itself as a personal being sometimes with visionary clarity . . . These facts show that spirit is not always merely a maxim or an idea that can be formulated but that in its strongest and most immediate manifestations it displays a peculiar life of its own which is felt as an independent being . . . , as a kind of higher consciousness, and its inscrutable, superior nature can no longer be expressed in the concepts of human reason.[44]

A higher consciousness, essentially superior, self-manifest, personal, independent, inaccessible to reason—such is exactly the *puruṣa.* However, as Jung goes on in his essay, the similarity with *puruṣa* is completely destroyed:

> One should, strictly speaking, describe this hypothetical consciousness simply as a 'wider' one, so as not to arouse the prejudice that it is necessarily higher in the intellectual or moral sense. There are many spirits, both light and dark. We should, therefore, be prepared to accept the view that spirit is not absolute, but something relative that needs completing and perfecting through life . . . a spirit which accords with our highest ideals will find its limits set by life. . . . The fullness of life requires more than an ego; it needs spirit, that is, an independent, over-ruling complex. . . . Life is the touchstone for the truth of spirit. Life and spirit are two powers or necessities between which man is placed. Spirit gives meaning to this life, and the possibility of its greatest development. But life is essential to spirit, since its truth is nothing if it cannot live.[45]

Spirit is again reduced to a complex, and put on the same footing as nature. This is not the realm of pure *puruṣa,* but that of *prakṛti.*

VI. Jung's Evaluation of Yoga

This analysis of Jung's concept of spirit will help to understand Jung's own evaluation of yoga:

> One hopes to control the unconscious, but the past masters on the art of self-control, the yogis, attain perfection in *samādhi,* a state of ecstasy, which so far as we know is equivalent to a state of unconsciousness. It makes no difference whether they call our unconscious a 'universal consciousness'; the fact remains that in their case the unconscious has swallowed up ego-consciousness. They do not realize that a 'universal consciousness' is a contradiction in terms, since exclusion, selection, and discrimination are the root and essence of everything that lays claim to the name 'consciousness.' [46]

"The ecstasy of *samādhi* is equivalent to unconsciousness." How should this be understood? First of all it should be remembered that the term "unconscious" has no pejorative meaning for Jung. "Jung defines the unconscious simply as that which is not conscious. He purposely never uses the term 'subconscious.' He attaches not the slightest valuation to the idea of the unconscious and leaves the question completely open whether the unconscious is above or below consciousness. He is to be taken as saying that the unconscious is as much above as it is below. Hence, in Jung's sense, spirit is enbued simply with the quality of the unconscious." [47]

Secondly, we should also remember, when Jung identifies "super-conscious" with "unconscious," what exactly Jung's definition of consciousness is. "Consciousness needs a center, an ego to which something is conscious. We know of no other kind of consciousness, nor can we imagine a consciousness without an ego. There can be no consciousness when there is no one to say 'I am conscious.' [48] Therefore, Jung's dictum that yogic superconsciousness is nothing but unconsciousness is not meant to be as condemnatory as it may sound: it implies no value judgment, and simply states that he cannot conceive of any consciousness without reference to an ego.

Yet, there are some texts where Jung goes further, and seems to envisage the possibility of a superconsciousness. "But as we cannot attain to such a state of wider consciousness or understand it, we do well to call that dark region, from our point of view, the 'unconscious,' without jumping to the conclusion that it is necessarily unconscious of itself." [49] He obviously accepts the possibility here of a superconsciousness with a new center, replacing the ego, and, speaking about yoga, he links this possibility explicitly with yoga: ". . . yoga is, I believe, the perfect and appropriate method of fusing body and mind together so that they form a unit that can hardly be doubted. They thus create a psychological disposition which makes possible intuitions that transcend consciousness." [50] "In the deepest sense, however, yoga . . . (means) the final release and detachment of consciousness from all bondage to object and subject." [51]

In another context, discussing Zen *satori,* Jung goes even further in describing this transconsciousness. "This tells us a good deal about the 'content of enlightenment.' The occurrence of *satori* is interpreted and formulated as a break-through, by a consciousness limited to the ego-form, into the non-ego-like self. This view is in accord not only with the essence of Zen, but also with the mysticism of Meister Eckhart. . . ." [52] And, further on, bringing Eckhart, Zen and yoga together, Jung affirms:

> This new state of consciousness born of religious practice is distinguished by the fact that outward things no longer affect an ego-bound consciousness, thus giving rise to mutual attachment, but that an empty consciousness stands open to another influence. This 'other' influence is no longer felt as one's own activity, but as that of a non-ego which has the conscious mind as its object. It is as if the subject character of the ego has been overrun, or taken over, by another subject which appears in place of the ego.[53]

These texts are very significant. The words "break-through into a non-ego-like self" recall the "rupture of planes" as experienced in the final stage of *samādhi.* And the new "self" that emerges, which is other than the ego, and yet is a center, seems so very much like the *puruṣa* described in the yoga treatises. Jung even says: "The goal of Eastern religious practice is the same as that of Western mysticism: the shifting of the center of gravity from the ego to the self, from man to God." [54] All this seems to suggest that any moment Jung is going to go one step further and say something more explicit about that baffling last stage of yogic *samādhi.* But he never does. On the contrary he usually withdraws and falls back to a position where the *samādhi* of *puruṣa* is simply reabsorbed into the unconscious processes, or identified with psychological processes of transcendence and individuation. The "break-through" which we mentioned as a possible parallel to the yogic rupture of planes is later on described by Jung as "an essentially compensatory relationship: the unconscious contents bring to the surface everything that is necessary in the broadest sense for the completion and wholeness of conscious orientation." [55] This constitutes a return to integration as opposed to isolation. This is strikingly evidenced by Jung's insistence that "the only movement inside our civilisation which has, or should have, some understanding of these endeavours (of yoga) is psychotherapy." [56] And even more strongly, "I have just said that we have developed nothing that could be compared with yoga. This is not entirely correct. True to our European bias, we have evolved a medical psychology, dealing specifically with the *kleśas.* We call it the 'psychology of the unconscious.' " [57] "Our Western psychology has, in fact, got as far as yoga in that it is able to establish scientifically a deeper layer of unity in the unconscious." [58]

VII. The Limits of Jung

So Jung seems again and again to approach an understanding of what the last rupture of *samādhi* means, but every time he retreats into the prior stage of cosmicization and integration. The reason for this is to be found in Jung's approach to the study of man. "Not being a philosopher, but an empiricist, I am inclined in all difficult questions to let experience decide. Where it is impossible to find any tangible basis in experience, I prefer to leave the question unanswered." [59] If yoga answers the questions, that is because "The Indian lacks the epistemological standpoint. He is still 'Pre-Kantian' . . . In India there is no psychology in our sense of the word. India is 'pre-psychological': when it speaks of the 'self,' it posits such a thing as existing. Psychology does not do this. It does not in any sense deny the existence of the dramatic conflict, but reserves the right to poverty, or the riches, of not knowing about the self." [60]

So the answer why Jung retreats at the last moment, is because he is an empiricist, post-Kantian. But there is more than just an "epistemological" difference here. Jung is a "healer," a psychotherapist, and his whole system is built for the function of this healing process. And this is where a judgment of value necessarily comes in. The healer must have his own idea of health, of "that which it is good to be like." Jung's ideal is "psychic wholeness," and he cannot conceive of a real "healthy self" which is not an integrated one. "If we conceive of the self as the essence of psychic wholeness, i.e., as the totality of conscious and unconscious, we do so because it does in fact represent something like a goal of psychic development, and this irrespective of all conscious opinions and expectations." [61] That is why Jung feels he must condemn "the depreciation and abolition of the physical and psychic man (i.e., of the living body and *ahaṁkāra*) in favor of the pneumatic man." [62] This abolition of prakritic man is unacceptable to Jung as constituting "wholeness," and this is exactly the final stage of *samādhi*. "Everything requires for its existence its own opposite, or else it fades into nothingness. The ego needs the self and vice versa." [63] Integration alone is acceptable to Jung, isolation as proposed and experienced in yogic *samādhi* is worthless annihilation.

Being an empiricist who must leave the ultimate questions unanswered, and a healer who had his own firm concept of the supreme value of the integrated personality, Jung was badly prepared to understand and appreciate the final stage of yogic *samādhi* and the doctrine supporting it. Patanjali belonged to a tradition which considered as natural the transition from experience and reasoning to metaphysical statements. Moreover, his function was not that of a healer, but of a *guru*, showing to very small numbers of possible adepts the method of realizing what he considered the acme of mystical realization. The student of mysticism is better prepared to understand *samādhi*, that rupture of planes where the "natural" order ends and the realm of the sacred begins. Jung constantly brings one to the portals, but one looks to the student of comparative mysticism to lead one across the threshold. R. C. Zaehner's proposed distinction between "nature mysticism" and "spiritual mysticism" may be helpful in that understanding.[64] What he calls nature mysticism seems to have close correspondences to the descent into the unconscious, the unification with the collective unconscious, and the cosmic inflation that accompanies it. His category, on the other hand, of spiritual mysticism often suggests a rupture of planes, a leap from the natural into the sphere of the sacred, "the wholly other." This seems to be applicable to the rupture and rapture involved in the final stage of *samādhi.* It is no wonder that Jung's analysis was extremely helpful at the beginning of our comparison, when the cosmic inflation of nature mysticism was discussed, the first stage of yogic meditation, and that Jung became more hesitant at the portals of the sanctum, opening doors but always withdrawing: here the empiricist and the healer must needs feel out of his element. Jung revels in the consideration of *prakṛti,* the totality of psychophysical reality, and in the study of the interaction of its forces, but the *puruṣa,* final goal of yogic *samādhi,* remains beyond his reach.

Notes and References

1. Cf. Jung's statement: "My point is naturally a psychological one, and moreover that of a practising psychologist whose task it is to find the quickest road through the chaotic muddle of complicated psychic states. This view must needs be very different from that of the psychologist who can study an isolated psychic process at his leisure, in the quiet of his laboratory. The difference is roughly that between a surgeon had a histologist. I also differ from the metaphysician, who feels he has to say how things are 'in themselves,' and whether they are absolute or not. My subject lies wholly within the bounds of experience." C.G. Jung, "The Structure of the Psyche," *C.W.* 8, p. 140.
2. J. Jacobi, *The Psychology of C. G. Jung* (New Haven: Yale University Press, 1951), p. 9.

3. For an exposition of the Sāṅkhya system, cf. S. N. Dasgupta, *A History of Indian Philosophy,* vol. 1 (Cambridge U.P., 1951), ch. VII; G. J. Larson, *Classical Sāmkhya: An Interpretation of its History and Meaning,* 2nd ed. (Delhi; Motilal Banarsidass, 1979).
4. Mircea Eliade, *Yoga, Immortality, and Freedom* (New York: Princeton Unversity Press, 1958), p. 24.
5. C. G. Jung, "Psychological Types," *C.W.* 6, p. 485.
6. Cf. Jung, "The Structure and Dynamics of the Psyche," *C. W.* 8, p. 384: "From this we can judge the magnitude of the error which our Western consciousness commits when it allows the psyche only a reality derived from physical causes. The East is wiser, for it finds the essence of all things grounded in the psyche." The parallel would be further strengthened by a study of the yoga concepts of *kāraṇa-vritti* and *vāsanā,* the latent potentialities of the mind, which in some ways correspond to elements of Jung's unconscious. However, a detailed consideration of these concepts is beyond the scope of this Chapter. Cf. Eliade, pp. 43–45.
7. This immediate aim must be distinguished from the ultimate aim, which will be considered under the heading "transcendence."
8. C. G. Jung, "Yoga and the West," *C. W.* 11, p. 537.
9. The method of classical yoga is generally divided into eight parts *(astanga): yama* and *niyama* (moral preparation), *āsana* (posture), *prāṇāyāma* (breath control), *pratyāhāra* (sense control), *dhāraṇā* (concentration), *dhyāna* (meditation), *samādhi* (trance).
10. *Yoga-Sūtras,* 11:46. For the *Yoga-Sūtras,* the edition used is *Patanjala Yoga Sūtras,* with the Commentary of Vyāsa and the Gloss of *Vāchaspati Miśra.* The Sacred Books of the Hindus, vol. 4, translation by Rama Prasada (Allahabad: Parini Office, 1974 first ed. 1912).
11. Eliade, op. cit., p. 54.
12. *Yoga-Sūtras* II:49; cf. Eliade, op. cit., p. 55.
13. *Yoga-Sūtras* I, 38, where dream and sleep are advised as proper objects of concentration.
14. Cf. Eliade, op. cit., p. 69.
15. Ibid., p. 83.
16. *Yoga-Sūtras* I: 45.
17. Cf. Eliade, op. cit., p. 97. The parallelism of macro- and microcosmos is a fundamental cornerstone of Indian thought, and has a long history going back to the famous *Purusha-Sūkta* of the *Rigveda.*
18. *Yoga-Sūtras* I: 40.
19. Cf. Vyāsa's commentary on *Yoga-Sūtras* III: 25.
20. Haridas Bhattacharya, "Yoga Psychology," in *The Cultural Heritage of India,* vol. 3, second ed., Calcutta, 1953, p. 62.
21. C.J. Jung, "Archetypes of the Collective Unconscious, *C. W.* 9, pt. 1, p. 36.
22. Ibid., pp. 21–22.
23. Ibid., "The Mother Archetype," p. 82.
24. Quoted in J. Jacobi, *Complex, Archetype, Symbol in the Psychology of C. G. Jung,* (New Jersey: Princeton University Press, 1959), p. 123.
25. R.C. Zaehner, *Mysticism, Sacred and Profane.* (Oxford: Oxford University Press 1961), p. 91.

26. Jacobi, *The Psychology of Jung,* op. cit., p. 66.
27. C. G. Jung, "Yoga, and the West," *C. W.,* 11, p. 532.
28. C. G. Jung, "Basic Postulates of Analytical Psychology," *C. W.* 8, pp. 349–350.
29. C.G. Jung, "The Personal as a Segment of the Collective Psyche," *C.W.* 7, p. 156.
30. Ibid., p. 160.
31. C.G. Jung, "The Assimilation of the Unconscious," *C.W.* 7, p. 141.
32. Jung refers to this where he writes: "In this line of research important parallels with yoga have come to light, especially with Kuṇdalini yoga and the symbolism of Tantric yoga, lamaism, and Taoist yoga in China." "Yoga and the West," *C. W.* 11, p. 537.
33. C.G. Jung, "Negative Attempts to Free the Individuality from the Collective Psyche," *C. W.,* 7, p. 163.
34. Ibid., p. 169.
35. Ibid., pp. 169–170.
36. C.G. Jung, "The Transcendent Function," *C. W.* 8, p. 69.
37. Ibid., p. 73.
38. Ibid., p. 88.
39. C.G. Jung, "Conscious, Unconscious and Individuation, A Study in the Process of Individuation," *C.W.,* 9, pt. I, pp. 275–354.
40. *Yoga-Sūtras,* I: 19.
41. Ibid., III: 50.
42. Eliade, op. cit., pp. 97–8.
43. C.G. Jung, "Spirit and Life," *C.W.* 8, pp. 319–38.
44. Ibid., p. 335.
45. Ibid., pp. 336–337.
46. C.G. Jung, "Conscious, Unconscious and Individuation, *C.W.* 9, pt. I, p. 287.
47. H. Schaer, *Religion and the Cure of Souls in Jung's Psychology,* (New York: Pantheon, 1950) p. 92.
48. C.G. Jung, op. cit., p. 283.
49. C.G. Jung, "Spirit and Life," *C. W.* 8, p. 334.
50. C.G. Jung, "Yoga and the West," *C. W.* 11, p. 533.
51. Ibid., p. 535.
52. C.G. Jung, "Foreword to Suzuki's Introduction to Zen Buddhism," *C.W.* 11, p. 543.
53. Ibid., p. 546.
54. C.G. Jung, "The Holy Men of India," *C.W.* 11, p. 581.
55. C.G. Jung, Foreword to Suzuki's Introduction to Zen Buddhism," *C. W.* 11, p. 551.
56. Ibid., p. 553.
57. Ibid., p. 572.
58. Ibid., p. 573.
59. C.G. Jung, "Spirit and Life," *C.W.* 8, p. 320.
60. C.G. Jung, '"The Holy Men of India," *C.W.* 11, p. 580.
61. Ibid., p. 582.

62. Ibid.
63. Ibid., p. 584.
64. Cf. R.C. Zaehner, *Mysticism, Sacred and Profane.* (Oxford: Oxford University Press 1961).

IX. Prāṇa and Libido: Prajñā and Consciousness

Jung has often shown particular interest in the Indian concept of *prāṇa:*

> The rich metaphysic and symbolism of the East express the larger and more important part of the unconscious and in this way reduce its potential. When the yogi speaks of *prāṇa,* he means very much more than mere breath. For him the word *prāṇa* brings with it the full weight of its metaphysical components, and it is as if he really knew what *prāṇa* meant in this respect. He does not know it with his understanding, but with his heart, belly and blood.[1]

Jung's keen interest was not purely academic, but through it he gave expression to some profound community of approach. This chapter intends to introduce the study of this similarity from a particular angle: by specifically comparing Jung's concept of libido with *prāṇa.* As exponent of the *prāṇa* concept, the *Kauṣītakī Upaniṣad* was chosen for the following reason. We want to catch the *prāṇa* doctrine at a stage where it is vigorously presented, but before it is caught up in the complex mythological and symbolic paraphernalia of later yoga and Tantra. Amongst the earlier *Upaniṣads* the *Kauṣītakī* offers the most coherent and extensive exaltation and investigation of *prāṇa:* it is the central theme of Chapters Two to Four.[2]

I. An Immanent Life-force: Biological, Psychic, Cosmic

The *Kauṣītakī Upaniṣad* starts its speculations on *prāṇa* from a consideration of the sensory powers of men: "The mind *(manas)* is the messenger, the eye is the protector, the ear is the announcer, and speech is the housekeeper of that *prāṇa*" (2.1). *Prāṇa* occupies a central position among those sensory powers, which link man with the outside world and constitute as it were a sheath around that center (2.2). This central position is more than one of *primus inter pares,* because the surrounding powers are said to "bring offerings to *prāṇa* without being asked" (2.1), a dependence similar to the dependence of man on the *devas.* In fact this power is more explicitly stated in reference to the magical practice of "dying around the holy power," which aims at the destruction of enemies around the sacrificer, symbolized by the absorption of the divinities or powers (fire, sun, moon, lightning) in the wind (*vāyu,* cosmic wind), and their re-emergence out of it.[3] The *Kauṣītakī* states that just as the cosmic powers are re-absorbed by Brahman (*vāyu* as the Absolute) and re-emerge out of it, in a similar way sensory-psychic powers merge into *prāṇa* and re-emerge out of it (2.12). However, in the case of *prāṇa* there is no direct reference to a sacrificial or cosmic operation, but to a psychic one: the re-absorption of sensory powers into *prāṇa* and their re-emergence out of *prāṇa* takes place in the state of deep sleep, and also in death (3.3; 4.20). *Prāṇa,* therefore, is the primary life-force out of which sensory-psychic life emerges, and which "has entered this bodily self to the very hairs and nails" (4.20).

However, this life-force is not a mere bio-psychic entity animating man; it is much wider than that. "As in a chariot the felly is fixed on the spokes, and the spokes are fixed on the hub, in the same way are these elements of existence fixed on the elements of intelligence, and the elements of intelligence are fixed in *prāṇa*" (3.8). The "elements of intelligence" here refer to the sensory-psychic powers previously mentioned, to which are added the organs which in fact put these powers into concrete operation (nose, tongue, hands, body, genitals, feet, etc.). The elements of intelligence, therefore, comprehend the inner and outer organs by which man comes into both cognitive and active contact with the outer world. The "elements of existence" are crudely enumerated as thoughts, form, sound, name, odor, taste, action, pleasure-pain, sexuality, movement. They are defined as *parastāt prati-vihitā,* "externally correlated" (3.5): those elements that correlate with man's experience and belong to the external objective world. The *Kauṣītakī* goes on to say that "if there were no elements of existence there would be no elements of intelligence, and if there were no elements of intelligence, there would be no elements of existence" (3.8). In other words, knowledge and being are essentially correlated and interdependent, the subjective and the objective must come together for the possibility of experience.

The *Kauṣītakī* declares that in the analogy of the wheel, the elements of existence are the felly, the elements of intelligence are the spokes, and the hub is *prāṇa* (3.8). The metaphor of the wheel recurs in the *Upaniṣads,* and the hub always refers to the essential central principle out of which the other elements emerge.[4] *Prāṇa,* therefore, is presented here as the total life-force, the source not only of subjective activity but also, in some way, of the objective field of that activity. No wonder that *prāṇa* is declared to be identical with *brahman,* the life-force that pervades the whole universe: as such *prāṇa* is sometimes called the cosmic wind, *vāyu* (2.1; 2.12). In this connection it is important to recall that in this particular *Upaniṣad, brahman* is presented as an immanent, intra-cosmic force, and is not referred to as transcendent, extra-cosmic, principle.[5] *Prāṇa,* therefore appears in our text as the all-pervading, immanent life-force, origin, and driving force of human life in all its aspects, and somehow also source of objective existence.

Jung's concept of libido is very aptly described by Munroe in the following words: "Jung retains the Freudian term libido, but gives it a different meaning that is at once more monistic and more pluralistic. He means by the term a life energy underlying all natural phenomena, including the human psyche—apparently rather similar to Bergson's *'elan vital.'* "[6] On the individual level, Jung calls the libido "an energy-value which is able to communicate itself to any field of activity whatsoever, be it power, hunger, hatred, sexuality, or religion, without ever being itself a specific instinct."[7] It is the driving force that initiates and sustains all human activity, from its lowest biological to its highest spiritual level, all-pervading.

Glover has eloquently summarized the meaning of libido as the individual's life-force in the following passage:

> It is a dynamic and creative element which streams in outer and inner directions, i.e., towards outer objects and towards the self. . . . It is what earlier psychologists called 'will' or 'tendency'; it is desire; it is wish; it is passion; it is interest; it is love; it is the joy of living; it comprises all human activities; it is the foundation and regulator of all psychic existence; it is the driving strength of our own soul; it is cosmic.[8]

There is evidently a striking parallel between *prāṇa* and libido as driving forces of man's activity. Jung, no doubt, would be the first to protest against this assertion of parallelism, because the *Upaniṣad,* he would say, speaks in "metaphysical" terms, whereas he himself is talking not about a vital life-force, but about a "psychological," hypothetical life-energy.[9] This methodological question will be discussed in the concluding section.

Since the libido is "the psychic energy, the totality of that force which pulses through and combines with one another all the forms and activities of the psychic system," [10] the libido is not only individual, but essentially cosmic. In the Jungian perspective, the psychic system includes, besides consciousness and the personal unconscious, also the collective unconscious, "the whole spiritual heritage of mankind's evolution, born anew in the brain structure of every individual." [11] Again and again Jung stresses the all-comprehensive cosmic dimension of the collective unconscious, personifying it as "a collective human being, combining the characteristics of both sexes, transcending youth and age, birth and death, practically immortal." [12] Dynamically it is "the living fountain of instincts, . . . the very source of the creative impulse. . . . like Nature herself-prodigiously conservative, and yet transcending her own historical condition in her acts of creation." [13] This world "possesses an energy peculiar to itself, independent of consciousness," [14] which is none other than the libido.

Thus we see that for Jung the psychic system is essentially cosmic in dimensions, and that the libido is the energy that drives this psychic system. But Jung goes even further in this parallel with *prāṇa.* We have noted that *prāṇa* is somehow the cause of the world as object; so is the libido. "Far, therefore, from being a material world, this is a psychic world. . . . The world-powers that rule over mankind, for good or evil, are unconscious psychic factors, and it is they that bring consciousness into being and hence create the *sine qua non* for the existence of any world at all. We are steeped in a world that was created by our own psyche." [15] "The psyche is the world's pivot: the one great condition for the existence of a world at all. . . ." [16] "The psyche is the greatest of all cosmic wonders and the *sine qua non* of the world as an object." [17] The parallel with the relation of *prāṇa* to the world as object is evident, and will have to be further analyzed later on.

II. A Purposive Force, Both Creative and Destructive

Prāṇa, as life force, is both creative and destructive. *Prāṇa,* indeed, is the force into which all other elements die and are absorbed, and out of which they re-emerge, be it on the cosmic scale, in the magic "dying around the holy power" (2.12–13), in deep sleep (3.3), or in death (4.20). Its driving force is not blind, but purposive. It directs all the psychic powers "to their respective stations" after the absorption of sleep (3.3) and death (4.20). Indeed, it is "like a chief among his own men, ordering and directing them" (4.20). It takes a purposive initiative: "He causes him whom he wishes to lead up from these worlds to perform good actions. He also causes him whom he wishes to lead downward, to perform bad actions" (3.8).

The unconscious, for Jung, is "the very source of the creative impulse," [18] and the libido, "the creative power of our soul" [19] also "has two sides: it is the power which beautifies everything, but, in a different set of circumstances, is quite likely to destroy everything." [20] "The libido is fructifying as well as destructive," [21] but this double-edged power is not a blind one, but one that is teleologically directed: "the libido possesses an intuitive faculty, a strange power to 'smell the right place,' almost as if it were a live creature with an independent life of its own (which is why it is so easily personified). It is purposive, like sexuality itself. . . ." [22]

Just as the creative and destructive (absorptive) movements of *prāṇa* are linked with the idea of cosmic and individual rebirth, so does Jung link the double movement of the libido with what he calls "the longing for rebirth." "It is as if the libido were not only a ceaseless forward movement, an unending will for life, evolution, creation. . . .; like the sun, the libido also wills its own descent, its own involution." [23] "If it is not possible for the libido to strive forwards, to lead a life that willingly accepts all dangers and ultimate decay, then it strikes back along the other road and sinks into its own depths, working down to the old intimation of the immortality of all that lives, to the old longing for rebirth." [24]

> Whenever some great work is to be accomplished . . . the libido streams back to the fountain-head. . . . But if the libido manages to tear itself loose and force its way up again, something like a miracle happens: the journey to the underworld was a plunge into the fountain of youth, and the libido, apparently dead, wakes to renewed fruitfulness.[25]

III. A Morally Ambivalent Force

Indra, who reveals himself as being *prāṇa* (3.2), says that he who knows him and who, therefore, knows *prāṇa* and is master of *prāṇa,* "by no deed whatsoever of his is his world injured, not by theft, not by the murder of an embryo, not by the murder of his mother, not by the murder of his father. And if he had committed a sin, the dark color does not depart from his face" (3.1). This transcendence of morality by the knower of *prāṇa* is later on clarified by the assertion that *prāṇa* itself is a morally ambivalent force, or rather a force which, though it pushes man to good and evil deeds alike, is in no way subject to the consequences of good or evil action.

> *Prāṇa* does not become great by good action or small by evil action. Indeed, he causes to perform good actions, him, whom he wishes to lead up out of these worlds. Indeed, he also causes to perform bad actions, him, whom he wishes to lead downward. He is the world's protector, its sovereign, its lord, he is my self (3.8).

This moral ambivalence, or moral neutrality of *prāṇa,* is in fact, but a corollary to its ambivalence as a creative and destructive force.

The same is true of the libido. Jung's statements are quite clear and unequivocal on this point. "This libido is a force of nature, good and bad at once, or morally neutral." [26] It is "the creative power of our own soul . . . . whose nature it is to bring forth the useful and the harmful, the good and the bad." [27] Sometimes Jung stresses the same idea very forcefully in more archetypical terms: "As a power which transcends consciousness the libido is by nature daemonic; it is both God and devil. If evil were to be utterly destroyed, everything daemonic, including God himself, would suffer a grievous loss; it would be like performing an amputation on the body of the Deity." [28]

There is a clear parallelism here between the moral ambivalence attached to both *prāṇa* and libido. But there appears to be some difference in the way in which this moral ambivalence is presented. *Prāṇa* is not described as being in itself morally ambivalent, but rather as a power which is not affected by good or bad actions. This is so because in fact it transcends the lower level of being where *karma,* good and evil, comes into play and produces its effects. On the other hand, Jung portrays the libido as a power which in itself is morally ambivalent, both good and evil, both God and devil. It is such precisely because it "transcends consciousness."

IV. A Divine Power

"Prāṇa is *brahman"* (2.1; 2.2). In this short statement, our *Upaniṣad* sums up the total importance of *prāṇa. Prāṇa,* which is mythologically also identified with Indra (3.2), is identical with the absolute ground of existence, the metaphysical absolute. But *brahman* means many things even within Upaniṣadic thinking, and it is important to remember here that in the *Kauṣītakī* there is nowhere any reference to a transcendent aspect of *brahman:* it is purely cosmic and immanent, the total world-soul.

If we bear in mind the all-encompassing cosmic meaning Jung gives to the libido, we should not be surprised to read, "If one honors God, the sun or fire, then one honors one's own vital force, the libido. It is as Seneca says: 'God is near you, he is with you, in you.' God is our longing to which we pay divine honours." [29] "The well-known fact that in the sun's strength the great generative power of nature is honoured shows plainly, very plainly, to anyone to whom as yet it may be clear that in the Deity man honours his own libido." [30] The libido, therefore, is God, and as in the *Kauṣītakī,* this divine power is both individual and cosmic, and wholly immanent. We shall have to discuss further on what Jung means by "God."

V. Consciousness and the World of Phenomena

So far we have concentrated upon bringing forward the many fundamental similarities between the two concepts, and before turning to the discussion of the deeper methodological issues, we have to consider a last important parallel: the meaning of consciousness and its relationship to the world of phenomena. The *Upaniṣad* declares that *prāṇa* is *prajñā.* (3.3) This is not a tautological statement, because *prāṇa* is a larger concept, including the "vital" principle of life: "as long as *prāṇa* resides in this body, so long is there life," (3.2) whereas *prajñā* refers only to intellectual processes. *Prajñā* is clearly differentiated from *manas,* which is the mind in as far as it coordinates, structures, and processes sense-data; as such it is always included as an item in the list of human "sensory" organs. What then does *prajñā* exactly mean in the *Kauṣītakī Upanishad?* A clear answer is given in chapter three: "Having obtained control over the speech by *prajñā,* one obtains all names by speech. . . . Having obtained control over the eye by *prajñā,* one obtains all forms by the eye." (3.6) The same is affirmed about all the ten organs. It is, therefore, the penetration of these organs by *prajñā* that enables them to obtain their object: the eye only sees forms when controlled by *prajñā,* etc. Therefore, *prajñā* here means consciousness in general, and this is confirmed by the following verse, which again goes through the list of ten organs saying, "Without *prajñā* speech would not make conscious *(prajñāpayet)* any name whatsoever." "My mind was elsewhere," one says. "I was not aware *(prajñāsisham)* of that name" (3.7). It is striking how the root *prajñā* is used here in two verbal forms, which obviously indicate the psychic factor of "awareness," "consciousness." On the other hand, as has been shown earlier, the *Upaniṣad* makes it quite clear that the *prajñā-mātrāh,* the elements of consciousness are fixed on *prāṇa,* and depend on that larger fundamental principle. In deep sleep and in death it is in *prāṇa* that even *prajñā* is reabsorbed. "Awareness," "consciousness," therefore emerges out of that larger principle.

To Jung, consciousness is very narrowly defined as that quality of being related to the ego. "Consciousness needs a center, an ego to which something is conscious. We know of no other kind of consciousness, nor can we imagine a consciousness without an ego." [31] The unconscious is simply that which is not actually related to the ego. This term, therefore, does not imply any valuation, and that is why Jung carefully avoids using the term "subconscious." In this context, it is not surprising to hear Jung say,

> . . . the truth is that the unconscious is always there beforehand as a system of inherited functioning handed down from primeval times. Consciousness is a late-born descendant of the unconscious psyche . . . it is . . . wrong, in my opinion, to regard the unconscious as a derivative of consciousness. We are probably nearer the truth if we put it the other way round.[32]

And more confidently, "The conscious mind is based upon, and results from, an unconscious psyche which is prior to consciousness and continues to function with, or despite, consciousness." [33]

Even here we are confronted with the striking similarity of the two approaches: consciousness and *prajñā* are declared to be in some way subordinate to, even derived from the libido and *prāṇa.* Consciousness wells up, in both systems, from a more original and basic life force.

This life force, together with the emerging consciousness, is moreover declared to be somehow the origin of the world as object, as we have seen earlier in our analysis of *Kauṣītakī* (3.8). No *rupa,* phenomenological appearance, can come about without the correlation of consciousness *(prajñā)* and the "elements of existence." The latter do not refer to abstract principles, but to the world as phenomenon, as involved in psychic activity: the enumeration of these elements make that quite clear: "name, odor, form, sound, taste, pleasure-pain, sexuality-procreation, movement, thoughts-desires" (3.5–8). This text makes it also clear that of the two correlates, *prajñā* is the primary one, being the spokes to the felly of the wheel. The same primacy is affirmed in a macrocosmic vein, when the same chapter describes the emergence after deep sleep: "when he awakes then—as from a flaming fire the sparks burst out in all directions—even so do the vital breaths proceed from the *ātman,* according to their domain, from them the gods (sense-powers), and from these the worlds" (3.3).

"Far from being a material world," says Jung, "this is a psychic world . . . The psychic alone has immediate reality. . . The world-powers that rule over mankind, for good or evil, are unconscious psychic factors, and it is they that bring consciousness into being and hence create the *sine qua non* for the existence of any world at all. We are steeped in a world that has been created by our own psyche." [34] First there is the force of libido, which brings forth consciousness, and hence arises the "world." The parallel with the *Kauṣītakī* is complete, and it is of the utmost importance to note that all levels, *praṇa*-libido, *prajñā*-consciousness, *rupa*-world, speak of both psychic realities and psychic processes.

VI. Fundamental Differences and Similarities

So far we have concentrated upon the parallels between Jung and the *Kauṣītakī,* postponing the discussion of important differences. Now we move on to these differences which will lead us to ask more basic questions of methodology. As we analysed the *Kauṣītakī* we took its statements mostly as statements of a psychological nature, which in fact they are, and as such they are most amenable to comparison with Jung. However, this is only part of the picture. Throughout the *Upaniṣad,* our philosopher constantly and without the slightest hesitation takes us one step further into the sphere of metaphysical statements. "That same *prāṇa* is the guardian of the world, its sovereign, its lord. He is my *ātman;* this is knowledge" (3.8). The emergence of consciousness out of *prāṇa* is, as we saw, a statement of psychic import, but it is immediately transformed into a metaphysical statement: *Prāṇa* is radically identified with *prajñā,* and hypostatized as *ātman. Prāṇaprajñātman* is the metaphysical absolute, intra-cosmic, and as such identical with *brahman,* cosmic life-force, cosmic soul. The reflections on the process of dying, on the sinking into and the emergence from deep dreamless sleep, on the awakening of consciousness and its creative reaching out from the inner to the outer world, are undoubtedly psychological reflections, but they are always transformed without hesitation into statements with metaphysical overtones. So we have throughout the *Upaniṣad* a continuous and imperceptible shift from psychological analysis to metaphysics.

The essential features of this metaphysic are the following. *Prāṇa* is life-force from a broad biological point of view; it is also consciousness or *prajñā* from a psychological point of view, and it is *ātman* from a metaphysical point of view; and *prāṇa* is all these both on the individual and the cosmic levels.[35] The transition between these points of view is not a difficult one, because there is no real gap between them; they overlap, in fact they merge into one another along the following lines. *Prāṇa* is not purely biological, since it is the center and source of sensation and mind, and thus it glides over into the psychological. *Prajñā,* we saw, is awareness, relatedness to a center. But this center is not merely the psychological ego, it lies beyond the ego,[36] and it is really the *ātman.* Thus we have a vision, very pre-Kantian indeed, as Jung has remarked,[37] where different disciplines merge, affirming very clearly an absolute comprising *prāṇa* and *prajñā* as two aspects of one reality. "*Prāṇa* is *prajñā* and *prajñā* is *prāṇa.* These two reside together in this body, and together they leave it" (3.3). "This *prāṇa* indeed is *prajñātman*" (3.8) is the strongest statement of identity of the three points of view, affirming a metaphysical absolute *(ātman),* which is fundamentally both vital force *(prāṇa)* and consciousness *(prajñā).*

Jung has made it quite clear, again and again, that he is neither a psychologist, nor a metaphysician, but an empiricist.[38] This assertion runs through his work to the point of seeming an obsession. In this, he is totally different from the pre-Kantian approach of the *Kauṣītakī.* However, can we accept this repeated affirmation at its face value?

How does his system view reality as a whole? Psychic reality, the only really empiric one, includes the fundamental, primordial collective unconscious, of which consciousness is but a late, precarious manifestation. This psychic reality includes all that is, the natural and the spiritual. "Just as, in its lower reaches, the psyche loses itself in the organic-material substrata, so in its upper reaches it resolves itself into a 'spiritual' form about which we know as little as we do about the functional basis of instinct." [39] "Matter and spirit both appear in the psychic realm as distinctive qualities of conscious contents. The ultimate nature of both is transcendental, that is, irrepresentable, since the psyche and its contents are the only reality which is given to us *without a medium.*" [40] "Between the unknown essences of spirit and matter stands the reality of the psychic-psychic reality, the only reality we can experience immediately." [41] Therefore, according to Jung, the psyche participates in both the material and the spiritual sphere. "Matter" and "spirit" are the abstract opposite poles, both inaccessible in their transcendence, constituting at the best *Grenzbegriffe,* limiting conceptual constructs. Some may call these "Absolute Spirit" and "Prime Matter," but Jung, the post-Kantian, will never accept these concepts to have metaphysical validity; he never acknowledges that man is capable of knowing that in actual reality something corresponds to them: for him the real is circumscribed by the psyche and only the psyche.

Whereas Jung refuses to accept the relevance of an "absolute" in any form, he does continuously speak about "God," and in many different forms. The collective unconscious, the libido, the spirit, the self, are all at some stage declared to be God. They are the God within, the archetypical idea and force, the experienced divinity, the symbol, which has nothing to do with the absolute reality of God. God is first the totality of psychic life itself, the collective unconscious. More specifically, within this psychic universe God is the creative and destructive vital force of the libido, driving all that exists. It is even more pointedly the "spirit," that "psychic complex full of creative beginnings and immense possibilities," [42] which is an intentional force of the unconscious. And finally it is that Self which emerges through the process of individuation, which "might equally well be called the 'God within us.' The beginnings of our whole psychic life seem to be inextricably rooted in it, and all our highest and ultimate purposes seem to be striving towards it." [43] The latter is the God-idea around which Jung's thought revolved more and more, putting the others in the shadow.[44] It has been most admirably described by Altizer in the following passage:

> Jung has chosen the term 'Self' to designate the totality of man, the sum total of conscious and unconscious existence. It is a totality which includes all the components of the psyche as symbolized in the quaternity or mandala symbolism. However, the Self as representative of the wholeness and totality of man defies conceptualization and must stand forth as an irrational symbol which is a product of the deepest reaches of the collective and universal psyche. The Self as a psychic symbol lies deeper than the God-symbol. It is the final symbolic consummation of the individuation process, and thus is the deepest and highest image of man and the universe. For the Self is a symbol reflecting the essential identity of macrocosm and microcosm in the final and ultimate reality of the *Anima Mundi,* the World Soul.[45]

Thus at the deepest level of his treatment, Jung speaks of God as the God that changes and emerges in the psyche of man, striving, from primeval forces, to become the fully integrated self, the focal point of the meeting of macro and microcosmos.

This negative attitude to the absolute claims of metaphysics, and this concentration on the theme of the changing and emerging God mark a profound difference between Jung's ideas and those of the *Kauṣītakī.* The latter is never afraid of plunging right into affirmation of the absolute as ultimate reality. This absolute is the world-soul, the vital force pulsating in macro- and microcosmos, but it is also *prajñā,* not just consciousness of the purely empiric type, but *ātman,* superconsciousness (which is not equivalent to unconsciousness and which is open to man's experience). Our Upaniṣadic philosopher does not see the pilgrim's progress here on earth as the surface reflection of the unconscious drama of the emerging God, but as the effort to discover in the soul, that all-encompassing *brahman. Brahman* to him is the absolute to be discovered, not the emerging God.

Although the differences pointed out are significant, the similarities between the two systems are sufficiently important to require some explanation. We think this explanation is to be found in the fact that there is a similarity in their respective approach as determined by some parallelism in basic presuppositions. The *Kauṣītakī* takes its starting point from an analysis of empiric consciousness: the close observation of the gradual retreat into deep sleep and of the process of dying suggest that phenomenal experience and empiric consciousness are rooted in the vital force of *prāṇa* from which they emerged.[46] However, this psychological analysis did not happen in a vacuum. It must be understood against the background out of which the very concept of *prāṇa* arose, because that background was bound to color the very interpretation of the psychological analysis. We agree with Eliade[47] that the origin of the concept of *prāṇa* is most probably to be found in a "mystical experience which was cosmic in structure." That is why the analysis itself and the subsequent interpretation took place within the assumption of a basic parallelism of macro and microcosmos. When the *Kauṣītakī* identified the superconscious realized in deep sleep and trance with *prāṇa,* this identification was bound to be transferred onto a macrocosmic scale: this superconscious was the ontological *ātman,* the "small" as well as the "great," the individual as well as the cosmic.[48] The conclusion was that reality in its most fundamental aspect was *prāṇa-prajñātman,* a world-soul both vitalistic and intelligent. Thus the psychological analysis, precisely because it took place within the assumption of the basic parallelism of macro-and microcosmos naturally moved on to the metaphysical assertion about the totality of reality, and had its end-point a monism of world-soul. It is only to be expected that within the bounds of such monism and its introspective analytical basis, the consideration of the intrinsic values of matter, empiric consciousness, and historical development would recede into the background.

Although Jung repeatedly and obsessively denies any metaphysical claims, one cannot escape the conclusion that some assumptions of a metaphysical nature frame his psychological analyses and explanations. He searches through dream, symbol, and myth for the depths from which empiric consciousness emerges. However penetrating his investigation into these may be, it always remains within the framework of some fundamental assumptions: that consciousness and phenomena, spirit and matter, are rooted in the basic reality of the collective unconscious; that this collective unconscious constitutes an original psychic identity, on which rests the conception of man as a microcosm corresponding to the macrocosm;[49] that in this collective consciousness the libido strives towards the emergence of the divine Self. Two commentators on Jung's work have expressed that same idea as follows. Jung "has always been very sensitive to the charge of being a metaphysician, but it can hardly be denied that in positing an undifferentiated libido he was, in spite of himself, asserting that the psychological data were unaccountable except on a postulate which was as metaphysical as could be." [50] "It must be apparent that Jung's very choice and definition of his data, and his intuitive method of exploring them, rest upon a theological-metaphysical system of panpsychism. It could not be otherwise as long as he accords his unconscious data with such high reality claims." [51]

The system of the *Kauṣītakī* and that of Jung are both forms of panpsychism. They are both based on a fundamental option in favor of the inner world, be it called the unconscious or the superconscious, that psychic realm where macro-and microcosmos meet. This option has a logical consequence: the very concentration on that inner world tends to divert attention from man's outside involvement, and leads to a devaluation of matter, empiric consciousness, and historic evolution and progress. How could two systems so distant in time, notwithstanding very marked difference in approach and conclusions, yet share so much? The *Kauṣītakī* represents a sphere of thinking which was still very close to the twilight experiences of man before the preoccupation with rational analysis and when mysticism had strong overtones of cosmic feeling. On the other hand, the mystics had developed highly sophisticated methods of introspection and mental control, which allowed them to monitor their descent into the inner world.

Jung has always been fascinated by such a mental outlook, and convinced that it was most favorable for revealing these essential structures of man's psyche which modern man with his outward-directed rationalism found it very difficult to rediscover. The *Kauṣītakī's* metaphysics are closer to Jung's conceptions than classical Sāṅkhya-yoga or Vedānta. Whereas the latter systems have as their apex an absolute spirit totally free from matter and cosmos, the *Kauṣītakī* remains immanentistic in its conception of the absolute *brahman* as world-soul. Whereas other Hindu systems such as Sāṅkhya have a very strong eschatological preoccupation, such concern is absent from *Kauṣītakī,* as it is from Jung's system. Both Jung and our Upaniṣadic philosopher do not seem to perceive any great need of explaining and evaluating the material cosmos, or human engagement in history and progress. Even their final aims are somewhat parallel: both are concerned with the liberation or fulfilment of the few. Jung sees the fulfilment of the basic drive for individuation as realisable only by exceptional individuals; the *Kauṣītakī,* more than other early *Upaniṣads,* heralds the esotericism of medieval Tantric sādhana; and for both the realization of the supreme goal means the recovery of the original psychic identity of macro and microcosmos, and the reconciliation or transcendence of all opposites. Most of these basic characteristic call up the epithet "Gnostic," and in the final instance that epithet may well be one of the most appropriate with which to describe the overall trend of Jung's thought, however repugnant it may have been to him.

Notes and References

1. C.G. Jung, "Yoga and the West," *C.W.* 11, p. 535.
2. For an edition of the text of the *Kauṣītakī* cf. *The Kauṣītakī-Brāhmana-Upaniṣad, with the "Dipika" Commentary of Shaṅkarananda,* ed., E.B. Cowell, The Chowkhamba Sanskrit Series, Varanasi, 1968 (first published 1861). We refer to the verse of the *Kauṣītakī* by putting the numbers of chapter and verses between brackets after the quotation. The translation throughout is our own, unless specified otherwise. We are naturally endebted to the translations of Max Muller, Hume, and Radhakrishnan, and especially to the edition and translation of Renou: *Kauṣītakī Upaniṣad,* publiée et traduite par Louis Renou, Adrien-Maisonneuve, Paris, 1948.
3. For an explanation of this magical practice, and its sources, cf. Renou, pp. 42–43.
4. For the Upaniṣadic use of the analogy of the wheel, cf. *Bṛhadāraṇyaka Upaniṣad,* 1.5.15 and 2.5.15; *Chāndogya Upaniṣad,* 7.15.1; *Praśna Upaniṣad,* 6.6.

5. The speculations on the "two ways" and on *brahmaloka* in the first chapter seem to form a section quite separate from the rest of the *Upaniṣad.* The doctrine of *prāṇa* is contained in Chapters 2–4, and there does not seem to be a close connection between these and the first. We feel we are justified, considering the very nature of most *Upaniṣads* to be compilations, to omit the first chapter for all intents and purposes from our discussion of *prāṇa* in the *Kauṣītakī.*
6. R.L. Monroe, *Schools of Psychoanalytic Thought* (New York: The Dryden Press, 1956), p. 541.
7. C.G. Jung, "Symbols of Transformation," *C.W.* 5, p. 137.
8. E. Glover, *Freud and Jung* (New York: Meridan, 1956), pp. 58–9.
9. C.G. Jung, "On Psychic Energy," *C.W.* 8, p. 17.
10. J. Jacobi, *The Psychology of C.G. Jung,* (New Haven: Yale Univ. Press, 1951), p. 66.
11. C.G. Jung, "The Structure of the Psyche," *C.W.* 8, p. 158.
12. C.G. Jung, "Basic Postulates of Analytical Psychology," *C.W.* 8, p. 349.
13. C.G. Jung, "The Structure of the Psyche," *C.W.* 8, p. 157.
14. C.G. Jung, "Analytical Psychology and 'Weltanschauung,' " *C.W.* 8, p. 376.
15. C.G. Jung, "The Real and the Surreal," *C.W.* 8, p. 384.
16. C.G. Jung, "On the Nature of the Psyche," *C.W.* 8, p. 217.
17. Ibid., p. 169.
18. C.G. Jung, "The Structure of the Psyche," *C.W.* 8, p. 157.
19. C.G. Jung, "Symbols of Transformation," *C.W.* 5, p. 121.
20. Ibid.
21. Ibid., p. 282.
22. Ibid., p. 125.
23. Ibid., p. 438.
24. Ibid., p. 398.
25. Ibid., pp. 292–293.
26. Ibid., p. 125.
27. Ibid., p. 121.
28. Ibid., p. 112.
29. C.G. Jung, *The Psychology of the Unconscious,* London: Kegan Paul, 1919, p. 52; this is rephrased without altering the meaning in "Symbols of Transformation," *C.W.* 5, p. 86.
30. Ibid., pp. 53–54. Rephrased in *C.W.* 5, p. 89.
31. C.G. Jung, "Conscious, Unconscious and Individuation," *C.W.* 9, part 1, p. 283.
32. C.G. Jung, "Basic Postulates of Analytical Psychology," *C.W.* 8, p. 350.
33. C.G. Jung, *The Integration of the Personality,* London, 1940, p. 13; the italics are Jung's. This is rephrased in "Conscious, Unconscious, and Individuation," *C.W.* 9, part 1, p. 281, as follows: "Consciousness grows out of an unconscious psyche, which is older that it, and which goes on functioning together with it or even in spite of it."
34. C.G. Jung, *"The Real and the Surreal,"* C.W. 8, p. 384. Cf. also references in footnotes 16 and 17 of this chapter.

35. Cf. R.D. Ranade, *A Constructive Survey of Upanishadic Philosophy*, Poona, Oriental Book Agency, 1926, pp. 91–2; J. Gonda, *Les Religions de l'Inde*, vol. 1, *Vedisme et Hindouisme Ancien*, Paris, 1962, p. 241.
36. In connection with this, an interesting connection between *prāṇa* and *mahat* is touched upon by H.H. Penner in his paper "Cosmogony as myth in the Vishnu Purana," *History of Religions*, vol. 5, no. 2 (1966), pp. 288–9.
37. C.G. Jung, "The Holy Men of India," *C.W.* 11, p. 580.
38. For instance, Jung, "The Structure of the Psyche," *C.W.* 8, p. 140.
39. C.G. Jung, "On the Nature of the Psyche," *C.W.* 8, p. 183.
40. Ibid., p. 216.
41. C.G. Jung, "The Real and the Surreal," *C.W.* 8, p. 384.
42. H. Schaer, *Religion and the Cure of Souls in Jung's Psychology* (New York, Pantheon 1950), p. 91.
43. C.G. Jung, "The Relations between the Ego and the Unconscious," *C.W.* 7, p. 236.
44. Cf. R.C. Zaehner, *The Convergent Spirit* (London, 1963), pp. 102–3.
45. T.J.J. Altizer, "Science and Gnosis in Jung's Psychology," *The Centennial Review* III (1950), p. 312.
46. For a short history of the idea of *prāṇa*, indicating how little *prāṇa* has to do with "breathing," cf. S. Dasgupta, *A History of Indian Philosophy*, vol. II (Cambridge, Cambridge University Press 1952), pp. 259–264.
47. M. Eliade, *Yoga, Immortality and Freedom* (Princeton: Princeton University Press, 1969), p. 337, n. 126.
48. Cf. J.A.B. Van Buitenen, "The Large Atman," *History of Religions*, IV (1964), pp. 103–114.
49. H. Schaer, op. cit., p. 106.
50. V. White, *God and the Unconscious* (New York: Meridan, 1961), p. 50.
51. T.J.J. Altizer, op. cit., p. 319.

X. Conclusion

Our study has revealed many similarities in the theories adopted by Jung and Eastern thought. Memory is understood by both as forgotten or repressed actions or thoughts which are contents of the unconscious. The continuity provided by memory is what generates one's sense of ego or I-ness. Knowledge of oneself is gained by bringing these memories up from the dark unconscious into the light of consciousness. 'Active imagination' and yogic meditation are techniques designed to do just this. Both Jung and yoga describe two levels of perception which in turn produce a two-level theory of knowledge.

Jung admits that he has been influenced by Eastern thought, as the above similarities show. But as one who follows modern Western scientific method, Jung finds it necessary to draw the line before accepting many of the yoga claims. The idea that memory and the unconscious are mainly composed of materials or traces stored up from past lives is in Jung's view scientifically unacceptable. While there is evidence for an inheritance of general psychic tendencies along the lines of the genetic factors that predispose our physical development, Jung has difficulty with the idea of the reincarnation of an individual soul along with its specific memory traces. Jung also rejects the yoga claim that through the technique of yogic meditation, memories can be brought into conscious awareness until all of one's past is known and nothing remains at the unconscious level. Since it is the continuity of memory that provides one's ego, the total destruction of memory claimed by yoga also means the complete loss of ego. Jung finds this claim to be unsupportable in both scientific psychology and philosophy. The error of Eastern thought in this regard is that it is not firmly grounded in the empirical method and instead has allowed itself to become lost in unsupportable metaphysical speculation. It is in this sense that Jung labels yoga as pre-Kantian and, with regard to scientific method, well behind modern Western scientific psychology. Yoga, claims Jung, is not really psychology but a form of precritical philosophical speculation which has in many of its claims become detached from the world of concrete particulars. The advance demonstrated in modern Western theorizing about cognition is that the empirical approach of modern psychology acts as an effective preventive against such speculative errors.

While both Jung and Patañjali generally agree on the cognitive processes involved in ordinary sense perception, they sharply disagree over the nature of a second level of perception. Here again the nub of the disagreement is the lack of an empirical basis in the yoga claims for *pratibhā* or supersensuous perception. Jung's study of intuitive perception indicates that it is totally dependent on sensuous processes. The reason that intuition differs from ordinary sense perception is that it occurs mostly below the level of conscious awareness. In Jung's analysis the 'hunches' which intuition produces do not come in any mystical way but arise from subliminal sense perceptions and unconscious inferences of the psyche. Jung's psychological theory of intuition is empirically based and is consistent with the analysis of the contemporary Western philosopher Bunge who defines intuition as rapid inferences to highly probably hypotheses.[1] Intuitive perception, from this viewpoint, is not really a second level of perception but simply regular sense perception and apperceptive processing which is occurring mostly below the level of conscious awareness.

In Jung's view it is precisely the lack of empirical grounding in the yoga notion of *pratibhā* or supersensuous perception that leads to the unsupportable Eastern claims of *prajñā* to omniscient knowledge. Although Jung applauds the holistic goal of *prajñā* (e.g., seeing the object under all conditions of space and time), he judges that it is a goal that will never be perfectly achieved. The limitations imposed by the inability of the ego to know the totality of the self mean that there will always be areas of both the unconscious and the external world yet to be discovered. In Jung's view the yoga idea that one individual through intense meditation could somehow achieve all knowledge is nothing more than a romantic wish-fulfilment that has seduced the Eastern intellect.

Jung's conclusion is that mankind's desire for greater knowledge of himself and the universe in which he lives will best be fulfilled through the approach of Western science. Jung agrees with the contention put forward by Gilbert Ryle that as long as psychology, philosophy, and the other modern scientific disciplines resist the tendency to narrow-minded imperialism and keep the larger perspective of one another's findings in view, the goal of increased knowledge will be achieved. It is here that Eastern thought can provide valuable confirming parallels, and pregnant insights. Our comparative studies show that several of Jung's major theoretical notions contain significant influence from the East. Joseph Henderson sums it up best when he suggests that Jung attempted to balance between the empirical considerations of Western psychology and the mystical tradition of self-centering in Being, as found for example in the *Upaniṣads.* Jung, observes Henderson, treated both traditions seriously but in the end remained true to his own "reality of the psyche."

Jung never thought of his own psychology as a closed theory. To his last years he remained open to new ideas that could come from either East or West. But throughout his life it was his activity as a psychotherapist that kept Jung skeptical of Eastern metaphysics and rooted in the tradition of Western medical science.

Note

1. Malcolm R. Westcott, *Toward a Contemporary Psychology of Intuition* (New York: Holt, Rinehart and Winston, 1968), p. 21.

C.G. Jung and Eastern Religious Traditions: An Annotated Bibliography

by John Borelli

This bibliography is divided into two parts. The first part includes several titles in *The Collected Works of C.G. Jung* and a few other titles by him which were published elsewhere, and the second part is a listing of studies by other authors. The bibliography follows the general theme of this volume and comprehends those writings which will be especially helpful for researching Jung's psychology and Indian religious traditions. Whenever necessary, I have added a note to an item for clarification or for cross-reference to another title. Often a title is a sufficient indication of the content of the work, and there is no justifiable need for a note of praise or caution.

In reducing a larger bibliography on C.G. Jung and the study of Eastern religions for this volume, I decided to include all of Jung's writings in which significant material can be found on Eastern religions. Very often Jung made general comments on several Eastern systems of thought or stated a feature of one Eastern religious tradition which he believed to be also true of others. A case in point is the imprecision of his use of the term "yoga," by which he generally meant any Eastern spirituality in some contexts. Hence anyone wishing to research

Jung's views on Indian religious traditions, symbols, and practices would do well to consult most of the material listed in the first part of the bibliography.

Because a work is a commentary on an Asian text or because it contains several pages of explicit discussion of a Hindu or Buddhist set of terms or doctrines, is not the only qualification for its being included in this bibliography. Quantity is not the only criterion for significance. For example, Jung devoted a lengthy work to psychological types, but throughout the book he made reference, in a sentence here or in a few sentences there, to *Brahman-Ātman* or to the introversion of Eastern spiritualities, which are important statements in the larger context of psychological types and Eastern spiritualities. Furthermore, it should be remembered that Jung made relevant statements in many more writings than those listed here. Even so, numerous repetitions occur. I believe that familiarity with the works listed in the first part of the bibliography gives as complete a picture of Jung's view of Asian traditions as can be drawn from his writings.

Dates have been added in brackets to the titles of Jung's works to give an idea of when Jung published each work and if it was revised. This is most important because his ideas passed through certain stages of development and his comments often should be considered in the context of his travels, interests, and work at the time. For example, Heisig's study of the image of God unfolds within a framework of the periods of Jung's life. Hence I recommend a biography of Jung too, the one which he approved and to which he contributed: *Memories, Dreams, Reflections.* The dates, therefore, do not refer to editions of his compiled writings (the most recent editions being used here) but rather to the appearance of Jung's writings in print.

The secondary literature involves several types of studies from brief notices or communications to books and theses. Some of the writings are comparative; others are works of synthesis; and still others are quite independent of Jung. The authors are from different backgrounds and possess varying expertise. There are analysts trained at Jungian institutes, friends and associates of Jung or of the institutes, orientalists, and historians of religions. Many of the writings are provocative, solid, carefully researched contributions, while others, in my opinion, are incorrect in part or in their main arguments. If I were to edit critically this bibliography and exclude those works which are superficial, ill-founded, or inaccurate, then approximately one-third of the titles would be absent in the second part. I have chosen to include all the titles since it is still worthwhile to be aware of the various opinions and to recall the differing approaches; but I hope that my notes will cue the reader as to the kind of work and scholarship behind the titles.

Several problems were evident to me as I reviewed the materials. For most Europeans and Americans, Asia is still undifferentiated. Nuances within interpretations of the *nirvāna* experience, the doctrine of *ātman,* the *karma* principle, mental constituents or impressions *(saṁskārās),* to name a few, are known only to specialists. On the other hand, Jung's writings and many by those trained at the institutes are difficult for outsiders to comprehend in a short amount of time. There is the additional dimension of one's own analysis. Often those who spend years in psychological training must rely on whatever materials are available to them on Eastern traditions, which they sometimes incorporate uncritically into their psychological research. Just looking at their published work, I have the impression that there is a lack of guidance in historical methodology. Rare indeed are the individuals who have met with approval among both Jungians and historians of religions: Campbell, Coward, Heisig, and Hillman. But even their work may be highly controversial within either camp. A characteristic Indian arrogance toward Jung's psychology, that is, the attitude that Indian wisdom is superior to the recent visions of Westerners, compromises the research of a few listed here: Deshmukh, Nath, and Vasavada. By "characteristic" I mean a position which many Indian thinkers have taken towards European and American thought in general. Also I should qualify that Vasavada has done much more than to pass judgment on Jung. He was trained in Zürich and has attempted to develop psychological studies in India. Finally, to name another problem, the long-standing belief that all final, mystical states are similar in kind but are only differently explained within the conceptual frameworks of the traditions keeps many studies on the superficial level: Coukoulis, Marlan, Parker, and Watts.

The general area of Jung's psychology and Indian religious traditions, and the larger area of Eastern religious traditions for that matter, is wide open. It is full of opportunities for both historians of religions and Jungians. Obviously one gains expertise in either camp, and then knowledge and assurance within the other field comes slowly after much study, discussion, and advice from counterparts. Dialogue and exchange of methodologies will precede future contributions. What psychologists have gained through their own analysis, clinical experiences, and studies, and what historians of religions can offer from their own careful studies need to be exchanged.

Many current works are useful developments within the general area but are in need of critical attention. For example, there are a number interesting and remarkable theses from the C.G. Jung Institut in Zürich: Baumgardt, Pascal, Wanner, and Wood. Of these four, two are in the field of dreams. Pascal and Wood, and represent a realistic step towards acknowledging and incorporating Asian materials on dreams and dream interpretation. Pascal is taking the time to expand his thesis to include as many Asian materials as possible before making it available. Studies by scholars, like Mishra and Wayman, should be consulted, and historians of religions have an opportunity to contribute further to the research too.

One curious field of intense study is comprised by the number of writings on particular Indian teachers in relation to Jung's psychology: Lauterborn, Linssen, Marsh, Parker, and Wanner. By far the most concise and profound study is by Wanner on Swami Muktananda Paramahansa. Lauterborn's work on Swami Omkarananda should be studied cautiously in view of the recent disturbances by the teacher and his disciples in Switzerland; Linssen's and Marsh's studies were done over twenty years ago but are still interesting, and Parker's incorporation of Paramahansa Yogananda's teachings unfortunately is disguised by the style of his book.

Much has been made of Jung's criticism of Westerners practicing Eastern spiritualities, and many authors have addressed it directly, referred to it indirectly, or composed responses: Borelli, Byles, Campbell, Coward, Frantz, and Parker. Views of historians of religions and analysts, considering both the variety of religious traditions and contemporary experience especially in the United States, should be exchanged on this issue. Their past articles are but the current step in the area by students of religions. Analysts trained at the various institutes are taking steps too in several directions. The hope is that this book and its bibliography will encourage and engender further comparative studies, discussions, and dialogues on many of the issues.

All of my research on this bibliography was done in New York. A few items were sent to me, but nearly all the works listed are available at either the Oriental Room of the New York Public Library on 42nd Street or at the Kristine Mann Library of the Analytical Psychology Club of New York on 39th Street. A special word of thanks to Doris Albrecht, the librarian of the Kristine Mann Library, without whose assistance and breadth of knowledge of published materials and authors this bibliography would have been more difficult to compile and certainly less complete.

Part One: C.G. Jung on Eastern Religious Traditions

The Collected Works of C.G. Jung. Edited by Sir Herbert Read, Michael Fordham, and Gerhard Adler. William McGuire, executive editor. Bollingen Series 20. 20 volumes. Princeton: Princeton University Press, the latest editions (1954–79).

1. *C.W.* 6, *Psychological Types* (1921; rev. 1960). This shows some influence, especially the *Brahman-Ātman* teaching, and contains comments throughout.

C.W. 8, *The Structure and Dynamics of the Psyche.*

2. "Synchronicity: An Acausal Connecting Principle (1952)." More references are made to Chinese philosophy, but this is one of Jung's fascinating speculations in parapsychology, an area to which Eastern religions and systems of thought can offer insight.

C.W. 9, 1, *The Archetypes and the Collective Unconscious.*

3. "Conscious, Unconscious, and Individuation (1939)." The essay concludes with a few remarks on *samādhi.*

4. "Concerning Mandala Symbolism (1950)."

5. "Appendix: Mandalas (1955)."

C.W. 10, *Civilization in Transition.*
6. "Good and Evil in Analytical Psychology (1959)."

7. "The Dreamlike World of India (1939)."

8. "What India Can Teach Us (1939)."

C.W. 11, *Psychology and Religion: West and East.*
9. "Psychology and Religion (1938; rev. 1940)."

10. "Psychological Commentary on *The Tibetan Book of the Great Liberation* (1939; 1954)."

11. "Psychological Commentary on *The Tibetan Book of the Dead* (1935; rev. 1953)."

12. "Yoga and the West (1936)."

13. "Foreword to Suzuki's *Introduction to Zen Buddhism* (1939)."

14. "The Psychology of Eastern Meditation (1943)."

15. "The Holy Men of India (1944)."

16. "Foreword to the *I Ching* (1950)."

17. C.W. 12, *Psychology and Alchemy* (1944: rev. 1952). This lengthy study of alchemy contains several references to yoga, the *Upanisads, mandalas,* and a short piece on the unicorn in Indian literature.

C.W. 13, *Alchemical Studies.*
18. "Commentary on *The Secret of the Golden Flower* (1929)."

C.W. 15, *The Spirit in Man, Art, and Literature.*
19. "Richard Wilhelm: In Memoriam (1930)."

C.W. 16, *The Practice of Psychotherapy.*
20. "Psychotherapy Today (1945)." Jung made specific comments on the practice of yoga and other Eastern techniques in the contemporary western world.

C.W. 18, *The Symbolic Life.*

21. "Foreword to Abegg: *Ostasien denkt anders* (1950)."

22. "On the Discourses of the Buddha (1956)."

23. "Letters to Oskar Schmitz, 1921–31." *Psychological Perspectives* 6 (1975): 79–95. Most of these letters were not included in the edition of Jung's letters, and they are quite helpful in explaining why Jung criticized the practice of yoga by Westerners.

24. *C.J. Jung: Letters,* vols. I and II, edited G. Adler and A. Jaffé. Princeton: Princeton University Press (1953 and 1974). Volume 2 contains an Index for both volumes which can be checked for Eastern topics.

25. *Memories, Dreams, Reflections.* Recorded and edited by Aniela Jaffé. New York: Random House, 1961. Contains important material on the role Eastern thought played in the development of Jung's psychology.

26. *The Process of Individuation.* Notes on Lectures Given at the Eidgenössische Technische Hochschule, Zürich, October 1938–June 1939. These are typed notes taken from twenty-two lectures by Jung, edited by Barbara Hannah, and cannot be taken as verbatim statements by Jung. In their present form they are still useful. They include a commentary on Patanjal's *Yoga Sūtras* and comments on two Buddhist texts. In addition, Jung discussed many Hindu and Buddhist teachings.

27. "Psychological Commentary on Kundalini Yoga." *Spring* (1975): 1–32 and (1976): 1–31.

28. *The Visions Seminars. From the Complete Notes of Mary Foote.* Zürich: Spring Publications, 1976.

In addition to *Memories, Dreams, Reflections,* the recently published biographical memoir, *Jung: His Life and Work,* by Barbara Hannah (New York: G.P. Putnam, 1976) should be consulted. It includes comments on Jung and Kuṇḍalinī Yoga, as well as a chapter entitled "Indian Intermezzo 1937–1938."

Part Two: Secondary Sources

29. Abegg, Lily. *Mind of East Asia.* Translated by A.J. Crick and E.E. Thomas. London: Thames, 1952. A psychological study attempting to understand the so-called "East Asian character," which includes all Asians, the article employs Jung's psychological types with two exceptions: an expanded meaning for the thinking type and a greater role for consciousness in introverts. One must first accept the overly generalized position that the characters of Easterners and Westerners differ. Jung wrote the foreword for the German edition, *Ostasien denkt anders,* which was republished in *C.W.* 18, pars. 1483–85.

30. Avens, Robert, "C.G. Jung and some Far Eastern Parallels." *Cross Currents* 23, 2 (Spring 1973): 73–91. More than a parallel study, it concludes that Jung's individuation process and several Eastern spiritualities share certain goals: self-awareness, transformation of ordinary consciousness, and transcendence. The insights are highly suggestive but should be more cautiously studied with an eye for greater differences of details and descriptions of states of "transformed consciousness." Avens presumes the religious nature of the collective unconscious about which he penned: "C.G. Jung's Analysis of Religious Experience." *Journal of Dharma* 1, 3 (January 1976): 225–45.

31. Baumgardt, Ursula. "Tibetisch-buddhistischer heilsweg und Jungscher Individuationsprozess." Thesis, C.G. Jung Institut, Zürich, 1977.

32. Borelli, John. "Jung's Psychology and Yoga Spirituality." *Riverdale Studies,* no. 4 (1977). An analysis of Jung's criticism of the practice of Eastern spiritualities by Europeans and Americans, the study identifies six interrelated reasons throughout Jung's writings why he argued against such practices.

33. Borelli, John. "Impression and Archetype in the Cognitive Theories of Classical Yoga and Analytical Psychology." In *Sāmkhya-Yoga: Proceeding of the IASWR Conference, 1981,* pp. 120–61. Edited by Christopher Chapple. Stony Brook, New York: The Institute for Advanced Study of World Religions, 1983. After a lengthy comparison of mental structures and processes within both systems, three conclusions are reached: 1) physical and psychic processes in an individual are connected through a basic subconscious patterning; 2) all depth experience is directed generally towards the spirit or the self; and 3) both systems provide techniques for understanding and manipulating psychic states as one seeks to experience the self.

34. Brunton, Paul. *Discover Yourself.* New York: Dutton, 1939. An influence on Jung, the author discusses typical errors of those who practice Oriental meditations in the west. A parallel work to Jung's is his: *The Spiritual Crisis of Man.* New York: Dutton, 1953. In addition, he wrote many other works commenting on Indian ideas for Westerners.

35. Byles, Marie B. "Vipassana Meditation and Psychologist Jung." *Maha-Bodhi* 68, 12 (1960): 362–66. A light and personal response to Jung's criticism that Westerners should not practice Eastern spiritualities, the article is favorable to that criticism for beginners but encourages Buddhist meditation after certain difficulties peculiar to Westerners are overcome. It would seem that the difficulties are the same for all uninitiates.

36. Campbell, Joseph. "The Separation of East and West." *Myths to Live By.* New York: Viking, 1972, pp. 61–81. The chapter is a reflection on possible differences in viewpoints implicit in mythologies with reference to Jung's observations.

37. Christou, Evangelos. "Complex Psychology and the Occidentalized Easterner: An Essay in Clarification." Thesis, C.G. Jung Institut, Zürich, 1954. Basing the thesis on the position that complex psychology is valid universally, the author develops through 134 pages of difficult reading a

logic of the soul from psychological experience, and then addresses the specific issue of the title. The thesis was expanded and later published posthumously as: *The Logos of the Soul.* Vienna Dunquin Press, 1963; Zürich: Spring, 1967.

38. Coster, Geraldine. *Yoga and Western Psychology: A Comparison.* London: Oxford University Press, 1934. One of the first good comparative works and still useful, very little direct reference is made to Jung.

39. Coukoulis, Peter. *Guru, Psychotherapist, and Self.* Marina del Rey, Ca.: DeVorss and Co., 1976. Through the relationships between guru and student and between analyst and analysand the self is experienced, and despite the verbal and conceptual differences, the author argues that the meaning and experience of the self is the same in Indian, Buddhist, and Jungian relationships.

40. Coward, Harold G. "Can Jungian Psychology be used to Interpret Indian Devotional Poetry?" *Studies in Religion,* 8, 2 (1979): 177–189. Keeping within the basic assumptions held in common between Jungian psychology and South Indian devotional poetry, a Jungian analysis of some devotional songs by the Tamil poet Tirunaavukkarasar is offered.

41. ———. "Cognition in Jung and Yoga." *Yoga Awareness* (Varanasi) 3, 1 (January 1979): 8–25. A comparative study of the processes of knowing as viewed by Jung and classical yoga, the article is a fine treatment of memory, perception, sense of ego, and self-knowledge.

42. ———. "Jung's Encounter with Yoga." *The Journal of Analytical Psychology* 23, 4 (1978): 339–57. This is a comprehensive study of the context of Jung's comments on Eastern religious traditions and of the role his encounter with those traditions played in his thought development. Also translated into French as "La Confrontation de Jung Avec le Yoga," in *Cahiers de Psychologie Jungienne* (Paris), 23, (1979): 19–40.

43. ———. "Mysticism in the Analytical Psychology of Carl Jung and the Yoga Psychology of Patanjali: A Comparative Study." *Philosophy East and West* 29, 3 (July 1979): 323–36. This is a comparison of mysticism in Jung with the notions of mysticism in *Yoga Sūtras* 1.42–51. Coward points out especially the difference in the degree of ego-loss.

44. ———. "Jung and Karma." *The Journal of Analytical Psychology* 28, 4 (1983): 367–75. The Indian notions of *karma* and rebirth influenced Jung, especially in his final years when his own dreams led to a fuller understanding of psychic inheritance. Coward shows that a general view of *karma* had a greater impact on the development of the archetypal theory than followers of Jung have admitted.

45. Deshmukh, C.D. "Some Clear Advantages of the Methods of Yoga over those of Modern Psychoanalytical Schools." *Philosophical Quarterly* (Amalner) 20 (1946): 193–98. A superficial understanding of psychoanalytical theory plagues this article.

46. Elder, George R. "Psychological Observations on the 'Life of Gautama Buddha.'" In *Buddhist and Western Psychology*, pp. 25–38. Edited by Nathan Katz. Boulder: Prajñā Press, 1983. A psychological interpretation of various Buddhist works treating the life of Siddhārtha Gautama, the study focuses on growth in wisdom by confrontation of certain psychological factors, which are identified by reference to Jung's psychology.

47. Faber, P.A. and Saayman, G.S. "On the Relation of the doctrines of Yoga to Jung's Psychology" in *Jung in Modern Perspectives*, ed. by R.K. Papadopoulos and G.S. Saayman. London: Wildwood House, 1984.

48. Frantz, Kieffer E. "Analytical Psychology and Yoga." *Professional Reports.* Sixteenth Annual Joint Conference of the Societies of Jungian Analysts of Northern and Southern California, March 14–17, 1968. San Francisco: C.G. Jung Institute, August 1968. Meditation and analysis are com-

plementary and may lead to wholeness when employed together.

49. Froebe-Kapteyn, Olga, ed. *Yoga und Meditation im Osten und im Westen.* Eranos-Jahrbuch, 1953. Zürich: Rhein-Verlag, 1934. The papers collected in these Eranos-Jahrbücher together present a somewhat unified study of the topic identified in each title. Often the reader must connect the various themes. Jung's contribution to this volume was: "Zur Empirie des Individuationsprozesses." Later his paper was completely rewritten, expanded, and published in 1950. The English translation is: "A Study in the Process of Individuation," *C.W.* 9, 1, pars. 525–626.

50. ———. *Ostwestliche Symbolik und Seelenführung.* Eranos-Jahrbuch, 1934. Zürich: Rhein-Verlag, 1935. Jung's contribution was: "Über die Archetypen des kollectiven Unbewussten." This was revised and republished in 1954, and the English translation is: "Archetypes of the Collective Unconscious," *C.W.* 9, 1, pars. 1–86.

51. ———. *Westöstliche Seelenführung.* Eranos-Jahrbuch, 1935. Zürich: Rhein-Verlag, 1936. Jung's contribution was: "Traum-symbole des Individuations-prozesses." It was revised, expanded, and published in 1944. It appears in English as: "Dream Symbols of the Individuation Process," *C.W.* 12, pars. 44–331.

52. ———. *Gestaltung der Erlösungsidee in Ost und West.* Eranos-Jahrbücher, 1936–37. Zürich: Rhein-Verlag, 1937–38. Jung's contributions: "Die Erlösungsvorstellungen in der Alchemie" and "Einige Bermerkungen zu dem Visionen des Zosimos." The former was revised, expanded, and published in 1944 and appears in English as: "Religious Ideas in Alchemy," *C.W.* 12, pars. 332–554. The Latter was revised, expanded, and published in 1954. The English translation occurs as: "The Visions of Zosimos," *C.W.* 13, pars. 85–144.

53. Heisig, James W. *Imago Dei: A Study of C.G. Jung's Psychology of Religion.* Lewisburg, Pa.: Bucknell University Press, 1979.

A provocative study, the work aims at disclosing the development of the idea of the God image by Jung and assessing his methods and arguments.

54. ———. "Jung and Theology: A Bibliographical Essay." *Spring* (1973): 204–255. This is an excellent essay and extraordinary list of sources. A few of the sources in this bibliography receive specific comments.

55. Henderson, Joseph L. "The Self and Individuation," in the *International Encyclopedia of Neurology, Psychiatry, Psychoanalysis and Psychology,* Vol. I (1975). An excellent analysis of the sources of Jung's concept of the "Self" highlighting the Hindu contribution.

56. Henderson, Joseph and Oakes, Maud. *Wisdom of the Serpent: Myths of Death, Rebirth and Resurrection.* New York: George Braziller, 1963. In the tradition of Jung, the authors explore the meanings and variations of Eastern and Western myths with special attention to contemporary experience.

57. Harding, M. Esther. "The Reality of the Psyche." In *The Reality of the Psyche.* The Proceedings of the Third International Congress for Analytical Psychology, pp. 1–13. Edited by Joseph B. Wheelwright. New York: G.P. Putnam's Sons, 1968. The author uses the *chakras* of Kuṇḍalinī Yoga tradition to illustrate the development of ego-consciousness and the stages of assimilation of levels of unconscious contents.

58. Hillman, James. "Peaks and Vales: The Soul/Spirit Distinction as Basis for the Difference between Psychotherapy and Spiritual Discipline." In *On the Way to Self Knowledge: Sacred Tradition and Psychotherapy,* pp. 114–47. Edited by Jacob Needleman. New York: Knopf, 1976. Hillman presents his well thought-out distinction between psychotherapy as concern for psychologizing, the *anima* as guide, and multivalency and polytheism, and spirituality as ascent, growing up, and becoming unified.

59. ———. *Re-visioning Psychology.* New York: Harper & Row, 1975. Throughout this synthesis, Hillman draws from a number of sources including Jung and Eastern traditions.

60. Jacobs, Hans. *Western Psychology and Hindu Sādhanā: A Contribution to Comparative Studies in Psychology and Metaphysics.* London: Allen and Unwin, 1961. Not really an honest comparative study, the work molds Jung's position to fit Indian thought.

61. Jones, Richard Hubert. "Jung and Eastern Religious Traditions." *Religion,* 9, 1979, 141–156. Asks whether Jung's psychological concepts are adequate to understand Eastern religions. Jones concludes that they are not.

62. Jordens, Joseph. "Jung and Yoga." *Journal of the Indian Academy of Philosophy* (Calcutta) 3 (1964): 1–21. One of the first good comparative studies, the article emphasizes practical comparisons in reference to the study of psychological states.

63. ———. "Prana and Libido." *Journal of the Indian Academy of Philosophy* (Calcutta) 6 (1967): 32–44. The early notion of *prāṇa* as found in the Upaniṣads, especially in the *Kauṣītakī,* is very close to the psychological notion of libido. Includes a careful analysis of Jung's attempt to avoid metaphysical claims.

64. Kenghe, C.T. *Yoga as Depth-Psychology & Para-Psychology.* Vol. II. Depth Psychology. Varanasi: Bharata Manisha, 1976. One of the best summaries of classical yoga's view of mind and its functions with comparisons mainly with Freud and Jung. A fair and general reading of Jung's psychology is presented throughout with only a couple of imprecisions. His main objective is to define mind from the view of Patanjali yoga, which he does and then contrasts with the essentially materialistic, in his opinion, views of depth psychology. Distributed by South Asia Books.

65. Krishna, Gopi. *Kundalini: The Evolutionary Process in Man.* 2nd rev. ed., Berkeley: Shambala, 1970. With a commentary

by James Hillman, the entire work is an interesting contribution to the area of yoga and archetypal psychology.

66. Lauterborn, Eleonore. *Swami Omkarananda und C.G. Jung: Der psychologische Schatten und das uberpsychologische Selbst.* Zürich: A.B.C., 1970.

67. Linssen, Rām. Etudes pszchologiques de C.G. Jung à Krishnamurti. Bruxelles: "Etre Libre," n.d. [ca. 1950]. An honest little book in regard to what it tries to do, certain general ideas are taken from Jung and then completed or improved through Krishnamurti's teachings.

68. Marlan, Stanton. "The Creative Tension of the Ego-Self Axis: A Jungian Psychoanalytical Critique of the Notion of the Transcendence of the Ego: Phenomenological and Religious Perspectives." Diploma Thesis Submitted to the Interregional Society of Jungian Analysts, Pittsburgh, 1980. In one section [pp. 53–63], the author treats the Eastern sources of Jung's idea of the self, tries to clear up some false ideas about Eastern views of the self, differentiates a number of Eastern schools of thought, but does not distinguish their exact positions with regard to the self. The first part of this thesis appears in *The Metaphors of Consciousness.* Edited by Ronald S. Valle and Rolf von Eckhartsberg. New York: Plenum Press, 1981.

69. Marsh, R. "A Comparative Analysis of the Concept of Individuality in the Thought of C.G. Jung and Sri Aurobindo." Unpublished Ph.D. Dissertation, University of the Pacific through the American Academy of Asian Studies, 1959.

70. McCully, Robert S. "Tantric Imagery and Rorschach Perception." *Rorschachiana Japonica* 15 & 16 (1974): 123–34. Arguing that Tantric imagery and Rorschach imagery are similar through process, the paper demonstrates that the psychological experiences that are concretized in the imagery are similar, and hence attention is paid to links and not differences.

71. McKell, Kimberley. "Psychology of the Tantric Chakras." Unpublished Ph.D. Dissertation, California Institute of Asian Studies, 1975.

72. Mishra, Umesh. "Dream Theory in Indian Thought." *Allahabad University Studies* (Arts Section) 5 (1929): 269–321. Not a comparative study with Jung, this article is useful to anyone doing comparative study of dream theory.

73. Mokusen, Miyuki. "The Psychodynamics of Buddhist Meditation", *The Eastern Buddhist,* 10, 2 (1977): 155–168. Relates Jungian analysis to Buddhist practices such as *Zazen* and *Koan* meditation.

74. Nath, Prem. "Patanjali's Yoga in the Light of Modern Psychology." *Philosophical Quarterly* (Amalner) 25 (1952): 53–61.

75. O'Flaherty, Wendy Doniger. "The Dream Narrative and the Indian Doctrine of Illusion." *Daedalus* III, 3 (Summer 1982): 93–113. Interpretation of the dream within the dream motif in the *Yogavāsiṣṭha-mahārāmāyana* in which a monk imagines himself to be another person and so on through a series of imaginations to the god Rudra who dreams a hundred dreams, among them one of a monk who imagined himself to be another person. References are made to dream interpretation theories, Indian religious ideas, and the importance of dreams in India.

76. ———. "Hard and Soft Reality." *Parabola* 7, 2 (May 1982): 55–65. A review of Indian sources containing the motif of dreaming another's dream with reference to theories of interpretation by Freud, Jung, and others. The author distinguishes three grades or strengths of the shared dream: 1) lovers who know one another and who dream of one another on the same night; 2) a man dreams of a woman or a woman dreams of a man, searches for the person in the dream, finds that person, and they marry; 3) a man and a woman, unknown to one another, dream of each other, meet, and discover that they dreamt of one another.

77. ———. "Illusion and Reality in the *Yogavāsiṣṭha,* or the Scientific Proof of the Mythical Experience." *Quadrant* 14, 1 (Spring 1981): 46–65. The stories of Lavaṇa who imagines a series of events and of Gādhi who imagines a similar set of events in that both live among untouchables. After the "daydreams," evidence is found that the events truly happened. Levels of perceived reality, fantasies, and imaginations become intertwined as psychological facts.

78. Pal, Kumar. "Yoga and Psychoanalysis." *Prabudha Bharata* (Calcutta) 52) (1947): 119ff.; 173ff.; and 204ff. A fairly competent study in most places, the article surveys psychoanalytic theories and Indian views of the self; unfortunately, the archetypes are viewed as purely racial.

79 Pascal, Eugene. "Jung and the Dream in Buddhism." Thesis, C.G. Jung Institut, Zürich, 1978. Not just on Buddhism, this thesis gives the Indian background of dream interpretation before proceeding with a treatment of various suggestions of interpretation throughout Buddhism. A major conclusion is the ambivalence displayed in both the Hindu and Buddhist traditions towards the interpretation and meaning of dreams.

80. Parker, Thomas E. "Analytical Psychology and the Science of Yoga." *Professional Reports.* Fifteenth Annual Joint Conference of the Societies of Jungian Analysts of Northern and Southern California, 1967, pp. 14–20. San Francisco: C.G. Jung Institute, 1967. After a brief review of the eight aspects of Patanjali's yoga, Parker asserts that expansion of consciousness is a common goal and takes exception to Jung's criticism of Westerners practicing yoga, since yoga is foreign even to many Hindus too and since there is not a loss of individuality, in his opinion, in either system.

81. ———. "Notes on the New Culture." In *The Shaman From Elko: Papers in Honor of Joseph L. Henderson on his Seventy-fifth Birthday.* San Francisco: C.G. Jung Institute, 1978. A comment on the current transitional phase of American culture is given in reference to the themes included in the symbol of the Indian mother goddess Kālī.

82. ———. *Return: Beyond the Self.* Saratoga, Ca.: Polestar Publications, 1979. A reflective and informal book, without notes, on meaning in the contemporary world, the piece represents a synthesis of analytical psychology and the teachings of Paramahansa Yogananda.

83. Raju, P.T. "Vṛtti or Psychosis." *Proceedings and Transactions of the All-Indian Oriental Conference,* 16th Session, October 1951 (Lucknow, 1955): 347–50. This is mainly a study of the Advaita Vedānta view of mental processes.

84. Roy, Manisha. "Animus and Indian Women." *Harvest* 25 (1979): 70–79. Hindu mythology as a projection of mainly familial relationships in contemporary India is discussed.

85. Schaer, Hans. *Religion and the Cure of Souls in Jung's Psychology.* Bollingen Series 21. New York: Pantheon, 1950. Originally published as: *Religion und Seele in der Psychologie C.G. Jung.* Zürich: Rascher-Verlag, 1946. The book offers a general, if not facile, synopsis of Jung's views especially in regard to Eastern traditions.

86. Schmaltz, Gustav. *Ostliche Weisheit und westliche Psychotherapie.* Stuttgart: Hippokrates-Verlag, 1953. Jung wrote a foreword to another book by Schmaltz, which was published in *C.W.* 18, pars. 839–40.

87. Schmitz, Oskar A.H. *Psychoanalyse und Yoga.* Darmstadt: n.p., 1923. Letters were exchanged by Schmitz and Jung on this book and related topics. See "Letters to Oskar Schmitz." Jung wrote a foreword to another work by Schmitz, which was published in *C.W.* 18, 1716–22.

88. Sharma, Jagdish and Siegel, Lee. *Dream-Symbolism in the Srāmanic Tradition. Two Psychoanalytical Studies in Jinist and Buddhist Dream Legends.* Calcutta: Firma KLM Private Limited, 1980. A study of Jain and Buddhist narratives of dreams by future mothers of Jinas or Buddhas. While the first part on Jain legends is claimed to be Jungian, it is so superficially. Sharma relies more on traditional Jain cate-

gories. The Buddhist portion by Siegel displays a Freudian orientation.

89. Skott, Prebeb. "The Unconscious: C.G. Jung and Buddhism." *The World Fellowship of Buddhists Review* 11, 5 (July–October 1974): 5–16.

90. ———. "Anatta: the Psychological Implications of the Doctrine of the Monk Gautama, Known as the Buddha." Thesis, C.G. Jung Institut, Zürich, 1980.

91. Sreenivasachar, S.M. "The Unconscious in Yoga and Psychoanalysis." *Philosophical Quarterly* (Amalner) 17 (1941–42): 261–68. This is a fairly good treatment of the impressions *(saṃskārās)* in yoga but involves a misreading of the archetypes.

92. Thomas, James Doyle. *The Self between East and West—Concepts of Self in Mead, Jung, and Mahayana Buddhism.* Thesis, Claremont Graduate School, 1974.

93. Thornton, Edward. "Jungian Psychology and the Vedānta." In *Spectrum Psychologiae,* pp. 131–42. Edited by C.T. Frey-Wehrlin. Zürich: Rascher-Verlag, 1965. By using Saṅkara's commentary on the *Māṇḍūkyopaniṣad,* the issue of Jung's empiricism is addressed as but one level of experience. In his autobiography, Thornton traced his personal development which included a few years of study with Jung: *The Diary of a Mystic.* London: George Allen & Unwin, 1967.

94. Valle, Ronald S. and von Eckartsberg, Rolf, eds. *The Metaphors of Consciousness.* New York: Plenum Press, 1981. In a section entitled "Beyond Psychology: East Meets West," four articles are listed which include comparisons of Jung and Buddhist theories of consciousness, thinking, and psychotherapy.

95. Vasavada, Arvind. *Dr. C.G. Jung ka nislesanatmaki manovijnan. Ek samksipth Paricay.* Varanasi: Chowkhamba Vidyabhawan, 1963.

96. ———. "Jung's analytische Psychologie und indische Weischeit." In *Abendlandische Therapie und östliche Weisheit,* pp. 236–44. Edited by Wilhelm Bitter. Stuttgart: Ernst Klett, 1968. English translation is: "The Analytical Psychology of C.G. Jung and Indian Wisdom." *Journal of Analytical Psychology* 13, 2 (1968): 131–45.

97. ———. "Philosophical Roots of the Psychotherapies of the West." In *Spectrum Psychologiae,* pp. 143–54. Edited by C.T. Frey-Wehrlin. Zürich: Rascher-Verlag, 1965. The concern of psychotherapies for the treatment of human ills is traced through several schools with comments that much may be learned from Indian spiritualities.

98. ———. "The Place of Psychology in Philosophy." Presidential Address to the 38th Session of the Indian Philosophical Congress of Madras, 1964.

99. ———. *Tripura-rahasya.* Varanasi: Chowkhamba Sanskrit Offices, 1963. Submitted earlier as "Tripura-Rahasya, or a comparative Study of the Process of Individuation." Thesis, C.G. Jung Institut, Zürich, 1956. His view generally is that Indian spiritual methods are superior to Jung's psychology, and the latter should give up scientific prejudices and become a spirituality.

100. ———. "Yogic Basis of Psychoanalysis." *Bhāratīya Vidyā* 2, 2 (May 1941): 239–43. Stylistically difficult to follow, the article tries to give prerequisites for an Indian psychoanalytic theory; however, certain common ideas from Indian philosophy are compared very simply with psychoanalytic terms.

101. Wanner, Armin A. "Visionen und Erfahrungen des zeitgenössischen Yogi Swami Muktananda Paramahansa. Versuch einer pszchologischer Interpretation." Thesis, C.G. Jung Institut, Zürich, 1978. An English translation is available at the Kristine Mann Library. The visions and experiences of Muktananda are subjected to amplification. Sections on Vedā, Sāṅkhya, and yoga provide background

material, and the study offers many carefully stated and provocative comparisons on methods of self-realization.

102. Watts, Alan W. "Asian Psychology and Modern Psychology." *American Journal of Psychoanalysis* 13, 1 (1953). This and the other two works listed here were written in the style of Watts' early writings, namely they are general, suggestive, but not too precise introductions to Asian materials.

103. ———. Legacy of Asian and Western Man: A Study of the Middle Way. London: John Murray, 1937.

104. ———. *Meaning of Happiness, the Quest for Freedom of the Spirit in Modern Psychology and the Wisdom of the East.* New York: Harper and Bros., 1940.

105. Wayman, Alex. "Significance of Dreams in India and Tibet." *History of Religions* 7 (1967): 1–12. Not a comparative study with Jung, this article is an excellent study useful for comparative study on dreams.

106. Welwood, John. "Meditation and the Unconscious: A New Perspective." In *The Meeting of the Ways: Explorations in East/West Psychology,* edited by John Welwood. New York: Schocken Books, 1979. Using Buddhist psychological theory, the author attempts a holistic model of the conscious-unconscious polarity over and against the depth psychological model, mainly constructed by Jung, which is criticized as dualistic.

107. Winter, F.I. "The Yoga System and Psychoanalysis." *The Quest* 10 (1918–19): 182–96; 315–35. A lucid and detailed study of how each system works with spontaneous manifestations of the unconscious, the article indicates the different views of libido yet stresses a unity of human mental processes evidenced by general symbols.

108. Wood, Dorothy Ann. "The Dream of Queen Trisalā: A Jungian Interpretation of the 14 Auspicious Signs of Foretelling the Birth of a Jaina Tīrthaṅkara Mahāvīra."

Thesis, C.G. Jung Institut, Zürich, 1974. An adaptation appears as: "Psychological Impressions from an Indian Dream." *Art Psychotherapy* 2, 3/4 (1974): 24–54.

109. Zaehner, Robert Charles. *Mysticism: Sacred and Profane. An Inquiry into some Varieties of Preternatural Experience.* Oxford: Clarendon Press, 1957. Comparisons are drawn between *buddhi* and the collective unconscious, *prakṛti* and the collective unconscious, and energy and *prāṇa,* and contrasts are made on the views of spirit and union.

110. ———. "A New Buddha and a New Tao." *Concise Encyclopaedia of Living Faiths.* London: Hutchinson, 1959.

111. Zimmer, Heinrich. "Indische Anschauungen über Psychotherapie." In *Zentralblatt fur Psychotherapie* 8, 6. Edited by C.G. Jung. Leipsig: Hirzel, 1935. An English translation by Violet de Laszlo ["Indian Views of Psychotherapy"] is in the files of the Kristine Mann Library. In Western methods the unconscious leads, but in India the *guru* directs. The *guru*-student bond is described and certain related views such as the sheathes, the soul, and parental relationships are discussed. Jung composed an introduction to Zimmer's *Der Weg zum Selbst: Lehre und Leben des indischen Heiligen Shri Ramana Maharshi aus Tiruvannamalai,* which appears in *C.W.* 11 as "The Holy Men of India."

112. ———. "Krishna and King Mucukunda: The Sleeper Awakened." Translated by Gerald Chapple and James B. Lawson. *Parabola* 7, 1 (January 1982): 52–55. An example of sleep as flight from *saṃsāra.*

About the Authors

John Borelli is Associate Professor and Chairman of the Department of Religious Studies, College of Mount St. Vincent, Riverdale, N.Y., U.S.A. His articles have appeared in *Philosophy East and West, Ecumenical Trends* and *Thought.*

Harold Coward is Professor of Religious Studies and Director of The Calgary Institute for the Humanities, The University of Calgary, Calgary, Alberta, Canada. He is author of *Bhartṛhari, Sphoṭa Theory of Language* and *Pluralism: Challenge to World Religions,* along with other books and articles.

Joseph L. Henderson is founding member and past president of the C.G. Jung Institute of San Francisco. Now in the private practice of Analytical Psychology, he was formerly Professor of Psychiatry, Stanford University. He is author of "Ancient Myths and Modern Man" in *Man and His Symbols,* ed. by C.G. Jung. His many articles appear in *Psychological Perspectives* and the *Journal of Analytical Psychology.*

J.F.T. Jordens is Dean, Faculty of Asian Studies, The Australian National University, Canberra, Australia. He is author of *Dayananda Sarasvati: His Life and Times,* and *Swami Shraddananda: His Life and Causes,* along with other chapters and articles.

Index*

* Items appearing in the footnotes and Annotated Bibliography are not included in the Index.

Whitney, W.D., 33
Wilhelm, Richard, 5, 29, 30, 42–43, 44
Wu-wei, 36–37, 50

Yab-yum, 20
Yang-yin, 17, 20, 44
Yoga, 3–91;
  as pre-Kantian or pre-psychological, 62, 188
Yoga Sūtras of Patañjali, xi, xiii, 3, 15, 30, 33, 34, 35, 46, 52, 61, 64–69, 74, 84–85, 95, 96, 105, 110–111, 134–142, 145–165

Zaehner, H., 154, 165
Zen, 20, 48, 67, 72–73, 89, 162
Zimmer, H., 79, 110–111